Gender, Geography and Empire

For my family,
with love

Gender, Geography and Empire

Victorian Women Travellers in West Africa

Cheryl McEwan

Ashgate

Aldershot • Burlington USA • Singapore • Sydney

Published by

Ashgate Publishing Ltd
Gower House, Croft Road,
Aldershot, Hampshire GU11 3HR
England

Ashgate Publishing Company
131 Main Street
Burlington, Vermont 05401
USA

Ashgate website: http://www.ashgate.com

ISBN 1 84014 252 9

British Library Cataloguing-in-Publication Data
McEwan, Cheryl
    Gender, geography and empire: Victorian women travellers in west Africa
    1. Women travellers – Africa – History – 19th century
    2. Africa – Description and travel
    I. Title
    916'.0423

US Library of Congress Cataloging-in-Publication Data
Library of Congress Control Number: 00-105244

This volume is printed on acid-free paper.

Printed and bound by Athenaeum Press, Ltd.,
Gateshead, Tyne & Wear.

Contents

List of maps and tables

List of plates

Preface

This book is largely a product of research I undertook while in receipt of a British Academy Scholarship in the Department of Geography, Loughborough University. It is also a product of my revisiting many of the original issues in the intervening years since I completed my thesis in 1995. My original intention was to trace, in some small way, the agencies of women hitherto hidden in histories of imperialism and geography, whilst retaining a critical eye on the production of their imperial and geographical knowledges. In attempting to do so, however, the realization that there are still other histories, other stories to be told, became apparent. This book does not attempt to trace all of these other histories – this would be more than a lifetime's work for a small army of researchers – but it does attempt to hint at where these other histories might lie. It also attempts to raise issues about the relationship between power and knowledge, issues that are of particular pertinence to academics in the contemporary world.

Many thanks and acknowledgements deserve to be made. I am particularly indebted to my supervisors, Dr Morag Bell and Dr Michael Heffernan, whose support, advice and encouragement during my time at Loughborough and in the years since has been invaluable. I also wish to thank Drawing Office Technician Ann Ankcorn (School of Geography, University of Birmingham) for redrawing the maps, and Cathrin Vaughan, Alec McAuley and Ruth Peters at Ashgate for their patience and advice. The research for this book would not have been possible without the assistance of many others in the various institutions in which I have worked. I am especially indebted to Janice Murray at Dundee Museum, who kindly allowed me to invade and colonize her office for three days and provided me with useful sources on Mary Slessor. I am also grateful to Gwynydd Gosling at the Highgate Literary and Scientific Institute, Christine Kelly at the Royal Geographical Society, Iain Flett at Dundee City Archives, Terry Barringer at the Royal Commonwealth Society, Miss K. Penney at Birmingham University Library, Reverend David Grainger (Principal of St Andrew's Hall, Selly Oak), Peter McKenzie (for providing information about Anna Hinderer in personal correspondence), and to the librarians at Rhodes House, Oxford, Cambridge University Library, the South Reading Room at the National Library of Scotland, and the Manuscripts Department of the British Library. I am particularly grateful to Alison Blunt for her characteristic generosity in sharing with me her 'discovery' (courtesy of Mona Domosh) of Beth Urquhart's collection of Mary Kingsley's correspondence in Oregon, USA. Having spent two years attempting to decipher Kingsley's notoriously poor handwriting, the transcripts of these letters were a great help to my research. I consider myself privileged to have had access to this archive, a product of years of conscientious research by Beth Urquhart.

Academic endeavour is not performed in a vacuum, and I am grateful to my colleagues at the University of Birmingham for their collegiality, friendship and support. I am especially grateful to Mike Bradshaw, John Bryson, Peter Daniels, Nick Henry, Jane Pollard, Alison Stenning and Terry Slater for comments and advice that assisted in the production of this book. Finally, and most importantly, I am eternally grateful to my family and friends, especially my parents, for their love, generosity, support and encouragement.

CHAPTER 1

Introduction

I can safely say that there is not a *petticoat* in the whole history (Haggard, 1885, 9).

Opening up a space for excluded voices and counter-traditions – extending the realm of 'legitimate' geographical knowledge – is, of course, a necessary task for any critical history of geography (Driver, 1995, 411).

Situated within the current academic theater of cultural imperialism, with a certain *carte d'entrée* into the elite theoretical *ateliers* ..., I bring news of power lines within the palace (Spivak, 1985, 360).

Rethinking histories of geography

The comment above by Alan Quartermain about the exploration of the African continent in Henry Rider Haggard's *King Solomon's Mines* could, until recently, have referred to the invisibility of women in histories of both geographical thought and British imperialism. However, in recent years there has been a proliferation of studies on the role of women in the British empire, mainly within anthropology, feminist history and feminist literary theory, but increasingly within geography. The role of women in histories of geography and geographical thought, however, remains a relatively neglected sphere of analysis within the discipline of geography. In this context, the aim of this book is to attempt to write a 'feminized' history of British geographical thought and imperial culture, using the specific example of women travellers in west Africa[1] during the nineteenth century.

Histories of geography are continually being recast and retheorized, with authors suggesting new ways of constituting, or challenging the very notion of, the tradition(s) of geographical thought.[2] As the quote from Driver suggests, much of the debate surrounds the definition of the boundaries of tradition. Thus, scholars are exploring the 'spatialization' of tradition (Rose, 1995, 415), and the implications for inclusion in/exclusion from these discursive territories. Of particular concern to feminist geographers, and a major focus of discussion in this book, is the explication of the gendered construction of 'the geographical tradition', the erasure of women and women's voices from histories of geography, and the potential for the recovery of the agency of women in these histories (Domosh, 1991a and b; Rose, 1993 and 1995).

Critical feminist approaches to histories of geography are, by now, well rehearsed.[3] However, Rose (1995, 413) suggests that the current rethinking of geographical traditions, and the questioning of what constitutes geographical knowledge in particular historical settings, has still yet to provide spaces in which women's contributions can be accommodated. Indeed, she writes, 'it seems that, even if we can no longer be certain exactly what geography was in the past, in virtually all histories of geographical knowledges one apparently incontrovertible fact remains: geography, whatever it was, was almost always done by men'. Rose argues that there is a critical dilemma for feminists trying to incorporate women into histories of geography. Women can be integrated into the discursive spaces of geographical traditions, only to become the same; the importance of gender difference is erased. Alternatively, women can be located outside the territory of tradition and their difference celebrated. The latter tends to reiterate essentialist definitions of masculinity and femininity. It is also one which, in its tendency to claim women travellers as proto-feminists, struggles to locate them in a critical, rather than celebratory, historiography. The erasure of the historical agency of the colonized subject in the production of imperial geographical knowledges further compounds these problems.

Much recent work on critical histories of geography has been inspired by the Foucauldian notion of the relationship between power and knowledge. In particular, as Barnett (1995, 418) argues, there has been 'an overwhelming, although not exclusive' fascination with the relationship between modern European geography and European imperialism. Arguments about constructing feminist histories have also drawn on examples from this period (Domosh 1991a and b). This work has been important in challenging the masculinist construction of histories of geography and suggesting the agency of white women in the creation of imperial geographies. It is clear that the masculinist nature of the discipline of geography has serious consequences for what is regarded as legitimate geographical knowledge and who can produce this knowledge. In order to create discursive spaces for the inclusion of women in histories of geography, it is therefore imperative to reconceptualize these histories. Stoddart (1991, 485) suggests that 'the contribution of women to the emergence and development of geography as a formal academic discipline' would be more relevant to a feminist historiography. There is certainly scope for this and increasingly work has been undertaken in this field (Bell and McEwan, 1996; Mander, 1995; Ploszajska, 1995). However, Stoddart's delimitation of the discursive boundaries of geography produces a definition that is both epistemologically narrow and contestable. As Blunt points out, institutions outside the academy were important in shaping views of women and their travels and produced a wider constituency for geographical knowledge. Rose's suggestion that a strategy is required to unsettle the traditional boundaries of geography and to create new spaces is both radical and holds out the potential of producing more inclusive histories of the discipline. The real problem, it seems, in (re)writing histories of geography lies with the apparent need to position women (and other 'subaltern' and marginalized groups) and their 'knowledges' at various historical junctures within or beyond the 'tradition', or within an alternative 'tradition'. The fact remains that women travellers, for example, were not geographers, nor did they define themselves as such. It seems illogical, therefore, to have to define alternative geographies to allow their voices to be heard. More important is the fact that they were writing and being read and, even more importantly, they were writing differently and often in highly original ways. Gregory's (1995) approach of exploring the constellation of power, knowledge and spatiality and, in the case of the nineteenth century, ideas about empire, race and femininity in various narratives suggests a more productive approach rather than the constant and laborious struggle to position these texts as 'geography'. The narratives themselves, their popularity and their consumption are of importance, not their position *vis-à-vis* the 'tradition' of geography, however the latter might be defined. A critical approach would eradicate essentialist approaches to 'women travel writers' and gendered genres of writing by exploring the gendered and racialized context of specific imperial encounters. In what follows I suggest strategies for how one might write a critical feminist account of geography and imperialism. These strategies not only attempt to deal with some of the problems and contradictions inherent in feminist analyses of empire, travel writing and geography, but also attempt to reveal the eurocentrism which is rarely problematized in these accounts. I wish not only to problematize the authority of colonial discourse, but also to detail some of the ways in which imperialism has constructed narratives of geography and gender. This account, therefore, is an attempt to combine feminist and postcolonial approaches in constructing a more critical version of geography and imperialism in the nineteenth century.

(Re)writing histories of geography: critical interventions

Moving beyond geography: women travellers as writers

Writers such as Driver (1990), Hudson (1977), Livingstone (1992) and Said (1990) have pointed out that the history of British geography during the late nineteenth century is intimately related to the history of British imperialism. During the nineteenth century the empire was perceived as a masculine preserve and the literature of empire was a male-dominated, heroic literature. Consequently, analyses of the history of the empire have often failed to account for the role of women as agents of British imperialism. As Melman (1992, 1) argues:

> Historians and students of culture alike relegate women to the periphery of imperialist culture and the tradition of 'empire', the assumption being that the

female experience of the Western expansion and domination outside Europe had been subsumed in hegemonic and homogeneously patriarchal tradition.

According to Callaway (1987, 3), the history of empire was very often the 'history of the greats'; its male figures were imbued with courage, fortitude and heroism. Empire was the preserve of the great explorers, the big game hunters and the adventurers who pitted their manhood against the hazards of unexplored lands (Oliver 1982, 189). As Russell (1988, 213) argues, there existed a powerful parallel between geographical conquest and sexual conquest; landscapes were feminized, penetrated, assaulted, conquered and subdued. The empire was also a sexual playground for European men, free of the stifling morality of Victorian Britain, a public, masculine domain exclusive of white women.[4] These imperial views on gender were informed by the belief system of a patriarchal Victorian Britain. Social Darwinism, evolutionary anthropology, medical tracts and treatises on psychology, the myth of chivalry, 'muscular' Christianity, boys adventure stories and the literary tradition of empire all contributed to the assumption of the superiority of the English gentleman (Callaway, 1987, 3). Attitudes in Britain towards race, social class and gender were intrinsic in this assumption; women, non-Europeans, the working classes, the deviant and the mentally ill all belonged to the realm of the 'other', metaphorically and physically excluded from the world of the Victorian gentleman. In the case of women, not only did Victorian notions of femininity and financial restrictions prohibit them from travelling abroad alone, the colonial governments and private businesses also prevented their access to the empire by refusing employment to married men. According to Ann Laura Stoler (1991, 61), marriage restrictions in Africa, India and South East Asia lasted well into the twentieth century.

Despite these restrictions, from the mid-nineteenth century onwards an increasing number of women took to travelling abroad, writing books about their experiences and presenting lectures at meetings of philanthropic, church and missionary groups, and very occasionally at some of the less formalized learned societies. Many Victorians viewed lone women travellers as oddities, eccentric 'globetrotteresses' with little to contribute to scientific and geographical knowledge. Even publishers and editors of the travel narratives were dismissive of the achievements of these women. For example, William Carey's introduction to Annie Taylor's diary of her journey to Tibet, which he edited and published, presents her trek as 'quaintly pathetic in its simplicity and ... richly amusing in its unpreparedness'. Taylor is reduced to 'a plucky and resourceful woman ... an unsophisticated pilgrim'.[5] As Callaway (ibid.) argues, where women were mentioned in contemporaneous accounts of British imperialism, particularly in the anti-colonialist literature, emphasis was placed on the wives of colonial administrators and officials as representations of the worst aspects of colonialism: its racism, snobbery and eurocentrism. Only those women travellers who were seen to remain within the boundaries of acceptable feminine behaviour, such as nurses and the wives of missionaries, were given any credence, Florence Nightingale being the prime example (Middleton, 1973, 66).[6]

The legacy of these attitudes is still to be seen in some relatively recent accounts of Victorian women travellers. For example, in her account of women adventurers, Maria Aitken (1987, 9) argues that although women did not travel frivolously, 'their vagaries are amusing now'. Accounts of such 'vagaries' add spice to already colourful biographies, but at the same time underestimate the contribution of women to British imperial culture and overlook the part they played in the production of imperial knowledges. The women remain amusing oddities on the peripheries of imperial experience, and it is their extraordinary lives that provide the context for analysis rather than their contribution to British imperial culture.[7] In addition, as Birkett (1992) argues throughout her biography of Mary Kingsley, women who travelled alone outside Britain are perceived by their biographers as victims of nineteenth-century attitudes towards women, as daring explorers, or as feminist heroines. The major achievement of women travellers in such accounts seems to be their apparent defiance of contemporary conventions regarding the supposed role of women; they are hailed as proto-feminists. Mills argues that although increasing attention has been paid to the texts of women travel writers, much of this has focused upon the women themselves as individual rebels against the constraints of Victorian society. There has thus been little exploration of the relations between the women and the territories through which they travelled, and their part in the production of imperial knowledges.

The restrictions on women's access to the empire were paralleled in Britain by restrictions upon their entry to learned societies. Many senior figures in the Royal Geographical Society were resolutely opposed to women Fellows. The Society flirted with the issue of women's admittance in 1892 and 1893, when a total of twenty-two women were elected, but the doors were closed again immediately; it was only in 1913 that the R.G.S. finally admitted women fellows on the same grounds as men.[8] George Lord Curzon in a letter to *The Times* succinctly expressed its attitude towards women fellows at the end of the nineteenth century:

> We contest *in toto* the general capability of women to contribute to scientific geographical knowledge. Their sex and training render them equally unfitted for exploration, and the genus of professional female globetrotteresses ... is one of the horrors of the latter end of the nineteenth century.[9]

It is not simply, as Domosh argues, that the legacy of such attitudes has meant that women have tended to be written out of, or peripheralized in, the histories of both geography and the British empire. The reason for this may also lie with the women themselves. As Stoddart (1991) has argued, it is difficult to incorporate women travel writers into histories of geography precisely because these women did not consider themselves geographers, nor were they remotely interested in anything that may be regarded as geography in the narrow sense. Furthermore, a particular problematic in writing feminist histories of geography has been the apparent need to claim women travellers in a disciplinary sense in order that they be located in the 'geographical tradition(s)'. A critical feminist approach need not concern itself with such myopic considerations. It is widely acknowledged that women, for the greater part, did not contribute to the 'heroic' history of economic and political imperialism. They did not discover, explore and conquer new lands, nor did they play a significant role in the establishment of academic geography towards the end of the nineteenth century. Despite recognition of their exclusion from the traditions and practice of scientific geography, however, the experiences of nineteenth-century women are nonetheless of relevance to the histories of geography and imperialism. On the one hand, British women were actively involved in the British empire as sponsors of expeditions or as critics in Britain, or as travellers, missionaries and the wives of administrators operating within the empire. In a few cases women were able to influence imperial policy.[10] On the other hand, women (and women travellers, in particular) made notable contributions to imperial discourse during the nineteenth century. Their status as writers, rather than their place in 'heroic' histories of geography, lends significance to the works of women travellers.

Recent years have witnessed a renewed interest, particularly in literary theory, in travel writing; as Kowalewski (1992, 6) argues, 'the signs of an invigorated contemporary interest in travel are everywhere to be seen'. Of particular relevance here is the fact that this interest has, to some extent, captured the attention of geographers, and several have made the case for seeing travel writing, both contemporary and historical, as a form of geography (for example, Barnes and Duncan, 1992; Bishop, 1989; Crush, 1995; Gregory, 1995). The inspiration for the recognition of both the enduring appeal of travel writing as a mode of representation,[11] and of the overlaps between geography as a discipline and travel-writing as a poetic, imaginative and occasionally 'scientific' genre of literature was Edward Said's *Orientalism* (1978). Said constructs a critical reading of what he refers to as 'imaginative geographies', the complex production of images of lands and peoples beyond Europe which were reproduced in accounts of the voyages of discovery and journeys of exploration, and in travel narratives. As Gregory (1995, 29) argues:

> For Said, imaginative geographies are discursive formations, tense constellations of power, knowledge and spatiality, that are centred on 'here' and projected towards 'there' so that 'the vacant or anonymous reaches of distance are converted into meaning for us here' ... This fed into his critique of Orientalism as a discourse that worked through a representation of space in which the Orient was constructed as a theatrical stage on which the Occident projected its own fantasies and desires.

Thus, the construction of imaginative geographies was fundamental to the imperial discourse of Orientalism, and travel writers played a significant role in the creation of these imaginative geographies. They were an important element in maintaining and affirming colonial relations. Blunt (1994, 30) argues that, 'Travel writing was particularly important in imperial literary traditions because individual Europeans travelled between colonized and colonizing worlds, perpetuating mythological otherness'. Drawing on Said's *Orientalism*, Bishop (1989, 3) makes the point that, 'Above all, travel accounts are involved in the production of imaginative knowledges. They are an important aspect of a culture's myth-making, yet this perspective is frequently overlooked'. To represent the world is a political as well as an aesthetic-cognitive activity. According to Porter (1991, 14–15):

> From the beginning writers of travel have more or less unconsciously made it their purpose to take a fix on and thereby fix the world in which they found themselves; they are engaged in a form of cultural cartography that is impelled by an anxiety to map the globe, center it on a certain point, produce explanatory narratives, and assign fixed identities to regions and the races that inhabit them. Such representations are always concerned with questions of place and placing, of situating oneself once and for all vis-a-vis an Other or others ...

Thus the discursive construction of places beyond Europe through such narrative forms as travel writings were located within the wider struggle by Europeans to redefine global geography and their own place within it. Furthermore, the operations of global capitalism during the nineteenth century cannot be isolated from colonial discourse. Indeed, Young (1995, 169–70) depicts capitalism as a 'territorial writing machine' which:

> ... describes rather exactly the violent physical and ideological procedures of colonization, deculturation and acculturation, by which the territory and cultural space of an indigenous society must be disrupted, dissolved and then reinscribed according to the needs of the apparatus of the occupying power.

The construction of imaginative geographies through such media as travel texts was fundamental to this process. Travel texts are of particular interest to geographers because of their role in territorial inscription and processes of othering, but also because, by their personal nature, 'they are a unique record of a culture's imaginative life' (Bishop, 1989, 7). Mary Louise Pratt (1992) has elucidated how imperial travel writing varied over time and space. Travel narratives draw together geography and literature, and the strategies of representation contained within nineteenth-century travel accounts thus present a valuable insight into the changing nature of British imperial culture.

In the wake of Said's *Orientalism* there is now a wide literature within geography which details the important role of travel writing in the creation of imaginative geographies of empire, and in strategies of imperialism (for example, Blunt, 1994, Driver, 1992, Gregory, 1995). As Richards (1993, 21) argues, '[G]eography was a necessary but not sufficient tool for realizing territory. It must always be accompanied by the imperatives of state ethnography, which territorialize a domain not only by mapping it but by producing all manner of 'thick' description about it'. Although they were excluded from academic geography and were, for a long time, denied access to the R.G.S., women travellers contributed to this 'thick' description of imperial territories, and to imperial discourses more widely. Their writings informed the imaginations of people who could not witness the empire at first hand. It is difficult to gauge the impact of narratives by women travellers on popular imaginations and opinions in Britain (this is discussed in detail in Chapter 3). Their narratives were not written to have any great bearing on imperial policy, although the women did occasionally express their views on British imperialism in west Africa. Ultimately most remained marginal within the sphere of British imperial culture. However, they contributed to a very popular body of imperial literature, and the narratives were of interest because they were written by women who had, in some way, transgressed accepted boundaries simply by travelling in west Africa and publishing their experiences. Their publications formed part of a much wider literature constructing the complex and enduring metaphor of the 'dark continent'. They are an invaluable source for the exploration of ideas about femininity, empire, race and so on at the end of the nineteenth century, and provide insight into the ways in which women played an active part in the construction of these ideas through the popular medium of travel writing. They are thus of significance in considering histories of geographical thought in the nineteenth century.

Moving beyond essentialism

Early feminist epistemologies of both history and geography have been roundly criticized for conceptualizing 'women' as a unitary category. It is imperative that analyses of the writings of women travellers avoid celebrating proto-feminist heroines and forsaking a critical understanding of the part they played in imperialism and the production of imperial knowledges. Perhaps most obviously, it is necessary to deconstruct the category of 'woman travel writer'. The women referred to in this account all travelled and wrote about their experiences, but not all were travel writers per se. It is important to recognize that the experiences of empire of British women were often distinct from their male counterparts, and were also very different to the experiences of colonized women. However, this should not construct a singular, essential 'feminine' experience to be contrasted with a singular, essential 'masculine' experience. As Mills (1994, 29–30) argues, it is possible to suggest that although the writing of women and men was not always fundamentally different, knowledges produced within a variety of imperial contexts, both in terms of how they were written and how they were judged, were profoundly gendered.[12] Femininity was a complex and contested arena, a fractured and disputed state in which women that travelled and wrote in the empire had an important and even formative role to play. Particular forms of British femininity arose in the late nineteenth century born of overseas, and in this case west African, travel. Thus, I would argue, it becomes more relevant to produce a nuanced reading of gendered imperial knowledges. Such a reading would acknowledge the importance of other relationships of power shaping the authorial identity (class, ethnicity, sexuality etc.), and draw out the differences between white women's experiences and narratives, rather than seek for similarities in order to posit a distinct genre of writing.

Travel writings by white women were positioned geographically, metaphorically and metaphysically between the dominant culture and the 'wild zone'.[13] While both men and women have occupied these margins in literary production, they have been positioned there in very different ways. In addition, there were differences between women in how they occupied these margins, which in turn produced significant variations in their texts. While there are similarities based on gender in the narratives of women travellers in west Africa, their writings were also shaped by class differences, and they varied according to the time period in which they were written. It is a misnomer to presume that overseas travel by women was exclusively a 'middle-class phenomenon' (Melman, 1992, 35). As this account demonstrates, aristocratic women travelled in the empire. Missionaries, missionaries' wives, and the wives of colonial administrators were not exclusively middle class. Differences in social class had profound influences on the ways in which women travellers related to the peoples and landscapes of west Africa, and on how these were represented in their subsequent publications. Thus, while I accept Young's proposition that colonial discourse was intimately related to the machinations of global capitalism, I would suggest that to depict it as a product of a particular (bourgeois) class, working to the benefit of that particular class, is to oversimplify matters. Women travellers of different class were positioned in very different ways within the British empire, and this had a bearing on the narratives they produced.

Mills (1994, 32) has argued that the stress on difference within colonial discourse is important in that it enables emphasis of the specificity of each imperial relation. As Said (1994, xxiv) argues, 'authors are ... very much in the history of their societies, shaping and shaped by that history and their social experience in different measure'. The recognition of this facilitates an understanding of the often quite marked differences apparent in the attitudes of white women travellers in west Africa, and in their representations of the landscapes and peoples that they encountered. It allows a recognition that their texts are gendered, but in ways that are more complex than merely as essentially 'feminine'. It also favours a deconstruction of the notion of the singular 'Other'[14] by allowing for the possibility of the textual construction of multiple others. However, while a stress on difference within colonial discourse is imperative for a nuanced interpretation, there is perhaps also a need to hold something(s) constant in order for realistic comparisons of the narratives to be made. As Bell (1995, 189) argues, studies which seek to reinterpret relations between geography, gender and empire benefit from a more geographical approach; emphasis should shift away from women travellers as a category to specific regions in their imperial setting and the activities of particular women in these settings. Such an approach allows an exploration of the complexities of both the travel narratives of women travellers and of the evolution of British imperial culture.[15] In focusing on west Africa, this book explores the intricacies in Britain's relationship with this part of the continent throughout the latter half of the nineteenth century, and how it was understood and represented in a variety of ways in Britain over this time period. It also attempts to avoid creating myths about the myths of the so-called 'dark continent'. As Youngs (1994) argues, critics of nineteenth-century images of Africa tend to elide the differences in representations of disparate parts of the continent. In their efforts to trace the genealogy of the myth of the 'dark continent', different historical and geographical relationships between imperial metropoli and their colonial territories are ignored. This study focuses upon west Africa, which had unique historical and geographical relationships with, in this case, Britain, and was represented quite differently to east, central and southern Africa. In addition, by recognising the numerous and ever-evolving contexts in which women travelled in and wrote about west Africa from the 1840s onwards, one can begin to explore the complexities in the narratives themselves, and to understand why differences and similarities exist in representations of west Africa by women travellers.

Representation, 'whiteness' and authority

As early feminist epistemologies of history and geography have been criticized for conceptualizing 'women' as a unitary category, so critics have argued that the feminist and post-imperial rediscovery of women's writing and history has effectively erased race from the arena of discussion (Haggis, 1990; Noor, 1996). Thus, the 'adding on' of women's experiences and knowledge has done little to disrupt the structural inequalities in the writing of histories of empire, nor does it challenge the ways in which the past is constituted discursively. It is crucial, therefore, while locating women in histories of geography to question the very basis of that history, and to remain critical about the knowledges that were produced. Much criticism of this nature has emanated from within postcolonial theory. [16]

Critical feminist histories can engage postcolonialism by exploring the racialized positions of white women. It is clear that white women were placed ambiguously within the process of imperialism. As McClintock (1996, 6) argues:

> Whether they were shipped out as convicts or conscripted into sexual and domestic servitude; whether they served discreetly at the elbow of power as colonial officers' wives, upholding the boundaries of empire and bearing its sons and daughters; whether they ran missionary schools or hospital wards in remote outposts or worked their husbands shops and farms, colonial women made none of the direct economic or military decisions of empire and very few reaped its vast profits.

However, white women travellers during the nineteenth century were, in many and varying ways, complicit in imperialism; their own liberation was facilitated by the oppression of others. Again, according to McClintock (ibid.):

> ... the rationed privileges of race all too often put white women in positions of decided – if borrowed – power; not only over colonized women but also over colonized men. As such, white women were not the hapless onlookers of empire but were ambiguously complicit both as colonizers and colonized, privileged and restricted, acted upon and acting.

The power, valorization and experience of whiteness of women travellers thus requires serious critical attention.[17] As Williams and Chrisman (1993, 17) argue, discussion of ethnicity is always also by implication a discussion of gender and sexuality. As the biological 'carriers' of the 'race' (Davin, 1978) women occupy a primary and complex role in representations of ethnicity, and it is often their sexuality which is a major concern underlying these representations. As this study demonstrates, women travellers were on occasions critical of British imperialism, but it must be borne in mind that their narratives were constituted by the imperial moment and by their experience of their whiteness. This point can be illustrated by white women's access to colonized women, and subsequent portrayals of the latter by the former (this is discussed in Chapter 7). Scholars have used these portrayals to destabilize assumptions of a homogeneous colonial gaze (Callaway, 1987) and to suggest alternative representations which were cross-cut by the shifting terms of race, nation and gender (Lewis, 1996). While there is obvious merit in such a strategy, particularly in bringing women to the centre of the historical stage as both actors and subjects, this needs to be woven with a more critical account that reveals colonialism as a problem of power, exploitation and oppression (see Haggis, 1990; Melman, 1992; Ong, 1988). The contact between white women and their colonized counterparts created the possibility of totally unequal and dependent relationships in which British women helped to define themselves, and to define and describe the conditions under which colonized women lived, as well as the nature of those women themselves. That British women had access to women in west Africa was important in claiming authority in the construction of the sexuality of the colonized other; the authority of the female gaze was thus grounded in its presumed gendered experience (Lewis, 1996, Melman, 1992, Ware, 1992).

Critical feminist strategies of reading the texts of nineteenth-century women travellers have proved to be problematic. As Gikandi (1996, 121) argues, 'students of colonial discourse and postcolonial theory do not know what to do with the women of empire'. Rose's (1995) critical dilemma for feminists trying to incorporate women into histories of geography (either by erasing gender difference or by locating them outside the discipline) is complicated by a further paradox when reading the feminine in the culture of imperialism:

> We want to read woman as the absolute other in the colonial relation so that we can unpack the universalism of the imperial narrative and its masculine ideologies, but the result (positing white women as figures of colonial alterity, for example) can be achieved only through the institutionalization of the dominant discourse of empire and the authority of colonial culture (Gikandi, 122).

The ambivalent location of white women in what Gikandi (122–3) terms the 'colonial economy of representation' has created a 'complicity/resistance' dialectic,[18] whereby the empire paradoxically became the setting for increased opportunities and liberation for women who, given their subordinate positions in the metropoles, found it impossible to unconditionally valorize the imperial voice. This paradox has created anxieties for much of the critical writing growing out of this dialectic. As Gikandi (123) argues, the desire to reclaim imperial women as subjects who challenged dominant gender norms in the nineteenth century (and this period is where much of the critical writing has been focused)[19] is 'haunted by the fear that by valorizing the positive function of empire in the constitution of female subjectivity, we might mitigate the ideologies of white supremacy embedded in the theory and practice of imperialism'. One of the foremost postcolonial theorists, Spivak (1986), has suggested that mainstream feminism has not found a way to resolve this dilemma.[20] One way in which this dilemma may be dealt with, however, is to read women's narratives both as products of colonial cultures and the discursive field of imperialism, and as instrumental in changing discourses on colonial spaces and, by extension, the domestic sphere. In this way, we can accept Mills' proposition that these texts 'both disclose the nature of the dominant discourses and constitute a critique from its margins' (1991, 23). Freed from the 'complicity/resistance' dialectic, one can begin to explore ways of producing critical feminist readings of the texts of

British women travellers, and it is this approach that I adopt in reading the narratives of British women in nineteenth-century west Africa.

Disrupting Eurocentrism: historical agency and the resistance of colonized others

One of the more significant challenges to white feminism has come from women variously described as 'women of colour', 'Third World women', 'black women' and 'indigenous women'. These groups of women have challenged the assumptions of western/white women's movements that all women share some universal characteristics and suffer from universal oppressions, which can be understood and described by a group of predominantly white, western-trained women academics. Issues of 'voice' and 'visibility', 'silence' and 'invisibility' have become increasingly important in debates about research and the emancipatory potential of research. As Tuhiwai Smith (1999, 166) suggests, it has been recognized that there is considerable work to be done in terms of undoing or deconstructing the dominant paradigms by which most academic research and writing is constructed. This involves critique, the development of new methodologies, and the possibilities of alternative ways of knowing or epistemologies. As suggested above, this challenge to western feminism, therefore, has greatly informed postcolonial strategies in both research and critical theory, and holds out potential for disrupting Eurocentrism.

Postcolonial strategies might be deployed in other ways to those suggested above in reading imperial travel narratives by British women. Recent interrogations of histories of British geography have articulated the need to disrupt either the patriarchal or the eurocentric construction of these histories. More broadly, just as western feminism often fails to recognize its Eurocentrism, so those postcolonial theorists critiquing eurocentrism very often do not account for the importance of gender.[21] Discursive space has not been created in which these two critiques can be combined, either within postcolonial theory or within geography. Histories of geography are not only masculinist in their construction, they are also Eurocentric.[22] Thus, in the light of recent critiques which fall under the broad rubric of postcolonialism, this book attempts to explore a problem which has yet to figure in any large measure in debates concerning critical histories of geography; that is, the question of the place of Europe's 'others' (especially colonized 'others') in histories of a putatively western discipline.[23] While feminist critiques have been important in challenging the masculinist construction of histories of geography and suggesting the agency of white women in the creation of imperial geographies, they are problematic in that they continue to privilege the 'west' as the site of the production of geographical knowledge. They thus deny the possibilities of the historical agency of the colonized. In order to counter these hegemonic histories we need to unsettle 'notions of the modern geographical enterprise being solely the product of metropolitan energies and initiative' (Barnett, 1998). As Sidaway (1997) argues, the narration of the history of 'western' geography tends to suggest that the origins of these knowledges are located solely in the west, and thus ignores the contribution of 'non-western' geographical knowledges in their formulation. Here, as with paternal renderings of the history of the discipline, the problem lies with the ways in which boundaries are drawn to determine what does and does not constitute geographical knowledge. Attempts to uncover the ways in which British women travellers, for example, contributed to the production of geographical knowledges within imperial culture runs the risk of re-privileging the former imperial powers as the producers of this knowledge. Colonial representations by white women might be read critically, but the imperial gaze is still privileged and the voice of the colonized 'other' remains silent. Thus, in Chapter 7, drawing on the intersections between feminist, postmodernist and postcolonialist debates in geography,[24] I present some suggestions on how discursive spaces might be opened up to reveal multiple agents in the production of imperial geographies, whilst simultaneously acknowledging the problems such a strategy presents. In doing so, I bear in mind Barnett's (1997, 137) caution that questions about institutional positionality and academic authority should be kept squarely in sight when discussing the problems of representing the struggles and agency of marginalized social groups. Thus, in addition to revealing the 'power lines within the palace' of academic geography which continue to construct exclusionary histories, I will also suggest ways in which the notion of a putatively western (and, by implication, masculine) geographical tradition might be disrupted, while acknowledging that this critique itself is situated squarely within western academia.

Spivak's concern with revealing the ways in which power and knowledge are intimately related and, in particular, the epistemic and actual violence of writing out the agency of the colonized in histories of imperialism, seems to have a great deal of resonance with the concern of feminists in recovering the agency of white women in the production of geography. A deconstructive reading of the narratives of women travellers in west Africa might allow, to some extent, for recovery of the agency of the colonized subject, both within the theatre of imperial culture and in the production of geographical knowledges. It might also reveal alternative layers of meaning rather than singular expressions of interests and desires. It is impossible to avoid privileging the authorial voice in exploring (albeit critically) representations of colonized peoples and landscapes by white women; however, this does not preclude the exploration of resistance to their presence, nor of subaltern agency in the formulation of their geographies, evidence of which is quite clearly contained in their narratives (see Chapter 7). This deconstructive approach also facilitates a response to the contemporary concerns within geography and related disciplines over the use and reproduction of both visual and textual images.[25] Several geographers, primarily those working on historical geographies of imperialism and on contemporary Third World issues, have been accused of 're-presenting' racist images, both visual and

14

textual, in the course of their presentations and publications, thus perpetuating racism, ethnocentrism and colonial productions of knowledge. David Livingstone (1998) has dealt with these criticisms, and his arguments are pertinent here. In exploring the texts of white women travellers and the imperial knowledges that they constructed, the aim is not to present the images they contained as 'authentic' or 'inauthentic', but to unravel, understand and explain the discursive strategies of power contained within them. It is only by recognising and analysing these discursive strategies, and challenging the manifestation of these in travel narratives, that a critical understanding of women's role in British imperial culture can be achieved.

Aims and context

In the light of the theoretical positions outlined above, the perceived relationship between travel narratives and geography, and of the differences in imperial travel writing over time and space, I use the example of women travellers in west Africa during the nineteenth century to explore three primary objectives. First, I consider the possibilities of transcending disciplinary boundaries to reveal the ways in which women writers may have contributed to geographical knowledge. Second, in the light of recent critiques of attempts to write feminist histories, I suggest ways in which one might produce a less essentialist and more critical reading of the geographies women produced. Finally, I suggest possibilities for recovering the agency of white women whilst simultaneously allowing for the agency of the colonial subject in the making of their geographies. In attempting the latter, I also confront the dilemmas and contradictions in acknowledging simultaneously the agency of 'first world' women and that of subaltern groups.

British imperialism in nineteenth-century west Africa

The nature of British imperialism in west Africa underwent fundamental changes in the course of the nineteenth century.[26] The motives behind economic and cultural imperialism evolved from campaigns to suppress slavery, to attempts by British traders to establish legitimate trade, by British missionaries and others to Christianize west Africa, and the establishment of a vast formal empire towards the end of the century. During this period the image of Africa in the imaginations of many Victorians was transformed. Brantlinger (1985) has referred to this transformation as the 'genealogy of the myth of the Dark Continent', and suggests that it said more about the needs and desires of Victorian middle- and upper-class society than it did about Africa. Brantlinger elides differences in representations of different parts of Africa (which, as discussed earlier, were represented quite differently according to different geographical and historical relationships). However, despite this tendency to assume a monolithic European myth of the 'dark continent', his arguments are still persuasive. The creation of myths about Africa were not only a part of a larger imperialist discourse that was shaped by political and economic pressures, they were also a product of the psychology of many Victorians and their desire to maintain a sense of cultural dominance. As Brantlinger (ibid., 166–7) argues, 'For middle- and upper-class Victorians, dominant over a vast working-class majority at home and over increasing millions of 'uncivilized' peoples of 'inferior' races abroad, power was self-validating'. In Britain, this power might have been threatened by Chartism, trade unionism and the working classes, but in imperialist discourse the culture of the 'conquering race' seemed unthreatened, since the voices of the dominated were absent and silent. Thus:

> Africa grew 'dark' as Victorian explorers, missionaries, and scientists flooded it with light, because the light was refracted through an imperialist ideology that urged the abolition of 'savage customs' in the name of civilisation. As a product of that ideology, the myth of the Dark Continent developed during the transition from the main British campaign against the slave trade, which culminated in the outlawing of slavery in all British territory in 1833, to the imperialist partitioning of Africa which dominated the final quarter of the nineteenth century (ibid., 166).

Myths about the 'dark continent' evolved in Britain in parallel with the changing nature of Britain's involvement in west Africa. Therefore, an understanding of evolving British imagery of Africa during the nineteenth century, and its complex relationship with the changing nature of British imperialism and of Victorian society, provides a useful context for a diachronic study of British women travellers in west Africa. The women of this study travelled in west Africa in every decade between 1840 and 1915, and their narratives can thus be considered within the context of the prevailing ideas of the time. This, in turn, provides a context for understanding the differences in their representations of west Africa, their contributions to popular images of west Africa, and their participation in British imperial culture.

British women travellers in west Africa

West Africa was a part of the British empire that seemed to have an extraordinarily masculine history. It was the setting for the great explorations of the mid-nineteenth century; it was not colonized in any large part until well into the twentieth century; and white women were not present in large numbers in west Africa during the preceding century. Few European women lived or travelled in west Africa, and fewer still wrote and published travel accounts during the nineteenth century. This fact made simple the selection of those women to be included in the study; the women included here are seven of only nine I have found to have travelled in west Africa between 1840 and 1915 and to have published accounts of their experiences.[27] The primary sources of the study are the written narratives by these women in which they recount their experiences. These include both published and unpublished narratives and, in particular, published accounts of their travels, journal articles, private correspondences, reports in missionary magazines, and newspaper articles. I include women labelled 'travel-writers' (in other words those who travelled purely for their own pleasure or to publish accounts of their experiences), and women who travelled to, and in, the British empire to undertake specific duties (missionaries, missionaries' wives, and the wives of judicial and military administrators), who also published books and articles about their experiences abroad. The distinction between the two types of woman traveller is an important one; for the former, travel itself was the primary goal, whereas for the latter, west Africa became a temporary home, their duties were paramount, and travel was of secondary importance.[28] The analysis centres on the travel narratives of Elizabeth Melville, Mrs Henry Grant Foote, Zélie Colvile and Constance Larymore, who were all colonial residents, missionaries Anna Hinderer and Mary Slessor, and the traveller and explorer Mary Kingsley.[29] As Table 1 illustrates, each of these women was very different. They hailed from varying backgrounds, had different reasons for travelling to west Africa and spent varying amounts of time there. Their narratives were informed by different geographical, temporal and imperial contexts.

In what follows I explore the visions of west Africa in these travel accounts in relation to contemporaneous constructions of Africa as the 'dark continent'. The discussion focuses on four principal themes recurring throughout these narratives: representations of landscapes, 'race', customs and women in west Africa. The study is organized around these themes because they represent some of the primary topics of discussion in the travel narratives concerned. The politics of imperialism are important in providing a context for the journeys of British women, and these women were clearly influenced by the imperial ethos of the time. However, politics do not form one of the themes of the later chapters because women travellers, on the whole, did not engage in political debates or commentary. The women of this study wrote in a manner that was acceptable to their readers and, for the most part, avoided entering into political and scientific debate. This, of course, is not to argue that these topics were completely proscribed; women could, and did, make mention of these debates. For example, there were occasional references in these travelogues to the positive effects of British economic and political imperialism on west Africa (see Chapter 2), and Mary Kingsley consciously transgressed the boundaries into the arena of political and scientific debate, although such transgressions occurred primarily in her later writings. Indeed, Kingsley adopted several masculine personae (explorer, trader, ichthyologist, anthropologist) to lend credence to her opinions and arguments on the state of British imperialism in west Africa. Mary Slessor also used her position in west Africa to become politicized in terms of her opinions of, and reaction to, mission policies. However, most of the women of this study, including Kingsley and Slessor, chose to produce passage after passage of description of the physical environment, racial characteristics and cultural practices of the peoples they encountered.

Of importance, therefore, are the external factors influencing the content of women's travel narratives. For example, unlike many male travellers, women travellers generally did not write in the 'quest' genre. They did not discover,

Table 1 Bibliographical information on British women travellers to west Africa, 1840–1915

Traveller	Dates	Destination	Dates of Travels	Reason for Journey	Social Class
Elizabeth Melville	? (no data available)	Sierra Leone	1840–46	Wife of colonial judge	Aristocratic
Anna Hinderer	1827–70	Ibadan (Yorubaland)	1852–69	Wife of missionary	Middle class
Mrs Henry Grant Foote	? (no data available)	Lagos	1861	Wife of colonial consul	Middle class
Mary Slessor	1848–1915	Calabar/ Southern Nigeria	1876–1915	Missionary	Working class
Zélie Colvile	? (no data available)	Oil Rivers and the West Coast	1889	Wife of Acting Commissioner (Uganda)	Aristocratic
Mary Kingsley	1862–1900	Sierra Leone, Gold Coast, European W. African territories	1892–95	Independent traveller/ explorer	Middle class (working class mother)
Constance Larymore	? (no data available)	Northern/ Southern Nigeria	1901–07	Wife of colonial military officer	Middle class

explore, and claim tracts of territory for Britain, and, for the most part, did not travel through uncharted land (although Mary Kingsley crossed uncharted territory between the Ogowé and Rembwé rivers, and Mary Slessor lived and travelled in the unexplored forests of northern Calabar). As Mills (1991, 7 and 106–7) points out, constraints on both the production and reception of the text ensured that the 'quest' genre of travel writing was not an option for women, and most chose to avoid this style of writing. If their narratives were to be credible within the confines of the conventions of the time, women travellers could not be seen to be adopting masculine roles in the course of their travels and there was a need constantly to emphasize their femininity in their accounts. This is a major reason for the absence of political observations and commentary in their accounts. The fact of their presence in west Africa, and of their position as travellers, could in itself have been construed as transgressive in terms of the construction of conventional gender roles during the nineteenth century. However, in order to emphasize their femininity and stress the credibility of their narratives, women travellers modified their texts by disclaimers and interjections of humour, or by stressing the difficulties of travel, rather than adopting the position of the adventure hero. Therefore, as is discussed in subsequent chapters, tensions and ambivalence often characterized the travelogues of white women in west Africa.

Chapter 2 explores the impact of women writers on British imperialism and their empowerment through travel and travel writing. This allows some judgement on whether white women travellers were marginal within the sphere of British imperialism or whether their views had some popular, if not political, impact. Subsequent chapters explore in detail the responses of white women travellers to west Africa and the visions they created in their travel narratives. Chapter 3 explores their relationships with the physical environments and the ways in which they challenged, confirmed or were ambivalent towards prevailing nineteenth-century images of the tropical environment as pandemonium. The prominence of landscape descriptions in travel narratives by women are explored, as are the reasons underlying the differences in their representations of west African landscapes. Chapter 4 examines the attitudes of women travellers towards 'race' during the nineteenth century. On the one hand it analyses how they responded to the wider philosophical and scientific debates about 'race' in general; on the other, it explores their opinions about west Africans. Closely related to the portrayals of 'race' by women travellers were their depictions of west African customs. The striking differences in responses between the women to various west African customs are made apparent in Chapter 5, from the condemnation of these customs as barbarous by some women, to the understanding and justification of even the most violent of customs by others. This chapter also explores the views of those women who wished to see west African customs preserved, despite their position as pro-imperialists. Chapter 6 explorers the relationships between white women travellers and their west African counterparts, and the descriptions of the latter by the former. It analyses the ways in which British women challenged or confirmed prevailing images of west African women. Finally, Chapter 7 explores the possibilities and the problematic of retrieving subaltern histories, and evidence of agency and resistance of colonized peoples in imperialism and imperial discourses, from within the imperial archive. As is discussed in Chapter 2, white women were certainly empowered in many different and complex ways within the theatre of empire, not least in their ability to publish narratives based on their experiences. It may be that these narratives also contain evidence of the will of the colonized. However, it remains a matter for conjecture whether the western academic, situated within the elite 'palaces' of knowledge production, could ever claim to reveal this without being tainted by the very same colonizing politics of power and knowledge. As Childs and Williams (1997, 23) argue:

> In terms of postcolonial knowledge production and the refusal of the tyranny of the expert, ... one would need to be critically aware of the power invested in the particular locations from which one speaks and writes, the need for a certain humility in making interdisciplinary judgements, [and] the need, as Spivak has said, to undertake 'the careful project of unlearning our privilege as our loss'...

Situated within academia, Spivak's theatre of cultural imperialism, 'western' critics are not free of the constraints of cultural experience, and herein perhaps lie the limits of 'western' knowledge.

Notes

1. For ease of reference I refer to west Africa. The term is certainly reductive and contestable. As illustrated by Mary Kingsley's narratives, references to 'West' Africa during the nineteenth century included areas of equatorial Africa (modern-day Democratic Republic of Congo, Gabon and the Republic of Congo). In recognition of the problematic of naming, I use the lower case when referring to west Africa. The spellings of place names appear here as they do in the original narratives.
2. See, for example, the essays in *Transactions of the Institute of British Geographers* (Barnett, 1995; Driver 1995, Livingstone, 1995; Matless, 1995; Rose, 1995).
3. See, for example, the debate between Domosh, 1991a and b and Stoddart, 1991; Blunt, 1994; Rose, 1995.
4. For further discussion of this, see Hyam (1990), 38–49. On the issue of masculinities and empire, see Gittins (1996) and Phillips (1997).
5. Shirley Foster (1990, 6–7) discusses this in more detail.

6. For a detailed analysis of Nightingale's travel narratives on Egypt, see Gregory (1995).

7. For other examples of portrayals of women travellers as essentially eccentric and odd, see Hammalian (1981), Keay (1989).

8. See Birkett (1992), 62–3; Domosh (1991a), 97; Middleton (1973), 67; Bell and McEwan (1996), passim.

9. In Middleton (1973), 68. An anonymous verse in *Punch Magazine* parodied the attitude of the R.G.S. towards women fellows:

    A lady an explorer? A traveller in skirts?
    The notion's just a trifle too seraphic.
    Let them stay at home and mind the babies,
    or hem our ragged shirts;
    But they mustn't, can't and shan't be geographic!

    (Cited in Birkett, 1989, 63, and in Blunt, 1994, 160)

10. Flora Shaw (Birkett, 1992, xix; Callaway and O. Helly, 1992, 79–97) and Gertrude Bell (Winstone, 1978) are examples of women whose first-hand knowledge of overseas lands gave them a public platform upon which to debate imperial policy.

11. See, for example, Mills (1991); Clifford (1992); Driver (1992); Kowalewski (1992); Pratt (1992).

12. See also Shirley Foster (1991) for a discussion of the debates about gendered genres of writing.

13. The term is Showalter's (Horner and Sloznik, 1990, 7).

14. A major criticism of Said's *Orientalism* was its construction of a singular Other; by suggesting that 'westerners' represented the Orient in standard ways Said effectively denied the fact that Europeans constructed many 'others'.

15. For a critical response to the anti-historical stance of many postcolonial scholars, and a reassertion of the importance of context, see Kennedy (1996).

16. It is perhaps pertinent at this juncture to explain the context in which I am using the term 'postcolonialism'. Many commentators have pointed out the difficulties in defining the term postcolonialism (see, for example, Childs and Williams (1997), Hall (1995), McClintock (1992), Mishra and Hodge (1993), Moore-Gilbert (1997)). As Moore-Gilbert (ibid., 11) suggests, the difficulty perhaps arises from it being so variously applied to such different historical moments, geographical regions, cultural identities, political problems and affiliations and reading practices. As will become apparent, the focus in this book is very much on the latter, drawing on the work of postcolonial theorists such as Edward Said, Homi Bhabha and Gayatri Spivak.

17. Since the late 1970s there has been an impassioned and compelling critique of white feminism and its claims to give voice to an essential universal womanhood (see Amos and Parmar (1984), Carby (1982), hooks (1982). In

particular, critics have berated the lack of interrogation of whiteness as an ethnicity (see hooks, 1989). One of the few texts dealing with whiteness in literary production is Coetzee (1988). See also Ware (1993, 1996) and, within geography, Bonnett (1997) and Jackson (1998).

18. This is discussed in greater detail in many of the essays in Chaudhuri and Strobel (1992).

19. See, however, Nussbaum (1995) for a consideration of issues of empire in relation to literary texts of the eighteenth century.

20. Indeed, it seems that western feminists often fail to recognize that the politics of first wave feminism were formed within the context of a particular moment in the history of imperial capitalism; herein lie the objections of many third world women and women of colour to hegemonic western feminisms.

21. For a critique of the works of Bhabha and Said, where gender is very much a lacuna, see Moore-Gilbert (1997).

22. In this account I focus specifically on histories of British geography within the context of European imperialism. There are, of course, other critical histories to be written of geography in contexts with which I am less familiar. One interesting example is Mizuoka (1998).

23. Among the few examples dealing with these debates are Sidaway (1997) and Barnett (1998).

24. The relationship between feminism and postmodernism has often been problematic, ambivalent and contentious (Bertens (1995), Elam (1994), Nicholson (1990)). The engagement by western feminists with postcolonialism has largely been in response to criticism from Black and Third World feminists (Amos and Parmer (1994), Carby (1983), Hurtado (1989), Mohanty (1991), Trinh (1989)), and 'subaltern studies' (Spivak (1985)). Recent publications deal with the often problematic intersections of feminism, postmodernism and postcolonialism (Ashcroft et al. (1995), 249–282; hooks (1991); Williams and Chrisman (1993)).

25. See, for example, Barnes and Duncan (1992, passim), Madge (1993); Sidaway (1992), Radcliffe (1994), Berman (1995).

26. There is a substantial literature on this topic; see, for example, Ajayi and Crowder (1974), Curtin (1965), Crowder (1981), Dusgate (1985), Fage (1961), Hargreaves 1966), Robinson et al. (1981). A brief summary of this history is given in McEwan (1995a, Chapter 2).

27. The two women not included in this study are 'Mary Church' and Mary Gaunt. 'Mary Church' is believed to be the pseudonym of Catherine Temple, who was one of several European observers of Sierra Leone in its early years as a Crown Colony in the 1830s. She published her book anonymously, entitled *Sierra Leone; or, the Liberated Africans, in a series of letters from a young lady to her sister in 1833 and 34* (published by Longman in 1835). She is not included in

this study because her work belongs to a different body of literature to the other women. Her publication owes a great deal to the era of anti-slavery endeavours in west Africa rather than to the era of travel and exploration post-1840. Furthermore, it proved impossible to find any biographical information on 'Mary Church'; her only legacy seems to be the thin pamphlet she produced recounting her observations of Sierra Leone. Mary Gaunt was excluded on two counts. Firstly, she was Australian and her narratives could not, therefore, be contextualized within British imperialism. Secondly, she began travelling in the twentieth century and her observations of west Africa were published in 1912. Gaunt, unlike the women of this study, thus travelled in west Africa after the unification of Nigeria and during the new phase of imperialism. A traveller who continued travelling until the 1930s, Gaunt belongs much more to the twentieth century than to the nineteenth. On both narratives, see Robinson (1991, 205–6 and 181–2 respectively).

28. To avoid slippage between the terms 'travel-writers' and 'travellers who wrote', I will use the term 'women travellers' when generalising about these women, since the one thing they have in common is that they all travelled abroad.

29. It should, perhaps, be emphasized at this juncture that there is very little biographical or circumstantial information available concerning most nineteenth-century women travel writers, and in many cases it is impossible to locate family archives. Not surprisingly most of the women in this study are not mentioned by name in the *Dictionary of National Biography* and other sources such as Public Records Office lists, even where entries are included on their husbands, such is their anonymity in official records. As Béatrice Slama (quoted in Monicat 1994, 63) argues, 'One knows very little about many women. If one has biographical notes on some of them, it is because they are often ... the daughters of ..., the wives of ... One can measure at once how much help is, when one wants to publish, the very fact of being the daughter of ... or the wife of ..., but also how difficult it is for women to make a name, indeed a first name, for themselves'. In many cases, any available information on women travel writers exists as a consequence of the documenting and recording of their husband's lives. However, the writings of these women survive as rich sources of information both about themselves and their visions of the world in which they lived. For more detailed biographies of the women mentioned here see McEwan (1995a, 43–73). There is scattered information elsewhere; on Melville see Fyfe (1962, 216), Walford (1874, 162), Thorp (1950, 62); on Hinderer see Church Missionary Society (1911), Odoyoye (1969, 41), Padwick (1916), Stock (1899, 144), Thorp (1950, 54); on Slessor see Buchan (1980, 1984), Christian and Plummer (1970), Livingstone (1916), Oliver (1982); on

Colvile see Colvile (1896), Walford (1874, 704); on Kingsley see Birkett (1987a, 1992), Blunt (1994), Frank (1986a), Stevenson (1982).

CHAPTER 2

Travel, text and empowerment

Travel – liberation or 'duty'?

During the nineteenth century there was a substantial increase in the numbers of women, particularly those from the 'leisured' classes, travelling throughout the world. This was a product not only of the widening of spheres of travel for Europeans in general as a consequence of the expansion of overseas empires, but also a result of the expansion of opportunities available to middle and upper class women who had acquired the means to travel. During the eighteenth century it became more acceptable for women to travel as tourists, and travel was no longer seen as a threat to femininity. Social restraints and lack of money limited most women's opportunity to travel. Early male explorers had wealthy patrons, and later were sponsored by the geographical societies; both these sources were denied women (Tinling, 1989, xxiv). However, many (wealthier) women had the initiative, fortitude and money to travel. Their freedom to travel was facilitated by improved communications and modes of transportation, and the gradual loosening of the restrictions on their movements, which made it easier for them to broaden their activities. With this freedom came independence. Expedition advisers, sponsors and bureaucratic decoys replaced male chaperones. Women embraced the opportunity to travel because it offered them autonomy and a redefinition of themselves outside the narrow confines of society. As Foster (1991, 8) argues:

> ... in undertaking their foreign journeys these women were, albeit unconsciously, asserting certain positions with regard to their status and abilities their right to do what men had done for centuries, their capacity to meet challenges while still maintaining their female integrity, and their claim to be regarded as individuals, choosing and expanding the channels of their lives.

Thus women travellers began to transgress the boundaries of social activities ascribed to them by much of British polite society. As Aitken (1987, 9) argues, many women travellers rejected the submissive position of women in Britain, and had no particular affinity with domesticity; 'but if they laid the foundations of women's liberation, most of them did it unwittingly, for they were motivated by the desire for self-improvement'. However, the increasing incidence of women travelling was also linked to the middle-class notion of feminine 'duty'. As Robinson (1991, 1) points out, prior to the imperial era women were perceived as too precious and biologically ill-equipped to travel, but with the advent of imperialism, and especially colonialism, they were required to undertake more and more travelling as part of their duty towards family and country. While travel for most women was a liberating experience, for many the motives behind their journeys were rooted in their sense of social and private duty. The desire to be useful was a particular concern for many nineteenth-century women, despite Ruskin's dictum that the role of women should be confined to reigning as 'Queens' over their own hearths.[1] The tensions between personal liberation and fulfilment and public and private duty are often apparent in the narratives of women travellers in west Africa.

All but one of the women of this study felt a need to justify their travels in west Africa and, to varying extents, all expressed this in terms of 'duty'. (The only exception was Zélie Colvile, the only true 'tourist' among the women, who took a holiday with her husband before he assumed his post as Acting Commissioner in Uganda in the late 1880s. Map 1 illustrates Colvile's journey around the coast of Africa.) As Frank (1986b, 70) argues, 'in an age when a woman could scarcely ride alone in a railway carriage from Brighton to London, she would certainly be called upon to explain why she was off to the mouth of the Niger or the source of the Nile'. Duty provided one such explanation; women travellers expressed this as 'feminine' duty, but the distinctions between public and private obligations were often obscured. For example, Slessor's motivation for travelling to west Africa was defined in terms of her duty to the Church of Scotland, an obligation which she herself felt was a public responsibility. Inspired by the death of Livingstone in 1873, she felt that it was her duty to continue his work in bringing Africans into the fold of the Christian religion. However, Slessor also considered this a private duty that was grounded in her own family. By becoming a missionary she fulfilled her mother's desire to see one of her children enter missionary work abroad. Slessor's mother had wanted to send her eldest son to Calabar as a missionary until his premature death in New Zealand. With the death of the second son, Slessor felt that it was her responsibility to contribute to the struggle to spread Christianity in Africa. Her motives for travelling to west Africa were, therefore, a combination of a sense of public duty to contribute to the work of the church, which for Slessor was also motivated by private, personal concerns, and a private duty to fulfil the wishes of her mother. This belief in self-sacrifice and duty was also apparent in Anna Hinderer's reasons for travelling to Africa, but her motives were also bound in with her role as the wife of a missionary. Hinderer's 'duty' was very much a public responsibility to the church; she wrote, 'I longed to do something. I had a strong desire to become a missionary to give myself up to some holy work, and I had a firm belief that such a calling would be mine' (in Ajayi, 1959, 87). However, her responsibility was also a private one to her husband, David Hinderer; wherever he went, she was obliged to follow, even if it meant risking her life during local internecine wars.[2]

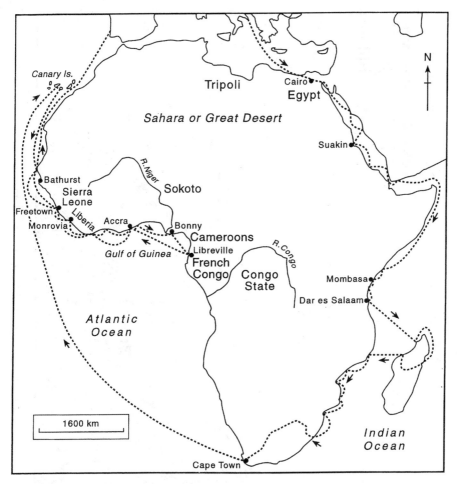

Map 1 Zélie Colvile's journey around Africa (adapted from Colvile, 1893)

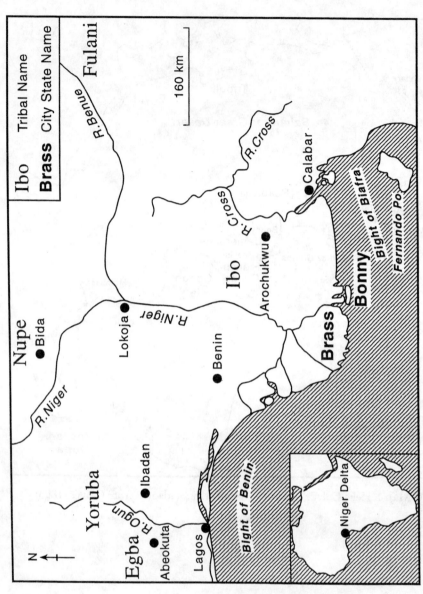

Map 2 Lagos and Yoruba in relation to the Niger and Benue river systems (adapted from McKenzie, 1976)

The sense of duty implicit in the role of 'wife' was of crucial importance to Melville, Foote and Larymore. In their narratives Melville and Foote did not question their responsibility to travel with their husbands on their assumption of posts in west Africa. Both believed it their personal obligation to support their husbands in the quest to end slavery; it was a duty grounded in the family, but at the same time part of a wider public burden to facilitate the 'civilizing' of Africa. Foote (1869, 155 and 172) even wrote of spending three months in Madeira awaiting a 'summons' from her husband to join him at Lagos (see Map 2). This was also the case with Larymore. She had travelled with her husband to India, and felt it her duty to uproot herself once more and follow him to west Africa. Although she was acting on an essentially a private, familial duty to her husband, Larymore also had a sense of public responsibility towards the British empire in Nigeria. As well as performing the supporting role of 'wife', she also undertook what she perceived to be the necessary public service of studying and observing life in west Africa, and passing on her advice to other prospective colonial wives through her publication.[3] She was concerned to inform other women how best to fulfil their domestic duties in an imperial setting, and to contribute to the cause of British imperialism in west Africa.

Thus the roles of these 'colonial wives' were defined by those of their husbands in west Africa; they were essentially 'incorporated wives' (Callan and Ardener, 1984). Their husbands' employment, changing responsibilities and new locations determined their travels; they had little personal control over the nature of their journeys. Furthermore, none of the women of this study were financially independent. Those who were married relied on their husbands to finance their travels. The missionaries obviously relied upon church funding and their travels were constrained to some extent by church policy. (Although, as discussed subsequently, Mary Slessor did her utmost to free herself from reliance upon church funds in order to attain the freedom to travel where she felt her work was most needed.) Mary Kingsley had a small inheritance that she used to finance her first journey, but her second journey was sponsored by the British Museum, which was interested in her ichthyological research. The need for funding imposed restrictions on where she could travel and how she could spend her time in west Africa.

Kingsley's motives for travelling to Africa were complex, manifold, and rooted in personal desire, but she also needed an ulterior motive to make her escape into the west African forests seem socially useful. As Blunt (1994, 64) points out, this motive changed over time as Kingsley became more famous. Freed from familial domesticity by the simultaneous deaths of both parents when she was nearly thirty, she could finally realize her dreams of travel. According to Foster (1991, 11):

... both the light-hearted explanation given at the beginning of her *Travels in West Africa* (it was undertaken on a kind of whimsical impulse) and the more serious ones offered later (she went to study tribal religions and customs in order to complete her father's anthropological work and also collect rare fish for the British Museum) are incomplete and misleading reasons for what she seems to have regarded on the one hand as an opportunity for personal spiritual expansion and on the other as a deliberate courting of danger and death.

Thus, when she was more famous, Kingsley couched her motives in terms of both a public duty to add to scientific knowledge,[4] and a private, 'feminine duty' to continue her father's work on sacrificial rites.[5] The expressions by women travellers of private family loyalty, missionary duty, a public responsibility towards the imperial effort, and the desire to add to scientific knowledge, covered their journeys with a veil of respectability. The use of duty as a reason for travelling to Africa, however, did not hide the inner impulses that prompted these women to travel, the personal motivations hidden beneath the veneer of both public and private obligations. These are most recognizable in the narratives of Mary Kingsley, the only truly independent women traveller of this study. The need to escape the stultifying social restrictions of Victorian Britain was most strongly expressed in Kingsley's narratives. However, even Kingsley did not transgress the strict dress code required to maintain her 'femininity'; whether in the depths of the rainforest, climbing Mungo Mah Lobeh, or canoeing up the Ogowé River (see Map 3), she remained highly conventional, dressed from collar to toe in her black mourning dresses (see Plate 1). On one occasion she fell into a game pit lined with ebony spikes and concluded triumphantly, 'It is at these times when you realize the blessings of a good thick skirt. Had I paid heed to the advice of a good many people in England who ought to have known better, and did not do it themselves, and adopted masculine garments, I should have been spiked and done for' (1982, 270). Kingsley also carried an umbrella, and argued 'one had no right to go about Africa in things one would be ashamed of at home'. She also had a strong aversion to trousers, and said she would rather have 'mounted a public scaffold' than have clothed what she referred to as her 'earthbound extremities' in them (Aitken, 1987, 175).

In this sense, therefore, Kingsley's 'liberation' as an independent traveller in west Africa was constrained by the demands of social etiquette imposed at home. This is true for almost all the women of this study. The practicalities of travelling over 3,000 miles on horseback[6] required Constance Larymore to wear riding breeches, but she insisted on wearing full-length skirts over these. Her chapter on 'What to Wear' gave women advice on how to maintain feminine dress in a tropical climate.[7] According to Callaway, a photograph taken in Nigeria showed her in an Edwardian floor-length gown with long sleeves and a high neck, a daunting prospect in the tropical heat with

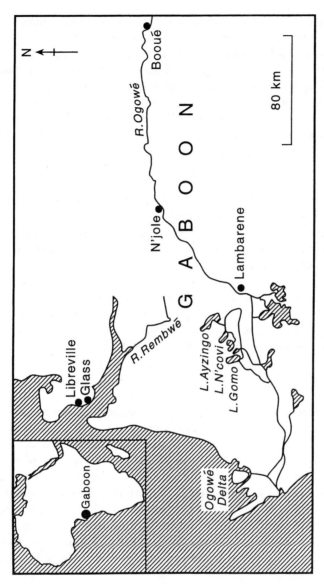

Map 3 Mary Kingsley's second journey, 1894–95 (adapted from Campbell, 1957)[8]

the necessary petticoats and underclothes. Larymore did not compromise on the need to wear a corset; she wrote, '*Always* wear corsets, even for a tête-à-tête home dinner on the warmest evenings; there is something about their absence almost as demoralizing as hair in curling pins' (Callaway, 1987, 169). Only Mary Slessor transgressed any boundaries concerning dress codes. She discarded European dress for a simple sack dress in keeping with the climate. On special occasions she wore a plain cotton dress (Livingstone, 1916, 125). She did not bother to wear a hat and frequently went bare-footed; her no-nonsense attitude did not allow social convention in Britain to dictate how she would dress in the tropics of southern Nigeria.

As Kearns (1997, 464) argues, despite their adherence to the demands of social etiquette, simply by being in west Africa white women travellers were 'doing something quite dangerous with imperial identities'. Furthermore, despite the constraints imposed by financial dependence and social mores in Britain, for most white women travel in west Africa was a liberating experience. As Foster (1991, 12) argues, their journeys were:

> ... the anticipated fulfilment of long-cherished dreams, often awakened in childhood; the desire to enter a fairy-tale or legendary world, glamorised by the romantic imagination; the lure of the unknown and the 'uncivilised', with their accompanying challenges; the search for a new self-hood, released from the narrow parameters of home life. But these were less easily articulated than the more obvious motivations, often merely hinted at or becoming evident indirectly.

For many women travellers, their journeys were psychological excursions of self-discovery as well as physical treks. Their horizons were widened both spiritually and geographically. Travel for some, like Slessor and Kingsley, was an escape from domesticity. However, for others, and particularly for the colonial wives, it was merely domesticity translocated in a foreign country. Although often constrained and compelled to travel by a sense of public and private duty, their journeys ultimately broadened white women's experiences and provided them with a new found liberation. Travel prompted these women to write, and gave them access to an audience they would not otherwise have acquired. Furthermore, they were all empowered to varying extents by their position as white women in colonial Africa.

Empowerment in west Africa

The fact of their whiteness meant that British women travellers assumed levels of authority and influence in west Africa that were not available to them in Britain; they were empowered by the fact that within the empire status was determined by skin colour rather than gender. Notions of gender were closely linked to notions of race; Africa as a continent and African people were commonly feminized by the literature of empire; women and Africans were both 'othered'. Drawing on the ideas of Foucault, Russett (1989, 63) argues that, 'Women and savages, together with idiots, criminals, and pathological monstrosities, were a constant source of anxiety to male intellectuals in the late nineteenth century'. In west Africa, however, British women often became 'honorary men', were treated no differently by Africans than were their male counterparts, and were often referred to by their African guides as 'Sir' (Kingsley, 1982, 502). The feeling of authority felt by these women manifested itself in a variety of ways. Most striking is the fact that they did not question their right to be in west Africa, or to appropriate what they saw. It is also apparent in their attitude towards, and treatment of, the indigenous peoples that they encountered.

That all the women of this study were imbued with the ethnocentrism and, in some cases, the racism of nineteenth century Britain is not in doubt. However, as with racist attitudes in Britain, their ideas about west Africans were formulated from notions combining theories about both race and class. This is particularly apparent in the narratives of Melville, Foote, Larymore and Colvile, whose attitudes towards west Africans were often predicated upon and informed by their own social status. It is argued in Chapter 4 that their ethnocentrism and upper- or upper-middle class status combined to produce a reaction to west Africans that was not wholly different from their attitudes towards servants in Britain. Their condescending responses to, and representations of west Africans were based on their social status, and their authority derived both from this and their white skin. Blake (1990, 348) argues that,

> ... the substitution of a sense of class superiority undermines the premises of empire. It transforms the cliché that Africans are childlike from a justification of imperialism to an attitude toward servants. It allows ... (them) to acknowledge the social distinctions Africans themselves make and to regard African society as parallel to English.

Blake's contention is that women travellers rejected racial superiority as a source of power because it was inseparable from gender superiority, and instead based their authority on class superiority. While this may have been the case for Mary Hall (the subject of Blake's article) and other women travelling in the early twentieth century, the women of this study present a slightly more complex picture. Their social status was important in their expressions of superiority and power, but they also seemed to have a sense of what they regarded as their own racial superiority. This is important when considering the attitudes both of Slessor, a working-class woman, and Kingsley, whose own mother was a housemaid before marrying into the Kingsley family. Neither Kingsley nor Slessor had the necessary social background to predicate their authority on a sense of class superiority; their influence in west Africa was based solely on their whiteness.

Both Slessor and Kingsley were aware of their authority among west Africans. Kingsley commanded and directed her own expeditions, hiring local men as guides and porters who were thus compelled to abide by her instructions. This level of authority, was not always straightforward and uncontested (see Chapter 7), but it was a novel experience for Kingsley. Slessor's behaviour towards west Africans was, on occasions, quite extraordinary. The Chief Magistrate of Okoyong, Maxwell, was astounded by her behaviour when he first met her in the early 1890s. He wrote (in Livingstone, 1916, 129–30),

> What sort of woman I expected to see I hardly know; certainly not what I did. A frail old lady with a ... shawl over her head and shoulders, swaying herself in a rocking-chair and crooning to a black baby in her arms. I remember being struck ... by the very strong Scottish accent. Her welcome was everything kind and cordial ... Suddenly she jumped up with an angry growl ... and with a few trenchant words she made for the door where a ... native stood. In a moment she seized him by the scruff of the neck, boxed his ears, and hustled him out into the yard, telling him quite explicitly what he might expect if he came back again without her consent. I watched him   and his followers slink away very crestfallen. Then, as suddenly as it had arisen the tornado subsided, and ... she was again gently swaying in her chair. The man was a local monarch of sorts, who had been impudent to her, and she had forbidden him to come near her house again until he had not only apologised but done some prescribed penance. Under the pretext of calling on me he had defied her orders – and that was the result.

This admonishment by Slessor of a local chief was not an unusual occurrence in Calabar. She would often rebuke elders, and physically assaulted chiefs if they ignored her wishes or allowed acts of violence such as twin murders to take place in her vicinity. It is clear that imperial power relations were mediated through Slessor. She was allowed such behaviour because of the respect that she commanded in Calabar, a respect that was predicated on her whiteness and her position within imperial power relations. As Matthews (1947, 5) argues:

> In many Oriental lands, in many parts of Africa, in the islands of the Pacific, the wife of a missionary [and, in Slessor's case, the single woman missionary] was the first white woman ever seen by the native peoples. We cannot easily exaggerate the importance of this fact or the influence which these Christian white women exerted over primitive peoples ...

At the same time, however, one cannot divorce the influence of the likes of Slessor from the violence of European imperialism. Kingsley's comments about Slessor are also revealing of her character and influence in west Africa:

> The natives round here have an upside down idea about white women because they have one of the most wonderful of them living among them – Miss Slessor – she came here many years ago built a mud house with a mat roof in their midst and settled down as missionary. She is now a white chief and has the whole tribe under her thumb, but not in the least converted. She herself has lost most of her missionary ideas and bullies the native chiefs in their own tongue ...[9]

Of all the women of this study, Slessor exercised the greatest influence in west Africa. However, it is also clear from Kingsley's comments that Slessor may have adapted more to local conditions in order to exercise this influence than locals did to her presence. As Chapter 7 suggests, imperial power relations were not straightforward, but were always complex and negotiated.

As with the other women travellers of this study, Slessor did not question her own, nor Britain's right to be in west Africa. Instead she believed that Britain's role should be one of improving education (albeit defined in ethnocentric terms) and the conditions of life, particularly for women, without damaging west African cultures. She often disagreed with both the church and the colonial government over their attitudes towards west Africa, and exercised considerable influence on both bodies. She attempted to distance herself from the church by trading, becoming self-sufficient and reducing her dependency on church funds. (Her mission houses at Okoyong and Enyong were built mostly from her own money.) In this way she could act independently of official church policy which she believed did not take enough account of indigenous cultures. As Maps 4 and 5 illustrate, she was a pioneer living on the frontier of European penetration into west Africa,[10] and her sense of individualism was particularly strong. She believed she understood the needs of the Calabar people better than the church officials back in Scotland. Her proximity to Africans, she believed, gave her a greater understanding of their lives and the less her dependency on church funds, the greater her freedom to implement her own policies. The church did not approve of her adopting an African lifestyle, especially her living in a mud-hut,[11] but Slessor ignored its complaints.

Slessor exercised considerable influence over church education policy. In the early days of the mission the least expensive methods of training were sought, avoiding technical and agricultural training which was costly in terms of personnel, money, and equipment. As Nair (1972, 66–8) argues, commercial education was gradually replaced by a system of quasi-religious education. Slessor believed this abandonment of technical and agricultural training inappropriate, and worked to

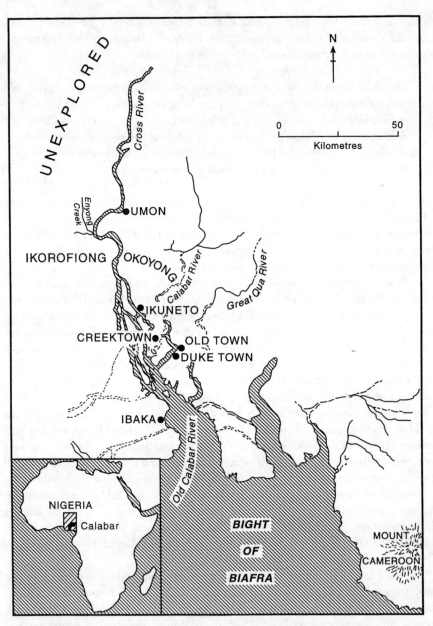

Map 4 The Calabar mission field at the time of Mary Slessor's arrival in 1876 (adapted from Livingstone, 1916)

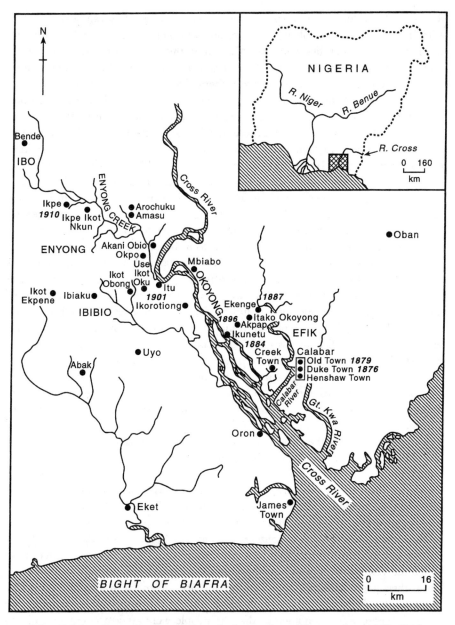

Map 5 Mary Slessor's advance into the lower Cross River region, 1876–1915
(adapted from Christian and Plummer, 1970)

rectify it. Her influence and command over policies in Okoyong can be detected in a letter to her about her plans, which pleads with her to reconsider her threat to sever completely her ties with the Mission if the church prevented her from carrying out her objectives.[12] The old imperial missionary did not appeal to her since there was too great a distance between themselves and the African peoples.

Slessor believed that British control was necessary to establish peace and justice in west Africa. However, she told the Consul-General of the Oil Rivers Protectorate, Sir Claude MacDonald, that the people at Okoyong were not ready to tolerate a government official in their midst, nor to accept without bloodshed the sudden introduction of new laws (Christian and Plummer, 1970, 124ff). She believed destruction would result from the imposition of British institutions upon the people of Calabar without regard for, or understanding of their customs. Her insight into African law prompted the colonial government to appoint her as the first female Vice-Consul in the British Empire in 1892, giving her the powers of a magistrate. However, her sympathy with west African customs brought her into conflict with the colonial administration. She constantly resisted policies that conflicted with local laws, and was often at odds with colonial officials. For example, in 1910, the people of Akpap complained to her that they were being compelled to build a road through a sacred grove of yams. Slessor was furious, and wrote a letter of complaint to the Assistant District Commissioner, accusing him of violating the sacred grove and ending with the valediction: 'I am 'Not' your obedient servant'.[13] By this time she had a considerable reputation for belligerence amongst the colonial officials.[14]

Despite her resistance to many of the decisions of the colonial government, Slessor's knowledge of the Calabar region was of undoubted importance to the authorities. She was often a mediator between the government and west Africans. On many occasions she brought officials and chiefs together to negotiate treaties. For example, in 1894 the villagers of Okoyong agreed to hand twin babies over to the Mission instead of killing them, and she was singularly responsible for establishing more peaceable relations between the Okoyong and Efik peoples. However, her major concern was to spread Christianity without completely destroying indigenous cultures. As a result, she was often critical of British policies. She resented Britain's destruction in 1901 of the sacred grove at Arochuku, the seat of the most powerful oracle in southern Nigeria, and home of the infamous Long Ju-ju. She felt that the violence that took place there could have been prevented using less force. She wrote, 'I can't bear those dreadful expeditions, the very sight of force raises their [west Africans'] apprehension and goes to make trouble'.[15] Slessor also resented the illegal arrests that took place without the necessary warrants in her districts. These were so numerous that the people were afraid to venture out, and previously prosperous markets were brought to a standstill.[16] She referred to this as a 'flagrant breach of law'.[17] Her animosity towards the colonial government erupted in a letter to a friend, where she wrote, 'This land belongs to the native and worked by the native, tho' our officers do not believe it ... I am not only writing rank treason, but I am doing so unrepentantly as we live in the bush under bush conditions, and I owe nothing to the government'.[18] At other times she described the government officials as 'iniquitous sometimes in their methods, or want of method, and heart'.[19] She found the lack of consideration for Calabar customs most irksome. She was instructed by the administration to take a census to the chiefs for completion, but scorned the idea. The people were too suspicious to complete it, and were too busy with consular and farm work during the day, and marketing in the evening, to comply. She wrote in her diary, 'So [I] was rather angry of white man's arrogant importunity. It is anything but dignified to natives'.[20]

Slessor acquired positions of authority that would have been unthinkable for a working-class woman in Britain. In addition to becoming Vice-Consul and magistrate for Okoyong, she was presented with a fellowship to the Order of Saint John of Jerusalem in 1913, primarily for her work in establishing the mission hospital and the refuge for women. As Buchan (1980, 304) argues, perhaps the greatest accolade came from west Africans, who named her Eka Kpukpro Owo – the Mother of all the Peoples. This epithet is indicative of the nature of Slessor's authority in west Africa; it was not based on the assumption of superiority in terms of class, nor was it based solely on race, it was in essence a maternal superiority. She tempered her role as a pioneer by assuming a maternal presence in west Africa. For example, she wrote of her excursion into Okoyong:

> I hope to get a room at several of the villages, so that they will feel they are looked after. At first they did not seem to know whether they should repulse me, but the medicine ... has made the whole place mine. Every chief, more or less, has been under my care, or some of his people have been, and they have expressed in various ways their appreciation of my services. No white person need fear to go anywhere now.[21]

Slessor was aware that her role as nurse and nurturer gave her the opportunity to exercise some influence over the chiefs and elders of Calabar.

Slessor's adoption of African children (see Plate 2) was symbolic of her wider adoption of the people of Calabar, who often referred to her as 'Ma'. She pictured herself as a mother figure, and her authority derived from this. Ramusack (1990, 319) refers to this as 'benevolent maternal imperialism', and the conception of the relationship between white women and west Africans in terms of mothers and children is one that was common to many of the women of this study. Anna Hinderer thought of herself as the 'white Iyalode' or mother of the town of Ibadan, and in this way was able to command the same respect as the Ibadani Iyalode, the maternal elder of the town (1872, 110–11).[22] The Ibadani people referred to her as 'Iya', meaning 'mother'. As with Slessor, Hinderer took local children into her home, particularly those that were former slaves whom she wished to educate; this was a symbolic expression of her maternal relationship with west Africans generally. Similarly, Constance Larymore became known as 'Uwamu', meaning 'Our Mother', which she herself referred to as her 'country' name. Her recognition of the authority implicit in such an epithet was clear when she wrote, 'the title is recognized as the highest expression of respect and affection that the African man can offer to a woman' (1908, 95). As Bell (1995) suggests, this 'maternalism' was also tied in to the notion of women's 'duty'. Post-Darwinian doctrine asserted that women had well-developed emotional and aesthetic skills that had evolved at the expense of their intellectual development, and which derived from the 'maternal instinct'. 'It was the role of women as active citizens of and in the Empire, to put these 'natural' skills to good use in the interests of imperial consolidation and expansion. It was, in effect, their imperial duty to fulfil the 'female civilising mission".[23] Thus, on the one hand, it could be argued that 'maternal imperialists' were more constrained by Victorian theories of biological difference than they were empowered. However, on the other hand, although their relationships with west Africans were often based on benevolence and philanthropy, the mother-child framework of these relationships was ultimately empowering for white women at the expense of subordinated west Africans. This 'maternalism' did not challenge imperialist depictions of Africans as 'child-like' (see Chapter 4). Furthermore, these unequal relationships raise questions about the motivations of the 'mothers'; Slessor, Hinderer and Larymore were all aware of their new-found authority in west Africa, which was mediated through their femininity, and they utilized it to their advantage.

Of critical importance in assessing and understanding the various ways in which white women travellers were empowered in west Africa is the notion of 'separate spheres'.[24] Independent women such as Slessor and Kingsley in some ways transgressed the boundaries of recognized 'feminine' spheres of activity, Slessor by becoming a single, female missionary (a rarity in the 1870s), and Kingsley firstly, by travelling alone and defining herself as a scientist, and secondly, by becoming involved in political debates about British imperialism. However, despite the new levels of authority they acquired through the process of travel, the influence of other women travellers in west Africa was still restricted to an essentially 'feminine', domestic sphere. That Slessor, Larymore and Hinderer were empowered by their 'maternal' presence in Africa is indicative of this, as is the fact that Foote, Melville and Colvile were empowered in the domestic sphere by their position as 'mistress of the house' vis-à-vis their African servants. These women were not involved in politics or in the administration of the colonies, they were empowered but only within their own separate spheres of activity. Obviously, their presence in west Africa had implications for the broader impact of British imperialism; they were, after all, responsible for transplanting British social values into the colonies. They also played a formative role in the complex and contested constructions of femininities during the nineteenth century. However, their sphere of activity remained an essentially domestic one. As the Honourable Mrs Joyce, President of the British Women's Emigration Association wrote in 1902, 'English women make homes wherever they settle all the world over ... [they are] the real builders of Empire' (Bell, 1995).

The notion of separate spheres was clearly expressed by the Church Missionary Society, which justified the employment of women as mission workers by arguing that far from threatening the ideal of womanhood, such work could even reinforce it. It described the separate realms of work of Anna and David Hinderer as follows:

> ... an observant eye will perceive she was always engaged in her own proper sphere. Her husband was the Lord's chief instrument for gathering disciples, organising the church, and exercising discipline for its government. Besides ministering in the congregation, he preached in the open places in the town, planted and watched over the new branches of the church, instructed the converts privately, diffused a knowledge of the Gospel among the teachers, quickened their zeal, and cultivated amongst them firmness and consistence of character, introduced to the inhabitants the art of reading and writing their native language, and moreover conducted exploratory visits to towns more or less remote.
>
> On the other hand her work, as will be seen, was chiefly within their own compound, among its few men and women, and frequent visitors, and still more amongst the happy children whom she was winning by her kindness and love, civilising, training, and teaching, and for whom perhaps she was even doing still more by the silent influence of her Christian character.[25]

Anna Hinderer had a strong desire to become a missionary, but in the 1850s the only way she could fulfil this wish was by marrying one. It was not until the late nineteenth century that single women missionaries were accepted. Mary Slessor (working for the Scottish Missionary Society, which had fewer restrictions for the employment of women than the C.M.S.) was able to transgress the boundaries of acceptable 'feminine' spheres of activity, and become a pioneer in the mould of David Livingstone. However, the work of Anna Hinderer, travelling to Africa almost three decades earlier, was confined to the domestic sphere. White women may have been empowered in west Africa, often on the basis of their race and class, but only a small minority were able to break out of their prescribed 'feminine' roles which were determined by social mores in Victorian Britain. Despite this, as has already been discussed, their presence in west Africa had broader implications for British imperialism; their 'separate spheres' were never truly disengaged from the public realm.

Empowerment through text

Travel was a liberating experience for many white women for it gave them the impetus to turn to print. This, in turn, gave them both a 'voice' and access to an audience that they would not otherwise have acquired. Women such as Foote, Melville, Colvile and Larymore may have been 'incorporated wives' whose social identities were drawn from their husbands' work and rank, and whose travels were structured according to their husbands' changing duties and re-postings. However, they managed to retain some autonomy by publishing books based on their own experiences. It is difficult to assess the extent of the audience that these women were able to reach with their views,[26] but it can be supposed that because of the popularity of the literature of empire during the nineteenth century, these women had access to potentially large audiences. Their audiences were, however, very different. Colvile broadened her audience by publishing an article in *Blackwood's Magazine*, and she also publicized her book by giving lectures.[27] However, like the travelogues of Melville and Foote, her narrative was aimed as light reading for the general enthusiast. Despite this, the potential for these works was considerable. There existed a fascination with empire among various leisured middle- and upper-class women in Britain, which was an extension of the desire among many people at the time for titillation by tales of adventure in far-off, 'exotic' locations. As Robinson (1990, 200) argues, the tales of 'the daughters of Albion' establishing little Englands around the world were extremely popular. In Slessor's case, her audience ranged across class barriers, but was probably restricted to Scottish Presbyterians. Although publication figures for the *Missionary Record* do not exist, it can be assumed that it was very widely read throughout the major industrial towns of Scotland where the Church of Scotland was particularly strong. Its sister publication, the *Women's Missionary Magazine*, for which Slessor was a prolific writer, had an average monthly publication for 1902 of 27,800 and gave her access to a considerable female audience.[28]

There is more evidence regarding the popularity of Mary Kingsley's work. Her audience was a varied one, incorporating those interested in travel narratives from the empire, and those engaged in commerce, science and politics. Birkett (1987a, 118–9) argues that Kingsley's inability to locate herself fully and be located in masculine discourses actually gave her greater freedom to address diverse audiences, and thus gave her greater influence. She writes:

> While the tensions of her adoption of white male status often curtailed her freedom of action, the temporary nature of her different professional disguises gave Kingsley a breadth of knowledge and expertise more rigidly identified Africanists of the period lacked. Not fitting easily into available professional categorizations, she could also swiftly adapt her assumed roles as the audience and circumstances demanded.

In addition to a varied audience, Kingsley's readership was quite a substantial one. The first edition of *Travels in West Africa* ran to 1,500 copies and was reprinted eight times up to 1904, the reprint runs totalling 7,500. *West African Studies* was published in 1899 in an edition of 2,000 copies. It sold 1,200 copies the week it was published.[29] It was reprinted in 1901 in an edition of 1,500 copies.[30] Both books were reviewed very widely by both the national and provincial press (the notable exception being *The Times*, which disagreed with Kingsley's stand on many issues concerning Britain's involvement in west Africa), and were also reviewed as far afield as France, Australia and the United States. Kingsley also published articles in the influential periodicals of the time, including *The Spectator*, *The National Review*, *The Fortnightly Review*, *Manchester Chamber of Commerce Monthly Record*, *British Empire Review*, and other learned journals such as the *Transactions of the Liverpool Geographical Society* and the *Scottish Geographical Magazine*. Kingsley broadened her audience further by embarking upon an exhausting series of lecture tours around Britain, lecturing most notably to the Scottish and the Liverpool Geographical Societies, but also to various audiences in Dublin, Glasgow, Dundee, Harwich, Halifax, Birmingham, Manchester, Newcastle, Durham, South Shields, and at various venues in London. She would often address over 2,000 people at these lectures. Potentially large audiences added to the influence that Kingsley, along with Slessor, commanded as a result of their publications.

Despite access to sizeable audiences, nearly all these women prefaced their narratives with some sort of apology for having written them in the first place, re-emphasizing their essential feminine reticence and denying the worth of their attempts at writing. For example, Melville (1968, v) wrote, 'In offering this little work to the Public, the Author craves indulgence for the trivial matter it contains'. Even Kingsley (1982, xix) felt the need to apologize for *Travels*, although her apology perhaps contained more irony than it did demureness:

> What this book wants is not a simple Preface but an apology, and a very brilliant and convincing one at that. Recognising this fully, and feeling quite incompetent to write such a masterpiece, I have asked several literary friends to write one for me, but they have kindly but firmly declined, stating that it is impossible satisfactorily to apologise for my liberties with Lindley Murray and the Queen's English. I am therefore left to make a feeble apology for this book myself ...

Although Colvile did not proffer an apology for her narrative, the preface was written by her husband in an effort to verify the experiences of his wife. The need to apologize for having written a book, or to have their publications authenticated by their husbands, is indicative of the fact that women were constrained by a set of literary conventions that were predicated upon gender. As Monicat (1994, 63) argues:

In this nineteenth-century discourse women are represented as 'naturally' emotional and primarily instinctive. When they are not deemed incapable of intellectual work, they are advised not to engage in it for the good of society. What women learn and write must therefore remain within distinctive boundaries.

Part of this process was the need to offer apologies in the prefaces of their travelogues. As Mills (1991, 83) argues, these disclaimers denied 'any scientific, academic, literary or other merit' of these travelogues. Any suspicion that travel in west Africa was transgressive of gender boundaries was also tempered, at least in Colvile and Larymore, by the inclusion of hyper-feminine images of the author in the preface (see Plates 3 and 4).

Mills highlights the constraints controlling the production and reception of texts written by British women, and suggests that the distinction between public and private writings is of some significance. The textual constraints that controlled and shaped published narratives were not present in private correspondence, where women were often freer to express their opinions regarding even the most taboo subjects in Victorian society. As discussed in Chapter 6, textual constraints shaped Kingsley's narratives; she was compelled to adopt masculine voices in order to describe the physiques of women in west Africa, and her allusions to female circumcision were restricted to correspondence with other women. Her views on miscegenation were also confined to her letters. Furthermore, Kingsley was constrained by politics. Hamalian (1981, 229) makes the point that 'though she travelled through the Congo Free State, she did not even hint at the terrible atrocities that the agents of King Leopold of Belgium were inflicting on the natives in a bloody regime of forced labour and monopoly'. At first glance this does seem a surprising omission by Kingsley considering her vociferous attacks on British taxation policies in Sierra Leone and southern Nigeria. However, Hamalian fails to consider the possibility that Kingsley, in order to gain permission to travel through the Belgian Congo, may have given an undertaking not to write anything of what she saw there. Although constrained not to describe the conditions of the Congo Free State in her narratives, there are intimations in her books that leave the impression that she was deeply shocked at what was happening. As Caroline Oliver (1982, 81) points out, she became a great friend of Edmund Dene Morel, leader of the campaign for reform in the Congo, and its seems clear that she supplied some of the evidence for his reports.

The tensions between public and private writings are even clearer in the work of Mary Slessor. In her reports in the missionary magazines she was a narrator, and as with Larymore, confined herself to describing her environment and her own work, without transgressing towards analysis and critique, politics and science. She made constant references to the state of her health, assuring her readers that she was well. The image she created was of a woman happily carrying out the work of the church in Africa, and enjoying some success. The picture of Slessor one gains from her correspondence, however, was very different. In the forty years she spent in west Africa, she was often sick with fever, and on occasions close to death. She suffered from erysipelas, lost her hair and had heart trouble. Her discomfort is evident in several of her letters, and in her surviving diaries. However, this was not reported in the *Missionary Record* or the *Women's Missionary Magazine*. This was partly because Slessor felt she had a mission to complete; she was aware of her tenuous position as a lone woman missionary and did not want to be recalled to Britain. On one of her few furloughs when doubts were expressed about her returning to west Africa she announced, 'If ye dinna send me back, I'll swim back' (Buchan, 1980, 24). She did not want her femininity confused with notions of weakness and unsuitability. Furthermore, Slessor did not wish to represent herself as a heroic figure in the mould of Livingstone. It was important that she was seen to remain within the bounds of acceptable feminine behaviour as defined by the Church of Scotland, which had already voiced its opposition to her proposal to travel inland.[31]

The focus on the domestic realm in the narratives of the likes of Melville, Foote and Larymore can be read as a product of textual constraints. However, as Monicat (1994, 67) argues, these narrative strategies may also have been empowering:

> By focusing on topics or aspects of life either forbidden to men (the harems) or not valorized by men (domestic life) women distance themselves from the values of masculine knowledge. This is one of women's most important intellectual victories as they present it – a victory materialized by their books, a victory which has crucial consequences on the ways in which they conceive and construct themselves as female subjects.

The act of describing in itself represented the authority assumed by women writers: they appropriated west African landscapes and peoples, filling their narratives with descriptions of those silenced by the imperialism that had facilitated their own liberation. As Hall argues (1992, 242), in the debates over Africans:

> English men and women were as much concerned with constructing their own identities as with defining those of others, and those identities were always classed and gendered as well as ethnically specific. Furthermore, their capacity to define those others was an important aspect of their own authority and power.

The critical point here is that women travel writers were empowered by their authority to represent other peoples and landscapes, and by being able to construct popular 'knowledges' about west Africa for consumption by audiences in Britain. Travel in the empire lent authority to the pronouncements of women authors. Their authoritative white voices were able to 'scrutinise, define and pin down' their black subjects (Low, 1996, 51). It was, perhaps, the production of textual images and the creation of 'knowledge' about west Africa and its peoples that was the ultimate source of empowerment, especially when juxtaposed against the silencing of colonized voices, for women travel writers in the British empire.

Published texts gave women travellers access to audiences that would have been difficult to acquire otherwise, and their own relative liberation in west Africa was achieved at the expense of the liberties of colonized west Africans. However, as several writers have discussed,[32] both imperialist and feminine discourses in nineteenth-century Britain constrained the ways in which women wrote, and the details that they were able to recount, thereby producing ambivalence and tensions within their narratives. Women travellers were caught between the conflicting narrative voices of imperialism and femininity. As Morin (1995, 195) suggests, they were part of the imperial system yet not totally of it because they were women; though they were women, in west Africa their whiteness gave them access to a broader sphere than that encompassed by the domestic realm. The result of these tensions was an ambivalence of narrative voice and a lack of straightforward authority in the text. As Mills (1991, 21–3) argues, 'through elements such as humour, self-deprecation, statements of affiliation, and descriptions of relationships, which stress the interpersonal nature of travel writing, these texts constitute counter-hegemonic voices within colonial discourse'. The women of this study were unable to adopt either voice (imperial or feminine) completely and successfully; they asserted and subverted both to varying degrees and at various times. Thus, the women of this study were ambivalent about their own authority and self-deprecation; they were both empowered by text and constrained by nineteenth-century discourses that governed the production and reception of their narratives.

Impact in Britain

As suggested in the previous section, it is difficult to gauge the impact of the views of most of the women of this study on opinions in Britain. One can assume, however, that although their narratives contributed to the body of literature pertaining to the empire, and are therefore of some import to an analysis of this genre of writing, most of these women had very little impact as individuals in Britain. Their narratives were not written to have any great impact on imperial policy, and ultimately white women travellers remained marginal within the sphere of British imperial culture. However, this was not the case with Slessor and Kingsley, both of whom transgressed the boundaries of feminine activity, as defined by an overwhelmingly patriarchal society, to have some impact on church policy (in the case of Slessor) and imperial politics (in the case of Kingsley).

Slessor was very much aware of her importance to the Church of Scotland in Calabar, but also of her own influence over mission policy formulated in Scotland. In an obituary, Hogg (1915, 53–4) suggests she was a modest and shy person, but had a great conviction that her own work in Calabar was indispensable. Thus she was at times critical in her letters towards the Church of Scotland for not providing the necessary support to allow her to continue her travels into the interior. She wrote, 'do you at home realize that while you are giving for extension, we are closing stations for want of workers?' (1908, 256). Her influence in Scotland was based primarily upon her publications in the *Missionary Record* and the *Women's Missionary Magazine*. It is significant that following her complaints over the lack of help she received in Calabar, many more single women travelled to west Africa during the final decade of the nineteenth century. Buchanan informed her that her reports were 'the means of awakening a new interest in Calabar in the minds of many of our people'.[33] The great interest that she inspired as a consequence of these reports, and because of her status as a woman alone in the forests of Africa, gave her significant influence within the Church of Scotland. The Foreign Missions Board was aware of the authority of her reports in the missionary magazines, and members wrote to her requesting more publications, 'a sketch of anything connected with your work – any of your observations or your experiences'.[34] Her knowledge of Calabar and her importance to the missionary work of the church meant that she was able to implement many of her own policies. If the church opposed her suggestions, her 'African' lifestyle and independence of church funds, which she deliberately fostered through trading, meant that she could go ahead with her plans regardless of protests from Scotland. This influence can be discerned from the fact that Slessor's journeys into the interior were mapped out by herself, rather than by the Mission; she decided where and when she went. On one occasion when the church opposed her ideas (possibly concerned with 'opening up' new villages in Ikpe) she threatened to sever completely her ties with the Mission. The response from the church was conciliatory, arguing that they were 'far too proud of you to dream of such a thing, and if there is a difference of opinion there will be many a solution thought of before that!'[35] Slessor got her own way, her colonizing presence was secured and she continued her progress in establishing stations in Ikpe.

Slessor's influence on church policy was based more on her position in west Africa than her standing in Britain. The views of Kingsley, more than any other woman of this study, however, had the greatest impact on public opinion in Britain, and were grounded on the status that she managed to acquire in Britain. Following her return from Africa in 1895 and the publication of *Travels in West Africa*, Kingsley became a celebrity in Britain. She also acquired a great deal of influence. Her first publication ensured that she was widely regarded at the time as the expert on the affairs of west Africa, and demands were placed upon her for further publications and lecture tours. She established contacts through a complex process of 'networking' with intellectuals such as Edward Tylor and James Frazer, colonialists such as Sir George Goldie, future colonial governors such as Frederick Lugard and

Matthew Nathan, representatives of the trading fraternity such as John Holt and Alfred Lyell, and members of the Colonial Office, including Joseph Chamberlain himself. She was also invited to meet the 'Balfour Set', which was well known among parliamentarians, and popular with the imperialists who ran the Royal Geographical Society (Flint, 1960, 304). This networking was enabled by the fame that she acquired through the publication of *Travels*.[36] It was also enabled by her gendered subjectivity. Kingsley referred to herself as a 'maiden aunt' in her relationship with, and influence over, the Liverpool traders.[37] On another occasion she wrote to the trader John Holt, 'you men will be men. A Frenchman would not listen to an Englishman talking to him about how to manage his colonies but he don't mind a woman doing so'.[38] Consequently, Kingsley came to exercise considerable influence within political circles, despite being outside them, particularly with regard to the debate surrounding the administration of the west African colonies and the formulation of Indirect Rule.[39] As Pearce (1988, 283) argues, 'Kingsley had a major impact on official views from the early years of this century onwards. She may be seen as having a seminal influence on all areas of British policy in Africa, and West Africa especially'.

By the end of the nineteenth century, Kingsley, Holt and Morel, began referring to themselves as the 'Third Party'. This they perceived as belonging somewhere between those who held imperialist ideas about the 'damned Negro', incapable of advancement without British rule, and those expounding the philanthropic but ethnocentric missionary approach to west Africans. Their alternative approach saw the administration of Africans as 'a challenging problem of world importance, demanding justice and wisdom but above all an appreciation of ethnological facts' (Nworah, 1971, 349). Although the significance of this 'sect' was small, and its proposals lacked any solid economic backing or wide public appeal, it was important in advocating reforms in the administration of west Africa at a time when the zeal for imperial expansion was at its highest. Nworah (ibid., 364) argues that even after her death, it was Kingsley's spiritual influence that compelled both Holt and Morel to fight for an imperialism based on moral duty rather than on jingoism. Morel himself referred to this 'moral' approach to imperialism as 'Kingsleyism' (Cline, 1980, 31).

Kingsley also had a major influence on debates about education in west Africa. Pearce (1988, 292) argues that education policy moved very significantly in the direction that she endorsed. The 1925 White Paper called for education to be:

> adapted to the mentality, aptitudes, occupations and traditions of the various peoples, conserving as far as possible all sound and healthy elements in the fabric of their social life; adapting them where necessary to changed circumstances and progressive ideas, as an agent of natural growth and evolution. Its aim should be to render the individual more efficient in his or her own condition of life, whatever it may be, and to promote the advancement of the community as a whole through the improvement of agriculture, the development of native

industries, the improvement of health, the training of the people in the management of their own affairs and the inculcation of true ideals of citizenship and service.

This was very much in line with Kingsley's own ideas. Although there were other influences on colonial educational policy, such as the Phelps-Stoke report of 1922, Kingsley's ideas were both anticipatory of later policy and of some influence upon them. As Pearce (ibid., 293) suggests, 'the unorthodox, radical stance which she had taken up in the 1890s had to a large degree become the orthodoxy of the 1920s'. She also laid the foundations for cultural relativism in the field of social anthropology.[40] Indeed, Porter (1968, 150) argues that 'in many ways she was the first English *social* anthropologist', and as such she exerted a considerable influence upon her successors. Following her premature death in 1900, having contracted enteric fever while nursing in South Africa during the Boer Wars, the renowned critic W.T. Stead wrote in the *Review of Reviews* (1900, 131):

> What a pity it is that Miss Mary Kingsley died before the Pan-African Conference was held! It is one more count of the indictment of Humanity against this hateful South African War, that it should have cost us the life of the only Paleface who could make the Black Man intelligible to Europe!

Despite the profound ethnocentrism of this comment, the role that Kingsley played in bringing west Africa to the attention of the British public, and the subsequent authority that she was able to command for her opinions, are apparent here. Kingsley positioned herself as an 'expert' on west Africa, and in this way was empowered by British imperialism. The effects of her writings were not immediately apparent in her lifetime, and she died with an enduring sense of failure. However, as Flint (1964, xxxvi) argues, in the years after her death she managed through her writings to 'revolutionise the attitude towards Africans of British Governments, British officials, and even that informed section of British public opinion which deigned to consider African problems'. Kingsley, therefore, was far from peripheral in the imperial debates surrounding west Africa. Although her legacy in terms of influencing imperial policy was small, she did succeed in inspiring many thinkers who carried on the work that she had started into the twentieth century. She was also responsible, alongside the likes of Lugard, for placing west African affairs firmly in the forefront of the public imagination. Perhaps of equal significance is the fact that she succeeded in propelling herself into the public arena, progressing from relative anonymity to become one of the most influential women in the 1890s.

Women travellers as pro-imperialists?

All the women of this study were empowered in various ways, and to differing extents, through British imperial culture and their travels in the British empire and all of these women were pro-imperialist in their attitudes towards west Africa. However, the term pro-imperialist is rather vague, spanning a variety of complex responses and attitudes that require further elucidation. Their travel narratives and the images contained within them were far from being 'only literature'; they were extraordinarily caught up in and indeed an organic part of the British imperial effort in west Africa. In many cases the readership may have been small, but narratives written by women about west Africa were rarefied, and this was often the closest that readers came to Africa. As Said (1994, 80) argues, such texts were, therefore, 'part of the European effort to hold on to, think about, plan for Africa'. That none of the women questioned their right to be in west Africa was not unusual for the times in which they travelled; their presence here was legitimated by British imperial culture. They identified with various aspects of British imperialism. Some supported cultural imperialism, others economic, political, or military imperialism; some saw Britain's efforts as paternalistic, others as potentially damaging to west African cultures; some were in favour of an informal type of imperialism; others wanted more a formal empire, governed rigidly and controlled by Britain. Each woman pictured herself contributing to what she believed was best for both Britain and west Africa. From this one can argue that to label these women pro-imperialist is too simplistic and their opinions require more profound investigation. The nature of their attitudes towards the British empire in west Africa, being so closely connected to the conventions of the periods in which they travelled, differed considerably.

Melville and Foote were clearly pro-imperialists, but the nature of the imperialism that they wished to see operating in west Africa was shaped by the philanthropic endeavours of the anti-slavery movement, and their belief in the responsibility of Britain to protect the freedoms of others. Both had an unerring confidence in the superiority of British morality and government. Melville expressed such beliefs in a poem, reproduced in *A Residence at Sierra Leone* (102), in which she welcomed the sight of an English ship sailing into the harbour at Freetown (see Map 6):

> Those upright masts, that hull's stout build, no foreign craft denote,
> Right proudly at her gaff I see the flag of England float!
> Oh! ever may that ensign bright all alien colours brave,
> And Britain reign triumphant still, the empress of the wave!

Both Melville and Foote were pro-imperialists but not colonialists. They saw their own presence, and the presence of British administrators and missionaries in west

Africa as a temporary sacrifice, there to eradicate slavery and 'civilize' Africans into a Christian way of life. Foote was almost resigned to the fact that it was Britain's 'burden' to assume responsibility for eradicating the slave trade; she wrote that slavery would endure in Africa 'until the civilising influence of Christianity has extended itself over those melancholy tracts of land' (1869, 220–21). To both women, the British effort in west Africa was a heroic one in the cause of freedom and the spread of 'civilization'. As Melville (1968, 303) wrote:

> ... while she may well mourn and lament over the fearful loss of human life sustained by her on this pestilent shore, let England at the same time take comfort in the testimony given by these reclaimed barbarians and converted pagans, towards the real and lasting good effected by her heroic and persevering endeavours in suppressing the slave trade.

In this sense, therefore, Melville and Foote supported British economic and cultural imperialism in west Africa because they perceived it in terms of a philanthropy and benevolence, which was in turn deeply inflected by ethnocentrism.

The missionaries, Hinderer and Slessor, were cultural imperialists in a similar sense. They believed it the duty of Britain to 'civilize' and Christianize west Africans, but they were drawn further into British imperial policy than were the wives of administrators. This is particularly the case with Slessor. Her progression from the coast to the interior can be constructed as a parallel to colonial conquest;[41] she was, to a certain extent, building her own 'empire' in Calabar, independent of both the British administration and the Church of Scotland. Here, Slessor 'reigned' as Eka Kpukpro Owo, mother, magistrate and vice-Consul. Not only did she assert her own influence in Calabar, but she (albeit unwittingly) laid the foundations for the future imposition of a British administration in this area. By helping establish the so-called 'native courts' in her districts, which combined both west African indigenous laws with British justice, Slessor ultimately aided the British imperial effort in southern Nigeria. As Adewoye (1977, 41) argues, the 'native courts' were very much part of the process of the subjugation of southern Nigeria by the British. They were not merely judicial institutions, but instruments for bringing large tracts of land under effective administrative control. Therefore, although Slessor was personally opposed to the extension of territory carried out for reasons of profit or aggrandizement, she found herself a reluctant advocate of British political imperialism. Similarly, by their very presence in Ibadan, Anna and David Hinderer helped lay the foundations for, and were therefore implicated in, British penetration into Yorubaland (see Maps 5 and 7). This area was one of the last in southern Nigeria to be 'opened up' to trade in the late nineteenth century; the presence of the missionaries and their stations facilitated the advance of the traders, which were succeeded by an administrative

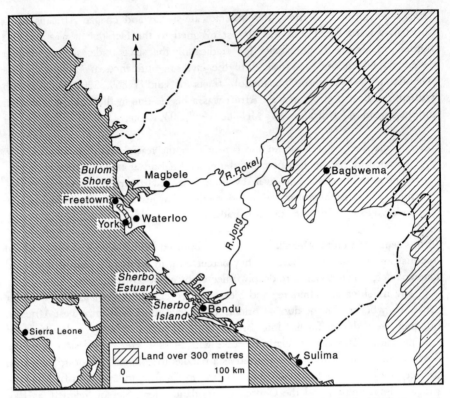

Map 6 The Sierra Leone Protectorate (adapted from Fyfe, 1962)

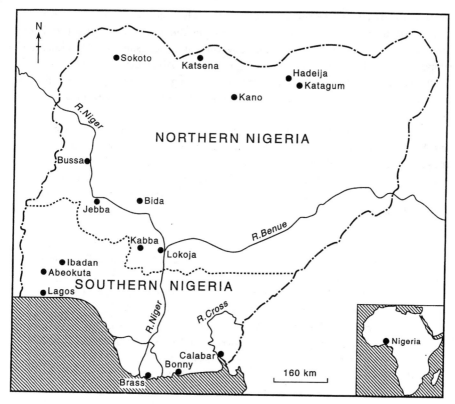

Map 7 The Protectorates of Northern and Southern Nigeria, 1900 (adapted from Orr, 1965)

framework based on British-style law courts. Their concern was the spread of Christianity in west Africa, which sometimes put them in direct conflict with the imperialist aims of successive British governments (for example, the Hinderers' support of the Ibadanis against the Egbas in the Abeokuta wars, and Slessor's obstructive attitude towards census-taking in Okoyong). However, paradoxically, the missionaries were unwittingly involved in aiding the British expansion into southern Nigeria.

Despite this, as intimated in this chapter, many of Slessor's personal opinions were revealing of an anti-imperialist attitude, particularly towards the abuses of the British administration in Nigeria. In later years, as George Eliot had bemoaned the increase in the pace of life facilitated by the steam engine, so Slessor, in 1903, bemoaned the passing of 'the romantic Old Calabar of my youth'. She wrote:

> What a rush of memories ... The changed conditions from the days when we lived among the natives, and they and we were free as the air to pursue calling under more than Bohemian licence, the advent of the steamers, with their old and kindly if rather rough and exaggerated criticism from skipper and man. The great hospitality on hulk, and in Mission House, the general bond of camaraderie and bond of friendship, which a stay on the Coast invariably conveyed. How changed it is now ... The advent of the British Government has brought all the freedom of the native and the European to an end, and just as if a cannonball had exploded and shattered us and scattered us as so many different particles, and sent us off into different locations, the old community of feelings is at an end, and the rush and competition and conventionality which makes life in Europe such a strain has come here to stay.[42]

This passage is revealing not only of Slessor's resentment of the more formal imperialism imposed on Nigeria and its peoples after 1900 but also, one would argue, of the erosion of her own influence as the British government took more of an active role in administering the Protectorate. Thus her anti-imperialist comments must be framed within the context of the loss of freedoms brought about by formal imperialism, both for the peoples of Calabar, and for herself.

Kingsley's position on imperialism was also complex, and she shared Slessor's ambivalence. She was undoubtedly an imperialist, but many of her opinions were in opposition to the prevailing wisdoms emanating from the Colonial and Foreign Offices. In *West African Studies* and other publications, she laid out her opposition to the plans for the British administration of Nigeria.[43] She believed that missionary propaganda provoked the government into a policy of destroying African states and the power of the African ruling classes through a policy of predatory wars. However, as Nworah (1971, 352) points out, it was not this destructive imperialism that she was opposed to, but the lack of constructive government and statesmanship in west Africa. Her opposition to the Crown Colony System emanated from these considerations. She wrote:

> I have attempted to state that the Crown Colony system is unsuited for governing Western Africa, and have attributed its malign influence to its being a system which primarily expresses the opinions of well-intentioned but ill-informed officials at home, instead of being, according to the usual English type of institution, representative of the interests of the people who are governed, and of those who have the largest stake in the countries controlled by it – the merchants and manufacturing classes of Britain (1899a, 314).

Kingsley also deplored the imposition of the hut tax on Sierra Leone, which she perceived as costly and interfering in local institutions. She understood that from an African perspective, payment for any item meant that it no longer belonged to its owner. She also questioned the legality of a tax where the authority of the British government was based entirely on treaties with local rulers which made no mention of taxation, but which did guarantee the protection of property. It was precisely this, in the eyes of Africans, which was being taken away.[44] Thus, between 1895 and 1900, she became the symbol of dissent from certain imperial attitudes towards west Africa (especially those expressed in *The Times*), championing the cause of the traders, by virtue of their experience, justice and humanity, as the best qualified men to govern British interests in this part of the continent. The wealth and prosperity of the traders and, subsequently, of the British economy, depended upon good relations with west Africans, and this notion shaped Kingsley's ideas on economic imperialism. Therefore, while standing in opposition to the jingoism of the 1890s, Kingsley retained conservative and traditional imperialist attitudes. However, what endeared her to the African intelligentsia of the time, men such as Edward Blyden and Mark Hayford,[45] was the fact that she insisted on the need to apply what she called 'the African principle', the idea of 'the government of Africa by Africans' as far as the conditions of the time allowed. This was certainly a radical break from much of the jingoism apparent in the 1890s, and anticipated Lugard's own visions for indirect rule in Nigeria, implemented after Kingsley's death in 1900.

Women travellers and women's rights

It is perhaps ironic that women who were themselves empowered on the imperial stage, both on a personal level and in the public realm, were often vociferously anti-suffrage. Despite their own liberation in the course of their travels and through the subsequent recounting of their experiences in their publications, none of the women of this study championed women's rights in Britain. This is perfectly understandable for those women travelling before the 1870s, when the campaign for women's rights had yet to gain any great momentum. However, it is perhaps more surprising of women such as Kingsley, who had acquired a public platform on which to air their views. Kingsley denied vociferously reports in the *Daily Telegraph* that she was a 'New Woman',[46] but this denial may have been further evidence of the constraints shaping her texts, and cannot be viewed without consideration of her great desire to be taken seriously in scientific and political circles. She felt that association with the women's rights movement would undermine her position of influence with the men of trade, science and politics that had become her acquaintances and allies. She could not afford to alienate her audience by being identified with radical 'shrieking females and androgens'.[47]

Kingsley also expressed her opposition to women becoming Fellows of the Royal Geographical Society and other learned societies, despite the fact that she herself was a member of the Anthropological Society. Despite being a popular lecturer, Kingsley was careful not to overstep prescribed boundaries of femininity. For example, she had her lecture to the Scottish Geographical Society read for her by a male Fellow, and her first lecture to the Liverpool Geographical Society was read by the trader James Irvine. When presenting her second paper in Liverpool she announced in her usual self-deprecating manner, 'Personally, I confess I wish what I have to say to you tonight was again being read by Mr Irvine, as my last address here was, and I feel certain that before I have finished you will wish it were so too' (1987b, 58). Kingsley was supportive of the distinctly female contribution to the imperial endeavour, particularly the role of the wives of administrators and, later, of overseas nurses (1890c, passim) but continuously agitated against women joining the élite ranks of male imperialists. From 1897 onwards, she began formulating ideas about forming an African Society, but she was adamant about not allowing women to become members. She wrote, 'I am not a Believer in women in learned societies ... Ladies *must* not be admitted'.[48] Despite being the inspiration behind the Society, she would not be present at its meetings; she wrote, 'I am not going to show my own petticoat in it but will be represented by a gentleman'.[49] In correspondence with Marion Farquharson, the botanist agitating for women's admittance to the R.G.S., Kingsley wrote:

> I feel I cannot add my name to your influential list. I have for many years heard this question about admitting ladies to learned societies discussed and my personal feeling is that I would not ask any society to admit me ... As for the Geographical Society I have never understood the desire of the ladies to force themselves on it as Fellows. I am myself excluded from it because I am a lady but I have received the greatest courtesy from it and have been told that any information at its command is at my service ... [50]

In order to indicate that she did not represent a threat to the male establishment, Kingsley sent a copy of her reply to Farquharson to Scott Keltie, Secretary of the Royal Geographical Society, and two days later wrote 'these androgynes I have no use for'.[51] However, Kingsley did argue that women were invaluable as 'ethnological bush workers' as they had access to knowledge denied to men. She wrote to Keltie:

> I sincerely hope that if the big Scientific [sic] ever let them [women] in they will make a separate Department – or let the ladies have a separate council-chamber in which they can speak their minds ... Women like your own Isabella [Bird Bishop] and myself know lots of things no man can know about the heathen and no doubt men do ditto.[52]

Kingsley was a firm believer in separate spheres for men and women; just as she believed that Africans were a separate species from Europeans, different in 'kind not degree', and able to progress along their own lines (discussed in Chapter 4), so she believed that women were different from men. She wrote, 'A great woman, mentally or physically, will excel an indifferent man, but no woman has ever equalled a really great man' (1896a, 71). She was also opposed to women's suffrage, believing that politics were the business of men; women's responsibilities were to exercise their influence upon these men in the private sphere. This mirrored her own engagement in politics, networking in order to exercise her own influence but without becoming directly involved in the politics surrounding the debates. She wrote (in Gwynn, 1932, 149) with typical humour, to Sir Matthew Nathan in 1900, 'I have been opposing women having the parliamentary vote this afternoon, and have had a grand time of it, and have been called an idealist and had poetry slung at me in chunks. Argument was impossible, so I offered to fight the secretary in the back yard, but she would not'. In terms of women's rights, therefore, Kingsley's attitudes corresponded with more conservative ideas about gender relations apparent among some intellectuals at the end of the nineteenth century.

Constance Larymore made no claims on behalf of women in her narrative, and encouraged other women to follow her example of remaining loyal to her husband, supporting him in his efforts on behalf of the empire, and making herself of some use whilst accompanying him on his travels. Mary Slessor perhaps did most to empower women in Britain, albeit within the constraining context of the missionary effort. As discussed, at the end of the nineteenth century it was still relatively unusual to find single women Protestant missionaries in Africa, and as Hunt (1990) argues, their presence was actively discouraged. However, not only was Slessor an inspirational figure to other Scottish women, she also vigorously encouraged them to work in west Africa. She complained in the missionary magazines about the lack of women volunteering to continue her work at the stations she had founded; it was imperative that others took over these stations in order that she continue her progress into the interior. As a result of such complaints, Charlotte Crawford at the Women's Foreign Missions Board agitated on Slessor's behalf in Scotland to send more women to west Africa. Several women answered Slessor's call, including her four protégées, Martha Peacock, Beatrice Welsh, Mina Amess and Agnes Arnot. Slessor believed that Africans should run their own out-stations, under the initial supervision of travelling white missionaries, and the presence of these women not only consolidated her own work but proved such ideas tenable. Moreover, she was able to provide a valid reason for other (predominantly working class) British women to broaden their horizons, take the opportunity to travel beyond the shores of Britain and assert their own independence. In defence of women missionaries she wrote, 'women are as eager to share in all the work and sacrifice of the world as men, and it is their privilege to share in it' (Christian and Plummer, 1970, 165).

Despite this, Slessor did not perceive the missionary's life as one of liberation, rather as one of service, and despite devoting a great deal of energy to the cause of west African women, she remained remote from debates over the rights of British women. In a letter to a friend concerning a book she had read, she wrote, 'I have enjoyed the old world gentlewomen, who after all are more to my taste than the new woman. I'm far too old for the new clever independent hand I fear'.[53] While not overtly opposing women's rights, Slessor, after thirty-five years in west Africa, simply felt too removed from the debates taking place in Britain to be able to comment on the subject.

Conclusion

Despite the existence of textual and societal constraints, to some extent the women of this study broke out of the mould prescribed for them by the mores of a patriarchal Victorian Britain. All were empowered to some extent through their travels. 'Duty' may have been a primary motivation, or, indeed, a justification for their travels in west Africa, but the experience of travel itself must have been in various ways a liberating experience. The very opportunity to travel beyond Europe was rare for Victorian women. Once in Africa, women travellers were empowered by virtue of their whiteness and, in some cases, by their social class. Furthermore, they exercised an authority, often based on their gender and their position as 'maternal imperialists', which they would not otherwise have had at home (except, perhaps, for the likes of Elizabeth Melville and Zélie Colvile who were used to exercising authority over domestic servants). Therefore, the basis of their empowerment in west Africa was not only predicated upon racial difference, but was also informed by class and gender difference.

Travel itself gave the women of this study the means to a 'voice' in the public realm, since all were inspired to recount their experiences in published narratives.

Slessor and Kingsley used their printed narratives to further their own ideas about west African affairs, and to have some impact on mission policy and political debate in Britain. Others, such as Melville, Foote and Colvile, merely added to the body of literature emanating from the empire, but their narratives were still of some significance since they were among the few written by women about west Africa during the nineteenth century. They were, therefore, of considerable interest at the time of their publication, if only, in several cases, for their novelty. More importantly for this study, the 'knowledges' constructed through the narratives provide an insight into white women's experiences and understandings of west Africa during the nineteenth century.

Notes

1. See Lewis (1991, 6). On the wider context of the gendered construction of public and private spheres, see Poovey (1989).
2. In 1860, the Hinderers were caught up in the Abeokuta wars, a product of Britain's annexation of Lagos and involvement in inter-tribal rivalries. Various branches of the Yoruba nation declared war on each other. The road to Lagos was blockaded, and the Hinderers were isolated in Ibadan for almost five years, during which time they almost starved to death. For further details see Church Missionary Society (1911), Stock (1899), McEwan (1995a, 47–8).
3. Larymore's book was unique amongst colonial narratives emanating from west Africa in that she devoted the final section to 'Household Hints'. This laid out the guidelines for other women travelling to west Africa with their husbands. It gave information on how to manage the home, the household, keeping dogs, poultry and cows, growing various types of garden, keeping a stable, coping with camp life, and 'what to wear'. It thus represented the transition from travel literature to tourist literature that took place at the beginning of the twentieth century (see Fussell, 1982). It also represented a dramatic contrast to the narratives of other women travellers, especially Mary Kingsley.
4. Kingsley contributed the following to the British Museum: one new species of fish (which Günther named after her), six modifications of known forms of fish, one fish for which only one specimen of its kind had ever been seen (forty years earlier from the Nile), one new species of snake, one species of lizard which the British Museum had waited ten years for, and forty-three different species of fish (see Gwynn, 1932, 112).
5. Blunt (1994) highlights the fact that despite Kingsley's claims, her father's unfinished book had not even begun to take shape yet, and she published two books of her own before she edited a collection of her father's work.

6.   Larymore accompanied her husband on most of his travels in (what was to become) Northern and Southern Nigeria with the Boundary Commission. She was the first white woman to experience at first-hand the harems of the emirs in the north, and her descriptions of these, and of the walled towns of Northern Nigeria, were unique for this period (see Larymore, 1908).

7.   Her basic list included: 'six cambric night-dresses, two flannel night-dresses, twelve cambric combinations, six pairs cambric knickers, twelve spun silk vests, six pairs tan thread stockings, six pairs black thread stockings, three white petticoats, two silk moirette petticoats, two dozen handkerchiefs, six pairs corsets, twelve camisoles ..., one woollen dressing gown, four linen skirts, two holland or drill skirts, two muslin dresses, one cloth gown, one tea gown, two evening gowns, blouses ad lib, one habit skirt, four riding coats, two pairs riding breeches, two panama hats ..., one sun-shade' (Larymore (1908, 290–91).

8.   Some of the place names have been altered to Kingsley's spelling. Campbell points out that the specific route cannot be clearly delineated as much of the country was uncharted at the time of Kingsley's travels, and there is great variation in the names given to places on different maps.

9.   Kingsley to Günther, Okoyong, Upper Calabar River, west Africa, 15/4/95, Günther Papers, British Museum Library (Natural History). Kingsley met Slessor at the end of her first journey to west Africa between August 1893 and January 1894. It was from Slessor that Kingsley learned much about indigenous customs in west Africa.

10. As in other parts of west Africa, trading and missionary endeavours in Calabar preceded the British flag. As Map 4 illustrates, little was known to Europeans of the Calabar region when Slessor arrived there in 1876. Only the coastal towns were known and much of the interior remained unexplored. By 1880, the European presence in west Africa was still confined to the coasts and valleys of navigable rivers, except for the British in the Gold Coast and Sierra Leone, and the French in Senegal (see Hargreaves, 1974). Even in 1900, the area between the Niger and Cross rivers where Slessor was based was still a blank space on the map and until the turn of the century Europeans were generally denied access to the interior by local resistance. Slessor was, therefore, very much a pioneer in the Calabar area, travelling from the coastal towns to live alone in the villages of the interior. As Map 5 illustrates, Slessor progressed from the coastal towns of Calabar into the Okoyong area in 1887, then moved westwards to Akpap in 1896 (which was coincidental with the spread westwards of the centre of the population of the Okoyong peoples). She reached the Enyong districts in 1910, where she stayed until her death in 1915.

11. See Buchanan's letters to Slessor 13/1/05 and 21/1/05, United Presbyterian Church Papers, Foreign 3, National Library of Scotland.
12. Stevenson to Slessor 4/6/12, United Free Church Papers, Women's Foreign Missions, National Library of Scotland.
13. Slessor to Falk, Assistance District Commissioner at Ikot Ekpene, September 1910, E.M. Falk Correspondence, Rhodes House, Oxford.
14. Falk to District Commissioner at Ikot Ekpene, September 1910; District Commissioner to Provincial Commissioner at the Eastern Province, 12/9/10.
15. Slessor to Charles Partridge, District commissioner for Eastern Nigeria, 20/1/08, Slessor Papers, Dundee City Public Library.
16. Slessor to Partridge 30/5/08.
17. Slessor to Partridge, 14/8/08.
18. Slessor to Mrs. Findlay 24/8/12, Cairns Papers, National Library of Scotland.
19. Slessor diaries, entry for 5/5/12, Macmanus Galleries, Dundee Museum.
20. Slessor diaries, entry for 3/4/12.
21. Slessor (1890), *Missionary Record*, October, 304.
22. This is discussed in greater detail in Chapter 6.
23. See also Russett's (1989) discussion of the post-Darwinian psychologist G. Stanley Hall, who identified altruism and an interest in aesthetics as 'feminine' characteristics (1989, 57–63).
24. There is a substantial critique of this concept within various strands of feminism, but for analyses of ideologies of 'separate spheres' in the nineteenth century, see Harrison (1978), Millett (1970) and Pateman (1988).
25. The quote is taken from Hone's preface to Hinderer (1872).
26. According to Frank Cass Publications, Melville's *A Residence at Sierra Leone* was reprinted in 1968 at around 400-500 copies, but there is no information for the 1849 edition. Similarly there are no records of publication figures for the books of Larymore, Colvile, Foote or Hinderer.
27. She wrote, 'I have hopes there may be a demand for Round the Black Man's Garden which I have been advertising by giving a lecture on Madagascar at Liverpool G.D. Society. My first attempt met with a most enthusiastic reception' (Colvile to Blackwood, 16/12/98, Blackwood Papers 1893–1900, National Library of Scotland).
28. Figures from the *Women's Missionary Magazine of the Free Church of Scotland*, July, 1903, 154.
29. Figures from Birkett (1992, 135). Compare this to Mungo Park's best selling *Travels in the Interior Districts of Africa* (1799). Its 1500 copies sold out within a few months, and three other editions were issued before the end of the year (Nussbaum, 1995, 74). Kingsley, and her version of Africa, was consumed with the same relish as her Scottish predecessor almost a century earlier.

30. Information courtesy of Macmillan Publishers Limited. Both books were reissued in the 1960s by Cass, and *Travels in West Africa* was reprinted in 1972, 1982, and 1987, the latter an abridged version.
31. Buchanan to Slessor, 13/1/05, ms. 7661, United Presbyterian Papers, Foreign 3, 394, National Library of Scotland.
32. See, for example, Blunt (1994b), Mills (1991, 21–3); Morin (1995).
33. Buchanan to Slessor, 10/11/02, United Presbyterian Church Papers, Foreign 1, National Library of Scotland.
34. Buchanan to Slessor, 7/7/02, 10/11/02, mss. 7658, 7659, United Presbyterian Papers, National Library of Scotland.
35. Stevenson to Slessor, 4/6/12, ms. 7952, United Free Church Papers, National Library of Scotland.
36. See Birkett (1987a, 219, 268; 1987c, 115–19).
37. Kingsley to Holt, 20/2/99, Holt Papers, Rhodes House, Oxford.
38. Kingsley to Holt, 13/12/98, Holt Papers, Rhodes House, Oxford. See also Blunt (1994), for a more detailed account of Kingsley's gendered subjectivity.
39. For accounts of Kingsley's influence in the political arena see Stevenson (1982); Nwabughuogu (1981); Nworah (1971); Pearce (1990); Porter (1961).
40. Pearce (1990, 145); Rich (1986, 30–1). Rich also points out that in the realms of politics and anthropology Kingsley, almost single-handedly, shifted attention away from India and Asia towards Africa.
41. For an analysis of the parallels between evangelical enterprise and colonial conquest in South Africa see, Comaroff and Comaroff (1988, 11).
42. Slessor to Irvine, Okoyong 12/12/03, Saint Andrew's Hall Missionary College Library, Selly Oak, Birmingham.
43. Kingsley (1899a, passim); (1899b, 63–5).
44. Throughout 1898, Kingsley contributed a whole series of articles on 'West African Property' to the Morning Post, in which she outlined her protests against the hut tax. She also detailed her objections in correspondence with Joseph Chamberlain (Chamberlain Papers, British Library) and John Holt (Holt Papers, Rhodes House).
45. See Blyden (1901); Hayford (1901). Both respected Kingsley for advocating the cause of African culture, reviewed her books, reproduced her speeches and constantly employed her ideas in attacks on missionaries (see Ayendele, 1966, 251).
46. *Daily Telegraph*, December 3 1895; letter from Mary Kingsley, *Daily Telegraph*, December 5 1895.
47. Kingsley to Holt, n.d., Holt Papers, Rhodes House, Oxford.

48. Kingsley to Edward Clodd, 7/1/98, Kingsley archive compiled by Beth Urquhart, Eugene, Oregon, U.S.A.. The African Society was formed in Kingsley's honour after her death by Alice Green.
49. Kingsley to Tylor, 10/12/98, Rhodes House, Oxford.
50. Kingsley to Farquharson, 26/11/99, Royal Geographical Society Correspondence 1881–1910, Royal Geographical Society.
51. Kingsley to Keltie, 27/11/99, 29/11/99, Royal Geographical Society Correspondence, 1881–1910, Royal Geographical Society.
52. Kingsley to Keltie, 01/12/99, Royal Geographical Society Correspondence, 1881–1910, Royal Geographical Society.
53. Slessor to Partridge, Use (West Africa), 1/1/08, Slessor Papers, Dundee City Library.

CHAPTER 3

Paradise or pandemonium?[1]

A wonderful stillness pervades these West African creeks. Except for the gentle ripple of the water among the mangroves, hardly a sound was to be heard, and the only sign of life was afforded by an occasional crane, which, startled by the sound of oars, reluctantly abandoned his fishing and flew heavily away (Colvile, 1893, 314).

[We] set out on our river journey, under a full moon, threading our way along one of the labyrinths of creeks – a liquid silver path, walled on each side with straight lines of mangroves, dense black shadows, and weird, bare white roots and stems – a scene suggestive of mystery, and full of a strange beauty of its own (Larymore, 1908, 5).

The West Coast of Africa is like the Arctic regions in one particular, and that is that when you have once visited it you want to go back there again; and now I come to think of it, there is another particular in which it is like them, and that is the chances you have of returning from it at all are small, for it is a *Belle Dame sans merci* (Kingsley, 1982, 11).

Introduction: British women travellers in west African landscapes

Landscape description was a subject to which women travellers chose to devote extensive passages. Textual constraints on the production and reception of the text may have influenced the construction of copious descriptions of the physical environment in the narratives of Victorian women travellers, but at the same time there was a certain amount of self-determination on the content of their narratives. The fact that Kingsley was able to enter into scientific and political debate suggests that, even if these textual constraints had not existed, many women travel writers would still have avoided more robust and modern, and by implication more directly political and, therefore, feminist forms of writing. What becomes important, therefore, is a recognition of the constraints on the production and reception of the texts, but also the significance of differences between white women travellers, based on personality and experience, and the ways in which these differences produced variations in their landscape descriptions.

The conventions of the time exercised some influence on the language employed in landscape descriptions by women travellers. For the most part, they did not employ in these descriptions the sexual metaphors often found in travel accounts by men at this time;[2] the language of penetration, conquest and domination was a language generally not employed by women, although not exclusive of them. Instead they 'attempted to combine the excitement of the unpredictable attaching to exploration' with 'the pleasure of knowing where one is' (Fussell, 1977, 39). From their narratives it is clear that white women travellers considered themselves observers and describers of the physical environment, rather than conquistadors and doing battle with their surroundings in an effort to establish dominion over them. However, as discussed in the previous chapter, the very acts of observing and describing have implications for the relative positions of authority attained by white women abroad; observation and description were also means of mastering and appropriating the landscapes of west Africa. Landscape descriptions in the travelogues of British women give an indication of the varying levels of their attachment to and involvement in west Africa, and the different ways in which these women related to the physical environments they described. There is a stark contrast between the women of this study. On the one hand, Melville, Foote, Larymore and Colvile placed themselves outside the physical environments they observed and on which they commented. On the other hand, Slessor and Kingsley positioned themselves very much within the landscapes they described. While the latter travelled into the interior of west Africa, the former were to some extent geographically removed from west African environments. Landscape descriptions in the narratives of Foote and Colvile were drawn mainly from their observation from the sea in the course of their travels around the coast, and both Melville and Foote lived in coastal towns (Freetown and Lagos respectively), rarely travelling inland. In the narratives of these women there is a strong sense of their externality to the landscapes they described; they did not appear to have felt comfortable in west Africa and seem not to have identified with the landscapes they encountered. West Africa was perceived as Other.

During the 1840s and the time of Melville's residence in Sierra Leone, a fear of the climate of west Africa and its supposed debilitating effects on Europeans was prevalent. This fear kept her indoors for much of the time, further enhancing her sense of distance from west African environments. She wrote (1968, 267), 'A person may live for years here, but ... return to Europe at the end of that time with the impression of having merely had for so long, a moving panorama of tropical scenery and figures before him ... This will be the case with me; for it is quite impracticable ... to tempt braving the climate'. When compelled to move to the hills outside Freetown in an attempt to find a more salubrious atmosphere, Melville's sense of distance and loneliness was intensified. She wrote after one of her few excursions outdoors:

> On coming within view of our own house again, the smiling plain below still open to our gaze, the house so strange and solitary, perched on the very pinnacle of that oddly-shaped hill, so unlike the social dwellings which shelter our fellow

creatures in the Sierra Leone capital, I felt more than usual what a complete out-of-the-world place our present habitation is, eight hundred feet above the level of the sea (ibid., 55).

Intrinsic to Melville's relationship with the physical environment was her sense of the imperial frontier. She believed that Sierra Leone was a small island of 'civilization' in a sea of barbarism and slavery, and that she and the other Britons in Sierra Leone were responsible for extending the frontier of 'civilization' further into west Africa. This notion of the imperial frontier amplified her sense of displacement and lack of identity with the surrounding physical environment; such feelings were often revealed in her landscape descriptions. On several occasions she contrasted the order and familiarity of the European settlements to the natural landscapes beyond. For example, she wrote:

> There lay ... immediately beneath us the race-course, ... the many little bays on our own side of the estuary, several villa-like mansions, with their cultivated grounds formed a pleasing contrast to the vast continent beyond, where, as far as the eye could reach, nothing was to be seen except forest and jungle, among which partial glimpses of creek and river shone like so many embowered lakes (ibid., 52–3).

For Melville, west African landscapes were attractive, but remained above all strange and unfamiliar.

Zélie Colvile was also struck by the strangeness of her surroundings. In the course of her voyage around Africa, one of her few excursions from the coast inland took her into the Oil Rivers and the creeks around the trading town of Bonny. Her descriptions of the mangroves along the Bonny River were almost Conradian in their evocation of mystery, otherworldliness and impenetrability: '[D]ark-green foliage, perched on top of a framework of earthless roots present a strange and unnatural appearance even by day; and in the twilight, magnified and rendered indistinct by the rising mist, these tangled roots look like bunches of some writhing reptile pendant from the dark walls that hem the narrow stream on either side' (1893b, 377–8). Although Colvile alluded to the 'wonderful stillness' of the creeks and the 'glorious vegetation' that lined their banks, she seemed less comfortable among the swamps and dense vegetation than she did when viewing west Africa from the decks of a steamer. She found the Bonny estuary bewildering and disorienting. She wrote, '[T]he creeks [became] narrower, and much more intricate; and in the utter absence of landmarks, one wondered how anyone could find his way about this watery labyrinth' (ibid., 319).

The sense of dislocation from the physical environment is also found in Constance Larymore's narrative. Larymore is somewhat unique among the women of this study in that she tended to adopt what Pratt (1992, 204–5) refers to as the 'monarch-of-all-I-survey' position in her landscape descriptions. Pratt argues that 'it is hard to think of a trope more decisively gendered' than this approach to describing landscapes; 'explorer-man paints/possesses newly unveiled landscape-woman'. The 'promontory descriptions' that Pratt sees as an inherent part of the 'monarch-of-all-I-survey' trope, however, occur throughout Larymore's text, and, on occasions, she made exaggerated claims about her achievements. For example, she described her procession through the forests of northern Yoruba as 'a very interesting experience, penetrating this silent forest, where no human being had passed before' (1908, 21). Larymore's adoption of this particular narrative style stemmed from the fact that she positioned herself as a female 'discoverer/explorer' of vast areas of Nigeria, especially Northern Nigeria. She wrote, 'It certainly was a step in the darkest dark; no Englishwoman yet had gone where I meant to go, or done what I hoped to do: we knew little or nothing of the conditions of life before us except that it was 'rough, very rough!'' (ibid., 1–2). As with Melville in Sierra Leone, Larymore positioned herself on the imperial frontier in Northern Nigeria, a frontier that her husband was partly responsible for rolling back through the imposition of a British administration. Although white men had travelled through Northern Nigeria for decades, Larymore emphasised her position as the first white woman to travel from the southern forests to the deserts in the north, and thus was able to depict herself as discover/explorer. In this guise, the 'monarch-of-all-I-survey' trope, which Pratt suggests is an essentially masculine genre of travel writing, became accessible to Larymore. The context of her journey was crucial to her attitude; as part of a military expedition to suppress indigenous populations, she was also aware of her relative position of authority within Nigeria. Her sense of superiority and of her presence on the imperial frontier is apparent in her landscape descriptions. For example, she described the view at Egga:

> I had a glorious and uninterrupted view of mile upon mile of grassland, flanked in the distance by the curious flat-topped hills at Padda. The distance was marked only by the 'wire road', the telegraph line leaving Egga and disappearing into the pearly iridescent Harmattan mists in an ever diminishing perspective – the one link with civilisation (ibid., 37–8).

Pratt argues that within the 'monarch-of-all-I-survey' trope three conventions can be identified which create qualitative and quantitative value for the explorer's achievement. These conventions are recognisable in Larymore's landscape descriptions. Firstly, the landscape is 'aestheticized', the view is seen as a painting and the description is ordered in terms of background and foreground, perspective and colouration. Secondly, 'density of meaning' is sought, particularly through the modification of nouns. Larymore's 'pearly' mists (and on other occasions, 'pearly blue haze' (71), and 'emerald green' plains (112)) tie the landscape to her home culture, 'sprinkling it with little bits of England'. Finally, the metaphor of the painting is important in terms of Larymore's 'mastery' of the scene. Larymore became a verbal painter reproducing a scene for others; what she saw was all there was. The landscape was ordered with reference to her vantagepoint. The 'ever-diminishing perspective' to which she referred privileged her position as observer. As Pratt (1992, 204–5) argues, the observer has the power 'if not to possess, at least to evaluate this scene'. These conventions are repeated throughout Larymore's narrative.

Despite Larymore's adoption of the colonial 'gaze', there is a certain tension within her landscape descriptions; she was obviously captivated by the landscapes through which she travelled, but she struggled simultaneously to maintain objective, even scientific rationality in her descriptions. As Rose argues, many explorers and travellers, in their quest to produce geographical knowledge, had to resist what J.K. Wright referred to as 'the sirens of *terrae incognitae*'.[3] Taking pleasure in viewing the landscape was often seen as a threat to the scientific validity of the observations contained in the narrative. This tension is apparent in Larymore's landscape descriptions. For example, she wrote, 'autumn is almost the best time of the year to 'see the country'; in the farms the guinea-corn was just beginning to ripen and droop its massive plumes of grain, ... and we got magnificent views of miles of wooded hill and plain unrolling themselves into the dim blue distance' (ibid., 69). Here, Larymore provided knowledge on when to acquire the best view of the landscape, and detail on the nature of the landscapes of Northern Nigeria, but she succumbed to the inherent pleasures of gazing upon the landscape. In the colonial context, Larymore's position as author-colonizer allowed her to adopt this 'gaze', which both Rose and Pratt argue is essentially a masculine gaze. Her descriptions thus contain the same tensions found in exploration literature between scientific narrative and the sense of almost voyeuristic pleasure the observer has in viewing the landscape.

Pratt suggests that the panorama is a device for seeing the country as a future colonized country, and thus by including panoramic scenes Larymore arrogated to herself the power of the colonizer.[4] She also used other conventions of exploration narrative that perhaps were not as readily available to the women who travelled in the nineteenth century. She described herself surmounting geographical barriers such as the rapids on the Upper Niger:

> At the worst point, where the whole face of the river appeared to be barred with a rush of falling waters, and no smallest passage was visible amidst the tumbling foam, the canoes were hauled under the steep bank, and their entire contents bundled out thereon, we, the passengers, clambering, by the aid of roots and branches, to a place of some security, where we sat on the warm sand and watched the manoeuvres down below (ibid., 159).

Here Larymore confronted the landscape, the rapids were obstacles which she must overcome in order to progress on her journey. On other occasions, she described herself as 'marching' into the towns of Northern Nigeria, identifying herself with the British military expedition that had facilitated her travels. Furthermore, whilst in Kabba she wrote, 'Outside the town, there is a little stretch of forest belt, and, as no one has ever disputed its possession with me, I am pleased to consider it exclusively my own property' (ibid., 118). She referred to this forest as 'my 'kingdom''. Significantly, Larymore 'claimed' this land not for Britain but for herself; she claimed it not for its potential wealth, but because of the beauties of both flora and fauna that were contained within the forest. Thus the convention of laying claim to territory, which Pratt views as a masculine convention, was tempered by her delight in the physical environment; her desire to possess was rooted in the aesthetic beauty of the landscape she encountered. However, this metaphorical claiming of land indicated how Larymore placed herself in a position of power and authority in relation to the landscapes that she described. This metaphorical claiming is not found in the narratives of those women travelling before the end of the nineteenth century and the advent of formal imperialism in west Africa.

Despite the presence of such conventions in Larymore's narratives, there are further ambivalences in her text.[5] For example, she wrote:

> Picture to yourself a green – truly emerald green – plain, holding an area of, roughly, ten square miles, dotted with palm trees, their tall slender stems crowned with crests of graceful drooping plumes, and bearing a respectable fortune in the palm-oil contained in the closely clustering bunches of nuts on each tree. Hundreds of acres are under cultivation ... Away, beyond, rise the blue hills, in a huge circle, jealously shutting in this little green paradise from the tiresome world of restless white folks, who would take count of time, make roads, try to introduce sanitation and otherwise employ themselves in fruitless and unnecessary works to the dire discomfort of the peaceful denizens of peaceful places! (ibid., 112–13)

Larymore's ambivalence is clear in passages such as this. As a wife of a military administrator in Nigeria she acquired freedoms and a degree of authority that would not have been available to her in Britain. Yet she expressed her worries about the impact of British economic and cultural imperialism, and the colonial administration her husband was helping to impose, upon the very landscapes and peoples she was observing. Larymore was clearly a romantic and wished to see the landscapes she encountered remain unchanged, yet she realised that British imperialism, in which she played a part, would have a drastic effect upon the pace of life in Nigeria.

As with Larymore, Slessor and Kingsley were also romantics, but their relationship with the physical environments of west Africa was on a more personal and spiritual level than the other women of this study. Whereas the likes of Melville, Colvile and Larymore were geographically distanced from the landscapes they observed, Slessor and Kingsley travelled deep into the forests of west Africa, placing themselves within the landscapes they described. A panoramic view was impossible in the dense rainforests of southern Nigeria. Slessor's movement away from the coastal towns into the unexplored forests of Calabar gave her the opportunity to construct epic visions of her local landscapes, and of her own achievements within these landscapes, much in the style of Larymore. Slessor envisaged herself on the frontier between 'wilderness' and 'civilization'. Beidelman (1982, 63) suggests that it was the overland progression from the coast to the interior that was the *rite de passage* into African reality and thus a journey that was constructed in epic terms. Missionary literature emanating from west Africa added to these heroic narratives; the epic accounts of missionary endeavours had, by the late nineteenth century, become an established European genre, alongside popular travel and exploration narratives. 'This was a literature of the imperial frontier, a colonising discourse that titillated the Western imagination with glimpses of radical otherness which it simultaneously brought under intellectual control' (Comaroff and Comaroff, 1988, 9). Reports told that, 'The print of the Missionary's foot is as yet only in the sand of Africa's shore. Oh there is not in the entire world a field more needful than this. Its numerous millions, lying in the blood, appeal to us for sympathy and help' (*Missionary Record*, January 1846, 3–4). Later, Livingstone came to embody the spirit of the frontier, combining both religion and commerce in his fight against the 'darkness' of Africa. The frontier sense of personal freedom and independence was of fundamental importance to Slessor. However, her accounts of her progression inland were rarely heroic and she seldom depicted the physical environment as a series of obstacles to be confronted and overcome. Instead, Slessor saw west Africa as a land of magnificent beauty, but with a climate of some hardship for Europeans. Her romanticism produced a view of the countryside as sanctuary, and the romantic notion of the 'wilderness'[6] was an important part of her thinking. Having lived in the slums of Dundee, she yearned for the peace of the countryside, and initially found it in Calabar. As discussed in the previous chapter, her mourning for the passing of 'the romantic Old Calabar of my youth' illustrated that there was an element of ambivalence in Slessor's position. Her presence in west Africa helped to 'open up' the interior to British officials, and she was part of the imperialism that had changed the pace of life in Nigeria that she now lamented.

Slessor arrived in Calabar for the first time during the rainy season, but the brilliant sunshine and the beauty of her surroundings misled her into describing the climate as 'delightsome' (Buchan, 1980, 27). As one of her biographers put it, 'The warm luxuriant beauty of Calabar contrasted strangely with the grey streets of ... Dundee' (McFarlan, 1946, 93). Though she would soon change her opinion of the climate, Slessor remained captivated by the effulgence of the natural environment.

During her first months in Calabar she took long walks into the bush and delighted at the tropical plants, brilliantly plumaged birds, flaming sunsets and the noises from the forest at night. The landscapes of Calabar appealed to the romantic side of Slessor's nature, and she was even moved to write poetry about her surroundings (Miller, 1946, 20). Her love of nature was deeply rooted in her upbringing. For her the countryside represented an escape, both from the demands placed upon the urban poor, and from the confines of an unhappy home.[7] As a Sunday school teacher in the slums of Dundee, she often took her charges into the countryside, which suggests that her training may have exposed her to Victorian ideas about the education of the poor and their relationship with their physical environment.[8]

Although she was a romantic, Slessor held contradictory views about the physical environment of Calabar. She wrote to friends, 'I feel drawn on and on by the magnetism of this land of dense darkness and mysterious, weird forests' (Miller, 1946, 97). Despite her delight in her surroundings, Slessor's descriptions of 'terrors' in the bush, and the 'dark' and 'mysterious' forests are reminiscent of depictions of west Africa as the heart of the 'dark continent', a land of intense beauty concealing hidden dangers to those attempting to penetrate its secrets. Furthermore, when describing her progress into Aro country Slessor wrote, 'First Itu, then the Creek, then back from Aro, where I had set my heart, to a solitary wilderness of the most forbidding description, where the silence of the bush has never been broken ...'[9] Here, Slessor constructed an epic vision of the landscape and framed herself within it. As with Melville, she envisaged herself on the imperial frontier, carrying the torch of enlightenment into the 'wilderness'. However, an important consideration in understanding Slessor's landscape descriptions is the fact that for almost forty years west Africa was her home. If Africa was a 'wilderness', it was also a sanctuary. Scotland had only ever been 'home' whilst her mother and sisters were alive; by 1895 all had died, and Slessor's home now, more than ever, was in Calabar. Her subjective responses to the landscapes she experienced were thus informed by her identification of these landscapes as 'home'.

Although Anna Hinderer lived as a missionary in west Africa for seventeen years, she did not share Slessor's identification of west Africa as 'home'. Hinderer is unique among the women of this study in that the landscape descriptions within her narrative are very few and far between. The reason for this is that for most of their stay in Yoruba, the Hinderers were preoccupied with their own survival in the midst of illness, wars and the threat of starvation. Hinderer's narrative, therefore, focused more upon the difficulties of everyday life than it did on observations of her surroundings. However, one gains a sense of her romanticism from her comments on first arriving in west Africa:

> Fancy the most lovely summer evening, our noble vessel at anchor in the stillest
> water possible, the little town of Bathurst lying before us, the most glorious

sunset behind those little old houses, the sweetest breeze that ever blew passing over us. Imagine all this, and then you will have a picture of me (1872, 24–5).

The romanticism informing white women's responses to the natural environment of west Africa had its roots in the wider philosophical trend that was developing in Victorian Britain. As suggested, within nineteenth-century exploration literature not only were the landscapes of west Africa depicted as wild and chaotic in opposition to the ordered and controlled landscapes of Europe, they were also among the few places that could still be referred to as 'the country' in contrast to an increasingly urbanized Europe (Williams, 1973, 281–3). However, it was in the works of Mary Kingsley that this romanticism was most strongly represented. Kingsley's beliefs were more akin to an eighteenth-century romanticism, which was characterised by 'the delight in, and wonder at, the beauty and beneficence of nature', and 'the ascendence of emotion and intuitive perception over reason' (Koster, 1975, 8) than they were to Victorian romanticism. Her responses to the landscapes were on a deeply personal and aesthetic level. Her claims to be an objective observer of west Africa were undermined by the subjectivity of her responses. However, as Blunt (1994b) argues, Kingsley claimed subjective authority by stressing the individuality of her response. For example, she wrote:

> To my taste there is nothing so fascinating as spending a night out in an African forest, or plantation; but I beg you to note I do not advise anyone to follow the practice. Nor indeed do I recommend African forest life to anyone. Unless you are interested in it and fall under its charm, it is the most awful life in death imaginable. It is like being shut up in a library whose books you cannot read, all the while tormented, terrified, and bored. And if you do fall under its spell, it takes all the colour out of other kinds of living (1982, 102).

The beauties of the natural environment were accessible to Kingsley because she was 'interested' in west Africa, and she allowed the landscapes to exercise their almost magical powers over her rather than seek to impose herself upon her surroundings. Kingsley located herself within the forests and attempted to blend with them instead of 'mastering' them. She was emotionally connected to the landscapes through which she travelled, and insisted, 'I am more comfortable there than in England' (ibid., xxi). Although raised by agnostics, her experiences in west Africa instilled within her a deep private faith in pantheism. Her favourite poem was Coleridge's *Ancient Mariner*, she had read the works of Spinoza, whom she claimed was the 'greatest European philosopher we have had' (1897b, 63), and she derived her spiritual beliefs from his works. For Kingsley, as with Spinoza, God was the immanent, not the transcendent, cause of all things; God was not the creator of things, but the things themselves. After her journeys, Kingsley identified these beliefs as 'firm African', and she maintained that she was happiest when among the 'non-human things' of nature. She wrote of the Ogowé rapids (present-day Gabon):

> The majesty of the scene fascinated me, and I stood leaning with my back against a rock pinnacle watching it. Do not imagine it gave rise, in what I am pleased to call my mind, to those complicated, poetical reflections natural beauty seems to bring out in other people's minds. It never works that way with me; I just lose all sense of human individuality, all memory of human life, with its grief and worry and doubt, and become part of the atmosphere. If I have a heaven, that will be mine (1982, 178).

Here, her experience was almost transcendental, and very often in the forests of west Africa she would, as Wordsworth wrote, be 'asleep in body and become a living soul'. As Claridge put it in the preface to the Virago edition of *Travels*, 'her innate pantheism attuned her to the spirituality of Africa; her innate loneliness was consoled by its solitudes' (1982, xiv).

Slessor and Larymore also experienced the transcendentalism evident in Kingsley's responses. Slessor delighted in the Enyong Creek area, perhaps the most luxurious part of Calabar. The banks of the creek were covered in lillies, orchids and ferns, and blossom sometimes cascaded down from the trees above. Slessor particularly enjoyed travelling up and down these waterways. Describing one such occasion she wrote, 'We turned the boat's head and glided into such a lake of aquatic plants and flowers as I believe could not be surpassed anywhere ... On we ran as if in an extravagant dream ...' (Christian and Plummer, 1970, 128–9) In less poetic moments, she described the scene as 'awful bonnie!' (Buchan, 1980, 175) Where a panoramic view was impossible, Larymore's responses to her surroundings were on a more subjective and personal level. For example, she described her experience by a pool in the middle of Kano as 'one of those special moments that come to us all, perhaps only once in a lifetime' (1908, 79). On another occasion while travelling upriver to Bussa, she described the Niger and its rich vegetation as 'bringing to mind that strange indefinable world that is neither dream-land nor fairy-land, but which very surely exists, and is sometimes momentarily revealed to most of us' (ibid., 152–3).

On occasions, Kingsley's landscape descriptions are revealing of her views on imperialism. For example, she wrote:

> [T]hese pioneer mangrove heroes may be said to have laid down their lives to make that mud-bank fit for colonization, for the time gradually comes when other mangroves can and do colonise on it, and flourish, extending their territory steadily; and the mud-bank joins up with, and becomes part of, Africa (1982, 90–91).

Inevitably, as other species colonise the mud-bank, the mangrove is doomed, but the great stretches of dead mangrove trees are the life-blood to succeeding generations of colonizers. To Kingsley, the traders were the heroic human embodiment of the mangroves, struggling to survive on the coasts of west Africa to establish a foothold upon which others could build, very often sacrificing their own lives in the process. In Kingsley's narratives, inanimate objects such as mangrove trees frequently take on human characteristics, reflecting her belief in animism and the living presences in nature. For example, she wrote of the Ogowé rapids:

> [I]t was a scene to make one believe in ghosts ... [T]here from Boue and Lope to Otala Amagonga are the fearful spirits of the rapids and the Okanda gorge, ever quarrelling with each other, and with the rocks and with the whirlpools in between; ever ready to kill the man who comes near them; but there are other spirits there who are kinder to him and who call him off from danger, and these are the singing sands of Okanda (1897c, 341).

Kingsley's personal identification with the landscapes of west Africa seems contrary to the imperial strategies contained in Larymore's narrative, and whereas the latter privileged vision, Kingsley's descriptions included other sensual responses such as sound. As Blunt (1994, 97) points out, Kingsley's descriptions were less likely to 'establish the landscape as a stage for the exercise of the imperial viewers' power' than they were to prompt self-questioning, 'further highlighting her personal and reflexive sensitivity to landscape'. For example, Kingsley wrote that while she was sitting on her verandah overlooking Victoria and taking in the scenery beneath her, she thought, 'Why did I come to Africa? ... Why! who would not come to its twin brother hell itself for all the beauty and charm of it' (182, 608). The extent to which she identified with the landscapes of west Africa was revealed in a letter written shortly before she died, where she wrote, 'I am no more a human being than a gust of wind ... My people are mangroves, swamps, rivers, and the sea and so on – we understand each other. They never give me the dazzles with their goings on, like human beings do by theirs repeatedly'.[10] However, as with Larymore, Kingsley's position in west Africa was often ambivalent. For example, in her ascent of Mungo Mah Lobeh, Kingsley sought a panoramic view. As Blunt (1994, 101) argues, Kingsley's account of her ascent 'illustrates the ambiguities of being constructed as inside and outside and moving between patriarchal and imperial discourses'. However, her ability to identify with the masculine, imperialist trope of the panoramic view was undermined by the obscuring of the vista by mist. Disappointed that her efforts to climb the mountain were unrewarded with a view from the top, Kingsley nonetheless appreciated the aesthetic effects of the mist which was 'exceedingly becoming to the forest's beauty' (1982, 570). As Blunt (op cit., 102) argues, the landscape was feminised, 'but its attraction lay in it being veiled rather than being unveiled'.

It is clear that differences existed in the ways in which various women positioned themselves in relation to the various landscapes through which they travelled. However, despite these differences, with the exception of Anna Hinderer, descriptions of the physical environment were of paramount importance in the narratives of all these women, and are often revealing of the personalities of the women themselves and their different positionings within imperialism.

Confronting 'chaotic' west Africa

The 'quest' genre of travel writing featured prominently in the works of nineteenth-century explorers, and within these narratives there was a common style of landscape description. As Hammond and Jablow (1977, 61) argue, 'though florid in style, the descriptions are matter-of-fact and more analytical than romantic', for many explorers the landscape was incidental to their exploits and provided only a backdrop for their adventures. Thus landscape descriptions were most eloquent when evoking the hazards and threats facing the explorer. For the explorers of west Africa, the image of the 'dark continent' was often used as the backdrop for the heroic deeds of the protagonist. The dangers and uncertainties facing the explorer meant that the physical environment was often depicted as a pandemonium lacking order and familiarity. It has been asserted that women travellers in west Africa were denied access to the 'quest' genre of travel writing, and, as a result, their relationship with their physical environment tended on the whole to be more harmonious and non-confrontational. As a consequence of this, their landscape descriptions offer up several challenges to notions of 'chaotic' west African environments.

A major feature of landscape descriptions by white women travellers in west Africa was their recognition of order in the natural environment, and this is particularly evident in the narratives of Mary Kingsley. For Kingsley, west Africa was not a homogeneous confusion of nature, but a series of ordered physical environments – coastal, riverine, montane and forest environments – each presenting its own hardships, but all dramatic in their beauty. In Kingsley's mind, the horizontal bands of colour in the landscape when viewed on approach from the sea – the blue of the ocean, the white of the surf upon the yellow of the sand, the brown and green of the mangroves, the deep green of the rainforest, and in the distance the purple of the mountains, were evidence of natural order rather than of pandemonium. Other women travellers remarked upon these bands of colour, which formed their first impressions of west Africa from the Atlantic, and, although bereft of the poeticism of Kingsley's descriptions, still conveyed the impression of order. Colvile noticed the 'long low line of palms, the strip of sand, and the fringe of breakers which are characteristic of this part of the African coast' (1893, 285); Larymore described the 'sunshine, sapphire water, the fringe of low grey coast-line ... [T]he huge swell swept shorewards, to break in its thundering surf, away by the grey palm-trees and the yellow sand' (1908, 4). The common perception was one of order and beauty rather than chaos. The layers of colour occur several times in Kingsley's descriptions, and even when she was in the rainforest she was able to recognize harmony in her surroundings. She wrote:

> [O]n either side there ... [are] banks of varied tropical shrubs and ferns, behind which rise, 100–200 feet high, walls of grand forest; ... behind this again are the lovely foothills of Mungo, high up against the sky, coloured the most perfect, dark, lambent blue. The whole scheme of colour is indescribably rich and full in tone; the very earth under foot is a velvety-red brown, and the butterflies that abound show themselves off in the sunlight with their canary coloured, crimson, and peacock-blue liveries to perfection (1896c, 40).

Kingsley intimated that she felt more comfortable in west Africa than she did back in the crowds and traffic of London, and once back in England she yearned to return to west Africa. She wrote:

> The charm of West Africa is a painful one. It gives you pleasure to fall under it when you are out there, but when you are back here, it gives you pain, by calling you. It sends up before your eyes a vision of a wall of dancing, white, rainbow-gemmed surf playing on a shore of yellow sand before an audience of stately cocoa palms, or of a great mangrove-walled bronze river, or of a vast forest cathedral, and you hear, *nearer* to you than the voices of the people around you, *nearer* than the roar of the city traffic, the sound of that surf that is beating on the shore down there, and the sound of the wind talking in the hard palm-leaves ... and everything that is round you grows thin in the face of that vision, and you want to go back to that coast that is calling you, saying, as the African says to the departing soul of his dying friend, 'Come back, this is your home' (1898c, 280).

It seems that it was her perception of the natural order and organization of the physical environment that Kingsley found most alluring about west Africa, and it could thus be argued that she employed a scientific, ecological 'trope' in her landscape descriptions (this is discussed in more detail subsequently). This can be observed in her descriptions of Corisco Island, off the coast of Angola. For Kingsley, Corisco Island was not only very beautiful, but was also an exquisitely ordered physical environment. She wrote:

I have heard much of the strange variety of scenery to be found on this island: how it has, in a miniature way, rivers, lakes, forests, prairies, swamps and mountains, and our walk demonstrates to me the baldness of the truth of the statement ... [Leaving the beach] we clamber up the bank and turn inland, still ankle deep in sand, and go through this museum of physical geography. First, a specimen of grassland, then along a lane of thickly pleached bush, then down into a wood with a little (at present) nearly dried up swamp in its recesses; then up out onto an open heath which has recently been burnt and is covered with dead bracken and scorched oil palms ... There is such an elaborate completeness about this museum, and we have not even commenced the glacier or river departments (1982, 385–6).

Similar descriptions are found in the narratives of other women travellers. Although Melville's landscape descriptions frequently alluded to 'wilderness', and she sometimes found the physical environment of west Africa threatening, she portrayed the landscapes around Sierra Leone as inherently harmonious. She wrote:

There are three distinct phases of landscape here. The first is hill and dale, clothed in all their original exuberance of stately forest, and appearing in their primeval grandeur, as it were, fresh from the hands of their Maker; the second is the first denuded and laid waste by fire and hatchet ... and that is the scenery I would gladly see changed; the third is the second rich in partial cultivation, and which, with the first, constitutes the peculiar beauty of the tropics, and in it I certainly desire no variety (1968, 225).

Melville perceived those landscapes that remained in their natural state, and those that were only partially cultivated, as the most aesthetically pleasing; those landscapes which remained untouched, or 'wildernesses', were equally ordered as those under cultivation. Larymore was assured by a friend that 'Nigeria was just like Accra – not a tree, not a blade of grass anywhere!' to which she responded, 'I have often smiled to myself over that pithy saying, while marching through magnificent forests, and miles of open, grassy, park-like country!' (1908, 2). Larymore used the adjective 'park-like' on several occasions to describe the landscapes of Nigeria, which suggests that she also perceived these landscapes as inherently ordered.

Women travellers further dispelled the myth of pandemonium by attempting to familiarise their readers with unfamiliar landscapes. These attempts to 'domesticate' west African wildernesses were by no means exclusive to women writers, but it is a theme that seems to run through many of the narratives by women travellers in west Africa. They alluded to familiar aspects of western art and literature in creating their imagery. For example, Kingsley wrote of the scenery of the forest of the Ogowé, 'It is as full of life and beauty as any symphony Beethoven ever wrote; the parts changing, interweaving and returning' (in Howard, 1957, 86). Her publications and lectures abounded with such descriptions of the forest, 'a vast, seemingly limitless cathedral with its countless columns covered, nay, composed of the most exquisite dark-green, large-fronded moss, with here and there a delicate fern embedded in it as an extra decoration' (1982, 570). In these forests climbing plants became 'coverlets' spread over the trees to keep them dry; bush-ropes and lianas became 'some Homeric battle of serpents that at its height had been fixed forever by some magic spell' (1898c, 272); sunshine lit up the red sand-banks which then glowed like 'Nibelungen gold' and the sun played with the mist in a vision of 'Turneresque' beauty (1982, 239). These frequent literary and artistic allusions provided a frame of reference through which her readers could familiarise themselves with the landscapes of west Africa. Kingsley also referred to popular authors of the time (Dickens, Twain, Dr Johnson, Stevenson, Goethe, Kipling), and made unfamiliar landscapes recognisable by comparing them to the works of Turner and the Pre-Raphaelites, again re-emphasising her own romanticism. She even compared the sounds of the forest to symphonies by Beethoven and Handel.

Although west Africa was strange and exotic to her, on occasions Melville's writing is similar to Kingsley's in relating the surroundings of Sierra Leone to her readers. She compared the 'soft quiet beauty' of the beach landscape to paintings by Claude and Poussin (1968, 6–7), and an approaching tornado was described as 'great fleecy clouds rising above Mount Oriel; their curled outlines forming many a Hogarth-like portrait against the sky' (ibid., 91). Like Kingsley, Melville sought to familiarise the sounds of the forest for her readers. Not all of the associations were pleasant or pastoral: she wrote, 'When darkness sets in, the hum of millions of insects arose – and a very unsentimental memory it brought along with it, being exactly like the noise of a large manufactory where spinning machines are constantly in motion' (ibid., 8). White women travellers also drew analogies between British and west African environments in order to render them more familiar. Melville compared the deforested hills around Sierra Leone to those in Scotland, 'where green herbage, heather, and furze appear in alternate patches' (ibid., 6), and Slessor compared the sunsets of Calabar with those in Scotland (*Missionary Record*, February 1887, 337). Colvile described a scene approaching Bonny Town in a similar manner: 'Two minute's walk brought us to the margin of a deep pool surrounded by gigantic cotton trees, whose heavy shade and buttressed roots would almost have made one imagine one's self in some early English cloister' (1893, 303). Larymore described a scene at Jebba in Northern Nigeria which:

> ... changed abruptly from low-lying grassy marsh land and warm sand-banks, where the wild duck and geese were wont to gather, to great beetling cliffs and walls of rock, which rose sheer from the still water, seemingly shutting in the river altogether, and giving the impression of one end of a highland loch (1908, 153).

Of course, the desire for order through the construction of familiar frames of reference is itself imperialist. Layers of meaning are imposed on the landscapes of west Africa by the roving, colonising eye. However, by painting their more familiar pictures of west African landscapes and making them recognizable to their readers, women travellers challenged the image of the exotic and frightening pandemonium which characterised many descriptions of west Africa during the nineteenth century. The landscapes in the narratives of these women were ordered and, to some extent, demystified.

The pastoral myth and west Africa as 'garden'

If there were similarities in the ways in which women travellers represented the physical environments of west Africa as ordered and familiar, there were also great differences in their designs upon their immediate surroundings. Kingsley and Slessor attempted to blend in with their surroundings, and related to them in a personal and subjective way. Kingsley, on occasions, felt that she was part of the landscape and identified with the physical environment on a deeply spiritual level. Mills (1991, 99) describes this more personalized form of writing as 'going native', arguing that it was a challenge to male Orientalism and a different way of representing non-European landscapes. In the case of Slessor, this phrase is particularly apt. She lived in African huts, grew and ate African food, drank unboiled water, and attempted to become assimilated into local ways of life as much as possible (McEwan, 1995b). Thus, Kingsley and Slessor envisaged themselves having as little impact upon the natural environment as was possible. This was not the case with some of the other women travellers in west Africa.

On occasions, and to differing extents, Larymore, Melville and Foote perceived west Africa as a potential garden in need of cultivation. In Victorian Britain suburbs were developing rapidly, and gardens came to be perceived as refuges amidst the enormity of urban sprawl, 'bowers and oases in a desert of brick and mortar' (Griffin, 1977, 171). In west Africa, the garden was a retreat from the surrounding 'wilderness', a small area of 'civilization' on the imperial frontier. Just as urban gardens in England could only be imagined in relation to the city, which shaped and defined them by surrounding and threatening them, gardens in west Africa could only be imagined in relation to the surrounding 'wilderness'. Both survived under siege, a passive persistence emphasised and symbolized by closure and concentration. Furthermore, 'the garden served as a rich metaphorical link; English order and productivity amid the tropical chaos of overgrown jungle or scrubby savannah' (Callaway, 1987, 178–9). Sections within the narratives of Larymore, Melville and Foote were illustrative of attempts by white women to impose their own personalities as well as British order upon the landscapes of west Africa. They were all impressed by the creation of gardens and farmland in the forests and remarked upon the contrast between these ordered features and the surrounding wilderness. Melville created a vision of west African landscapes that was consistent with anti-slavery depictions of an earthly paradise. She particularly delighted in the gardens in Freetown that, despite their exoticism, reminded her of home:

> I was enchanted by the luxuriance of the trees ... Innumerable blossoms shone in all directions; one resembling a branch of red coral; another, still more gorgeous, with its festoons of orange and scarlet, reminded me of the feathers of the bird of Paradise; while the pale lilac colours of a third recalled the image of more northern gardens, and claimed a kindly remembrance of old familiar flowers, although the perfume of orange and lime trees was all around us (1968, 8).

Here, Melville derived pleasure from a landscape that had been appropriated and transformed by the agents of British imperialism, but she also delighted in the more natural landscapes. For her, the beauties of the surrounding vegetation were a consolation for what she perceived as the vagaries of the climate, and a source of comfort to her during her frequent illnesses. She found both the natural vegetation and the gardens and cultivated hillsides alluring. She wrote of the richness of her surroundings where:

> [F]ruits and flowers, which attain to but a dwarfish height when coaxed in our home hothouses, spring up and flourish spontaneously in all their own native loveliness ... [W]here the broad-leaved plantain and banana form a natural arcade that breathes coolness even under the sun of Africa; there the paw-paw raises its slight shaft, which you wonder can support the green and golden load at top, while its yellow blossoms perfume the air ... But it is not *here* and *there*. Mingled in one rich mass of harmonious colouring, and flinging their sweet scent to the welcome sea-breeze, orange and lime trees, spangled with snowy flowers, and bending under the weight of their gorgeous fruit, vie with those of the luxuriant mango, the bay-leaved coffee, the pale-stemmed guava, the densely-foliaged rose-apple ... and many hundred others in the bush (ibid., 226).

The profusion of references to flowers in Melville's descriptions is significant. Rose makes the point that flower painting was the one genre in which women were well-represented as artists during the nineteenth century. She writes (1993, 186):

> Women were accepted as artists in this area because there was thought to be some sort of reciprocity between artist and subject; women were often described as flowers by Victorian gallants, and the flower analogy places both women and their work in the sphere of nature. The encoding of nature as feminine not only

gave rise to a series of visual representations of women as passive and fertile as nature itself then; it also limited the possibilities for women as artists.

The same argument can, therefore, be applied when considering the landscape descriptions of women travel writers. By placing an emphasis on verbal portraits of flowers, Melville was ensuring that she did not transgress acceptable boundaries, and that she maintained a vision of her own femininity. Floral description was a particular narrative style that was accessible to her, and acceptable to her audience, and she used it extensively where other narrative styles, such as political discussion or scientific considerations, might have been deemed inappropriate by the conventions of the time. However, this form of writing was by no means innocent; instead it contributed to the imperial 'science' of animal and plant geography (McEwan, 1998b). Both Pratt and Mills point out that this type of description, and the emphasis on naming vegetation and assembling knowledge about it, was a product of the process of imperial expansion. There was a close relationship between this kind of natural history, cartography and the geographical enterprise of naming which were central to the emergence of Europe's 'planetary consciousness' (Pratt, 1992, 38) and the construction of global meaning. Travel writing, and the observational enterprise of documenting geography, flora and fauna, was fundamental to this. Therefore, white women travellers such as Melville and Foote depicted the landscape of west Africa as a 'storehouse of random flora and fauna waiting for the civilizing ordering of the narrator with her Western science' (Mills, 1994, 41).

Foote's narrative also draws heavily on the theme of the garden. She wrote, 'Sierra Leone looks like one large garden, with its broad, red gravel walks, and groups of trees'. Like Melville, she could admire both the forests (albeit from a distance) and the cultivated and 'tamed' landscapes. She also took pleasure in her garden at Lagos, 'full of oleander and acacia trees' (1869, 7). That both Melville and Foote portrayed the natural vegetation as 'garden-like' in its appearance may be linked to the fact that they both travelled to west Africa with husbands who were involved in the anti-slavery effort. A good deal of anti-slavery literature tended to invoke images of an Arcadian Africa. Both Melville and Foote were of the opinion that, were it not for indigenous slavery, Britain would have little reason to be in west Africa; British administrators would no longer have to suffer in a climate unsuited to Europeans, and west Africans could be left alone to live in peace. The romance inherent in the anti-slavery movement thus informed the landscape descriptions of Melville and Foote.

Larymore had rather a different attitude, which was reflective of her presence in Nigeria at the beginning of the colonial period. To her, west Africa was not a 'garden' but a 'wilderness' which required taming. She took the theme of the garden a step further than both Melville and Foote, insisting that it was the duty of every Englishwoman resident in Africa to attempt to grow a garden as a constant reminder of England amid this 'wilderness', if only for the benefit of future residents. She wrote whilst looking over her Preperanda at Lokoja, 'I then and there took to heart the lesson which I have tried to practise ever since – the absolute duty of planting trees everywhere for the benefit of one's successors' (1908, 7). She even attempted to grow gardens in the most inhospitable of surroundings, such as her residency in Kano during the dry season. Certain parallels can be drawn at this juncture between those women, such as Larymore, living on the imperial frontier in west Africa and the experiences of women living on the North American frontier. As Kolodny (1984, xiii) writes:

> After initial reluctance at finding themselves on the wooded frontiers ..., women quite literally set about planting gardens in these wilderness places. Later, they eagerly embraced the open and rolling prairies of places like Illinois and Texas as a garden ready-made. Avoiding for a time male assertions of a rediscovered Eden, women claimed the frontiers as a potential sanctuary for an idealized domesticity. Massive exploitation and alteration of the continent do not seem to have been part of women's fantasies. They dreamed, more modestly, of locating a home and a familial human community within a cultivated garden.

Larymore certainly attempted to create a 'sanctuary for an idealized domesticity' on the imperial frontier of Nigeria. As mentioned in Chapter 1, she devoted an entire section of her book to advising her readers how to grow a flower garden, a verandah garden, a vegetable garden, a lawn, and trees and shrubs in the climate of west Africa. The imposition of English order upon the physical environment appealed to Larymore. She described the changes at Lokoja from her first visit, when the white settlement was surrounded by 'a waste of swampy ground, thickly covered with coarse, rank grass', to her visit five years later, when she found, 'numbers of neat bungalows, well-tended little gardens, the swamp drained and converted into recreation ground, containing tennis courts, cricket pitch etc., good roads, and flowering trees and hedges, it is as pretty a little cantonment as one could wish to see ...' (1908, 9).

Larymore's intention was to create 'little Englands' wherever she went in Nigeria, and believed it was the duty of the wife of the Resident to ensure that this task was undertaken, both for the increased comfort of their husbands, and for the wider benefit to British imperialism in Africa. In her chapter on creating a lawn, she wrote:

> It is said to be very dear to the heart of every Englishman to own a lawn, and it certainly should be doubly so to John Bull in exile; in a tropical country well-kept turf is much to be desired, there is nothing as cool and refreshing to tired eyes dazzled with the glare of the sunshine and baked earth, and perhaps, nothing that

gives such a home-like and cared-for look to a West African compound (ibid., 224).

Such responses to the landscape were in marked contrast to the more harmonious relationships sought by Kingsley and Slessor. Although both responses were imperialist they were very different, and they highlight both the complexities within imperialist representations of west Africa and the importance of the spatial and temporal context of the journey.

'Edenic' west Africa or 'The Land of Death'?

This chapter has argued that the descriptions of the physical environment by white women travellers were extremely complex, and it is virtually impossible to define a singular 'feminine' response to west African landscapes. However, despite the preoccupation with the notion of the 'garden' amongst some women travellers, most, with the exception of Larymore, avoided the Western preoccupation with establishing control over the physical environment. They also avoided what Greenstein (1982, 138) refers to as the 'Conradian appropriation of Africa as a metaphor for Western decadence'. Popular authors such as Henty, Haggard, Conrad and Cary sent their heroes to Africa to find a career, to make their fortune, to hunt big game, or simply to have fantastic adventures. As the work of the great explorers and the diaries of colonial administrators testify, historically Africa was the playground in which European men could fulfil their pre-pubescent fantasies. The protagonists of the literature of empire sought to test their manhood in the wildernesses of Africa, and they always returned victorious. This chapter has argued that, on the whole, white women travellers did not depict the landscapes of west Africa as a series of tests and obstacles to be overcome on their adventures. In general, women travellers also avoided depicting west Africa as an earthly paradise, a facet of the myth of the pastoral which was particularly prevalent in the works of anti-slavery advocates and the early missionaries.

The women of this study were aware of the vagaries of the west African climate, and one can derive from their descriptions their perception of the beauties of the physical environment, but also of the hazards they held for Europeans. For example, Colvile's chapter on west Africa was entitled rather sensationally 'The Land of Death'. Slessor spent the greater part of her thirty-nine years in west Africa suffering from fever and disease. Melville, whose descriptions of the cultivated hillsides of Sierra Leone perhaps came closest to evoking Edenic images of the landscape, was convinced that disease and death were the price to be paid for the exquisite beauty of west Africa. As a consequence of illness she was often homesick. Despite her pantheism and, at times, transcendental relationship with the physical environment,

Kingsley recognized the psychological malaise that could affect Europeans in west Africa, and although she felt at home in the forests, she realized that for those who could not identify with their surroundings, life there could be intolerable. She wrote:

> A more horrible life than a life in such a region for a man who never takes to it, it is impossible to conceive; for a man who does take to it it is a sort of dream life ... Mind you it is intensely beautiful, intensely soothing, intensely interesting if you can read it and you like it, but for a man who cannot and does not it is a living death (1899a, 39).

Hinderer captured the dangers of the climate when she wrote, 'It's like a tiger, the way it leaps on one' (1872, 91). After five years in west Africa she wrote, 'It seems at times almost a question whether we can still be in the land of the living ... the heat and oppression is terrible'.[11] The climate of west Africa, which was believed during the nineteenth century to be the cause of fever, disease and death, was the one aspect of the physical environment which drew the darkest descriptions from women travellers.

Sickness was often the cause of these sour meditations on the climate. As a consequence of their long duration in west Africa, the missionaries suffered most from the effects of the climate, and Slessor particularly so. Her final destination was Ikpe, located on a mosquito-laden creek. Slessor's house was too close to this creek and, consequently, she was constantly fever-ridden. Her discomfort was exacerbated by periodic affliction with erysipelas; on one occasion she lost all of her hair as a result. On another, when she was covered in boils from head to foot, she wrote, 'Only sleeping draughts keep me from going off my head' (Livingstone, 1916, 253). Her spirits were often low during the wet season, and at these times her descriptions of the physical environment lost their enthusiasm. She wrote:

> The rain is drizzling down again, and I have a heavy dose of cold on my chest, and must go inside. One blink of sunshine comes, then a drizzle of rain and then a blink, and again a downpour, and all the time we are in a mist for it is never dry under the bush ... I wish this month were past, to let us get a dry day now and then.[12]

However, the dry season brought greater hardships, with the dust-laden harmattans blowing down from the Sahara and draining her energy. She wrote of her longing for a 'wee blink of home', and then declared, 'But though the tears are coming at the thought, you are not to think for one moment that I would take the offer were it offered to me! A thousand times no!'[13] Her homesickness never lasted long, and despite the insalubrity of her surroundings she could still evince the beauty of Ikpe. The town was surrounded by stately palms, of which Slessor wrote, 'These palms are my first joy in the morning when the dawn comes up, pearly grey in the mist and fine rain, fresh and cool and beautiful' (Miller, 1946, 123). At other times she compared Africa favourably to Britain. She wrote, 'how would you feel if you never had a breath of wind? never a leaf stirring, and everything reeking with heat? It is very trying, but infinitely more preferable to your cold'.[14]

Although the climate was often a source of fear and trepidation for women travellers, there was sometimes a certain fascination with its emanations. For example, the typhoons on the coast were particularly hazardous but at the same time beautiful. Melville wrote that the tropical storms 'now make me tremble, though at first I used to watch their progress with admiration' (1968, 69). Foote described them as 'a wonderful and beautiful thing to witness' (1869, 214–5). She wrote:

> The sky became inky black, and the sea was of the same murky hue, making the crested waves gleam like snow. I stood on the verandah watching the approach of the wild wind, and was lost in awe and admiration of the beautiful sight presented by the harbour. In a moment the wind seemed to burst from above and lash the waves into fury. They sped before the typhoon at lightning speed, in a white line of foam, and the whole sheet of water, before so dark and quiet, became violently agitated. I was so absorbed in the beauty of the spectacle that I forgot how near the wind was upon us, when suddenly it clapped against the side of the house with a rushing sound, indescribably grand, and I found myself nearly blown off the verandah.

Therefore, even the supposedly deadly climate of west Africa produced spectacular sights and beautiful experiences that were recounted in travel narratives by British women. Although all these women had deeply aesthetic and personalized responses to the landscapes they encountered, they did not gloss over the very real dangers they believed the climate posed for Europeans. To them, west Africa was neither paradise nor pandemonium.

Conclusion

White women travellers were exposed to images of the 'dark continent' before they travelled to west Africa through various media, including colonial fiction, exploration literature, late-nineteenth century photography, imperial art and scientific treatises, and these often informed their descriptions of the physical environments of west Africa. This is particularly evident in their comments on climatic conditions, and the supposed links between climate and disease. However, their representations of west Africa were complex. This chapter has illustrated that various literary traditions in Victorian Britain influenced the ways in which women travellers wrote about the physical environment of west Africa. Victorian romanticism, ideas about the imperial frontier, and notions of the 'wilderness' and 'sanctuary' all exerted powerful influences upon the narratives of these women, and it could be argued that these were standard ways of representing the physical environment in travel literature at the time. The ambivalence apparent in these narratives was common to many colonial texts. However, to a certain extent women's descriptions of the physical environment were different from standard Victorian travel texts. Their romanticism was overtly expressed because they were constrained to emphasise their landscape descriptions rather than to engage in scientific observations or political comments. As Mills (1991, 77–8) suggests, the scientific narrator figure was not unavailable to women travel writers, but was constantly undermined by other elements within their texts. Nineteenth-century convention held that women's travel narratives were not supposed to be 'scientific' and authoritative, but, rather, supposed to be amateurish and subjective. It is for this reason that travel narratives by women were often prefaced with disclaimers denying scientific, academic or literary merit. Furthermore, an emphasis on landscape description was a means of maintaining this amateurish style. This is recognisable as a common characteristic in travel literature by women travellers in west Africa (only Hinderer did not dwell to any great extent upon descriptions of her surroundings), as are their attempts to familiarize landscapes rather than exoticize them.

Women's experiences on the imperial frontier were different from those of male travellers; on the imperial frontier they confronted not only unfamiliar Others (vegetation, landscapes and peoples), but also 'unfamiliar selves' (Pratt, 1985, 121). For many of these women, travel was a liberating experience, and their travels were psychological journeys of self-discovery as well as physical journeys in west Africa. The most obvious example of this was Kingsley and her deeply spiritual meditations on, and identification with, west African environments. Furthermore, the depiction of west Africa as a 'garden' in travel texts written by women after 1840 was unique to women travellers such as Melville and Foote. In contrast, by mid-century west Africa had come to be popularly perceived within Britain, and particularly by explorers, travellers and the formulators of imperial policy, as the heart of a dark and dangerous continent. While the vagaries of the climate steered women travellers away from Arcadian visions of west Africa, they also tended to avoid depictions of west Africa as pandemonium, and relied more upon evoking the intricate beauties of their surroundings. However, although they 'shied away from paradisal projection, they nonetheless seemed eager to tend the garden' (Kolodny, 1984, 47). Therefore, although they often portrayed west African landscapes in standard ways, white women travellers also made important contributions to popular images of the physical environment of west Africa in Britain.

Despite the common emphasis on landscape description in the narratives of white women travellers, it cannot be argued that there was a singular 'feminine' representation of west African environments. This chapter has highlighted some of the major differences in the responses of women travellers in west Africa. Some of the women, such as Larymore, Foote, Colvile, and to a certain extent Melville, felt the need to maintain a distance between themselves and the landscapes they observed. Others, such as Slessor and, particularly, Kingsley, had much more personal relationships with the physical environment. Indeed, Flint comments on Kingsley, 'No other writer, in my estimation, has so successfully evoked the beauty of the African forest, the steady tempo of the rivers, or the sounds and stirrings of the African night' (1965, 156–7). The clarity and depth of Kingsley's imagery was inspired by her intimacy with her surroundings. Landscape descriptions were often revealing of the different circumstances in which the women travelled, and their views on British imperialism in west Africa. Melville's attitude was typical of the 1840s, and philanthropic perspectives on Africa heavily influenced her landscape descriptions. Her west Africa was almost Edenic, but she believed its climate to be unfit for Europeans, who were making sacrifices for the sake of eradicating slavery. Foote and Colvile shared Melville's feeling of not really belonging in west Africa. Larymore was the only women to adopt the 'monarch-of-all-I-survey' trope in her landscape descriptions. She metaphorically claimed territory as her own in her writings, and was able to do so because, unlike the other women, she travelled in a part of west Africa which had been conquered by the British and formally incorporated into the British empire. In effect, she was surveying aesthetically territories that were about to be colonized and surveyed for military and economic purposes. She was part of a colonial expedition, and she was perhaps more aware of her power as a white woman in west Africa. Her attempts to impose British style gardens upon the landscape were an emanation of this feeling of power. Furthermore, the miasmatic theory of disease in west Africa had almost died out at the time of Larymore's travels, and there was less fear of the physical environment. It was now perfectly feasible to encourage the creation and enjoyment of gardens in west Africa. Kingsley's landscape descriptions were also unique, not only in their great abundance and poeticism, but also because they challenged many of the images of west Africa which prevailed during the 1890s, defying the conventions of the time. Unlike Colvile, who portrayed west Africa as the 'Land of Death', Kingsley drew on earlier romantic depictions in order to challenge negative representations of west Africa, and to raise interest in the possibilities for British imperialism there. She believed that if she could convince the British public that west Africa was not a land of darkness this would encourage the government to increase Britain's trading interests in the region.

It is possible to detect a certain amount of ambivalence towards the physical environment in the narratives of some women travellers, particularly in those of Larymore, Kingsley and Slessor. All these women expressed a desire to see the landscapes of west Africa remain unchanged. In her narratives, Kingsley even attempted to disguise her own presence in these landscapes by discursively placing herself within them and attempting to blend with them. However, these women could not blend into the landscapes through which they travelled simply because they were British and white. Their very presence in west Africa was facilitated by the same British economic, cultural and political imperialism that was altering the landscapes of west Africa. Furthermore, British women did not question their right to be in west Africa, nor the implications of their description and textual appropriation of the landscapes through which they travelled. It must also be emphasised that representations of west African landscapes, poetic or otherwise, were not innocent. These representations are noteworthy for their absence of African presence, and for their naturalization of human agency and vision. As Low (1996, 40) suggests, landscape descriptions in imperial discourse 'naturalise the historical and material contexts which enabled the Western observer's presence and commentary on the African world'. The absence of African people in landscape description draws directly upon the colonial fantasy of virgin territory (McClintock, 1995, 28–31). This is perhaps ironic, given the density of population in some parts of west Africa during the nineteenth century. However, it was an imperial 'trope' that white women travellers did not disrupt. As the next two chapters demonstrate, descriptions of the peoples of west Africa were dealt with in separate parts of their travel narratives. Furthermore, the ambivalence evident in white women's relationships with west African landscapes is also apparent in their relationships with west African peoples.

Notes

1. A shorter and revised version of this chapter has been published elsewhere (see McEwan 1996).
2. See, for example, Stott (1989, passim); McClintock (1995, 21–31).
3. Rose (1992, 8–18) explores the geographer's 'gaze' at nature in terms of the distinction between the feminization of the landscape, which requires interpretation, and the masculine, scientific gaze which produces this interpretation.
4. See also Mitchell (1988), for further discussion on the 'imperial gaze'.
5. Bhabha (1994, 85ff) argues that ambivalence is a marked feature of many colonial texts. It was not, therefore, exclusive to white women travel writers.
6. As Short (1991, 5–27) argues, there are two dominant themes in European depictions of wilderness. Until the eighteenth century, a classical view prevailed, which saw the wilderness as a place to fear. As wilderness became increasingly threatened by industrialization, this idea was superseded by

romantic constructions of the wilderness as a place to revere. Slessor's representations of Calabar draw heavily on this romantic view of wilderness.

7. Slessor's father was an alcoholic prone to violent outbursts.

8. See Matless's (1991) discussion of Vaughan Cornish.

9. Letter from Slessor at Ikot Obon, 28/2/06, *Women's Missionary Magazine*, June 1906, 142.

10. Kingsley to Matthew Nathan, 12/3/99, Nathan Papers, Bodleian Library, Oxford.

11. Hinderer to C.M.S., Ibadan, 17/5/55, David Hinderer Collection, Yoruba Mission/C.M.S. Papers, Birmingham University Archives.

12. Slessor to Mrs Findlay, 19/8/13, Cairns Papers, National Library of Scotland.

13. Slessor, 'A missionary's testimony', extract from a letter to friends, *Women's Missionary Magazine*, March 1910, 67.

14. Letter from Slessor at Ikot Obon, 25/1/14, *Women's Missionary Magazine*, February 1915, 78.

CHAPTER 4

White women and 'race'

With this final experience of the simple black man we bade adieu to the confines of his garden (Colvile, 1893, 341).

A few negroes came on board, but they seemed a far more civilised set than those farther down the coast, and therefore not half so amusing and interesting (Foote, 1869, 175).

One boy, who was a slave said 'You can't kiss me, because I am black and you are white', and I gave him immediately two or three kisses, which amused him immensely (Hinderer, 1872, 124).

Introduction: distance and proximity

In order to elucidate the different portrayals of west Africans by women travellers it is necessary to compare how they related to those whom they observed. As with their relationships with the physical environment, enormous differences existed in the amount and form of contact that Victorian women had with the various peoples of west Africa. For example, the missionaries, Hinderer and Slessor, had by far the most contact with west Africans over a long period of time, and they lived in close proximity to them. This is in direct contrast to the residents, such as Melville, Foote and Colvile, who tended to be more physically removed from local populations. In the course of their travels, Larymore and Kingsley had more direct contact with west Africans who acted as their guides and, on occasions, both women lived in African settlements.[1]

Mary Kingsley, in particular, advocated close contact with the peoples of west Africa in order to comprehend more their cultures and customs, and this was facilitated by her status as an independent traveller. Unlike, Constance Larymore who travelled with military expeditions, or Zélie Colvile who travelled in the company of other tourists on board steamers around Africa, Kingsley only ever travelled with a small entourage, her guides never exceeding nine men (Birkett, 1987a, 98). This meant that she had greater opportunity for direct personal contact with the peoples she encountered on her travels. She believed that it was only through this proximity that an accurate understanding of west African peoples could be formulated. She wrote, 'how impossible it is to understand the African, how unjust it is to judge him unless you will go and tackle him on his native bush-path' (Kingsley, 1898c, 264). For Kingsley, the only way for Europeans to understand African peoples was to abandon any preconceived notions spawned by the rhetoric in Britain, and to observe from the inside. She wrote of the intricacies of west African cultures (1982, 103), 'Unless you live among the natives, you never get to know them; if you do this you gradually get a light into the true state of their mind-forest. At first you see nothing but a confused stupidity and crime; but when you get to see – well! as in the other forest – you see things worth seeing'. Kingsley, therefore, argued that many of the prevailing views about west Africans were based on misconceptions through a lack of intimate contact. The preconceptions that she had of peoples in west Africa, which had been formulated in the context of the post-Darwinian debate about race in Britain, and from reading the accounts of the likes of Richard Burton, were soon dispelled when she encountered west Africans first hand. Fyfe (1962, 505–6) argues that Kingsley did not spend as much time among west African peoples as she herself liked to claim, instead spending the majority of her time at European trading and missionary stations. However, she did travel with west African guides and stayed in the villages of various indigenous peoples, including the Fang, living in close proximity with some west Africans. Many of her observations were based on this close contact.

As mentioned previously, missionaries, by the very nature of their motivations for travelling to Africa, had the greatest proximity to indigenous peoples. Mary Slessor, in particular, made efforts to increase her contact with the peoples of the interior of Calabar. While she was in the coastal towns she visited the women's compounds, and often found herself sleeping overnight in one of the overcrowded huts. As discussed in Chapter 1, to increase her contact with the Calabar peoples, she moved from the coastal towns of the Cross River estuary into the villages of the interior, firstly to the Okoyong areas and then further north into the Enyong villages. She quickly became assimilated into the pattern of life of the villages in which she relocated. She abandoned European clothing in favour of a simple sack dress, and cut her hair short for convenience. She ate indigenous foods, drank unboiled and unfiltered water, and lived in an African-style dwelling. As one source writes: 'she quickly became a native ... The old imperial type of missionary did not appeal to her and she was determined to get near to the natives. How better to accomplish this than becoming one' (Grampian, 1965, 482). Slessor's policy of living as near as possible to the peoples she was attempting to convert allowed her to live in the villages of Okoyong and Enyong for almost all of her forty years in west Africa.

Anna Hinderer lived for seventeen years in the Ibadan area of Yoruba, and also lived in close proximity to the Ibadani people. On several occasions, when David Hinderer was stranded in Ijebu and Lagos as a consequence of the Abeokuta wars, she was completely dependent upon the towns-people for food. Without a strong relationship with the Ibadani people she would probably have starved. She wrote, 'So here I am alone. I think it says much for a town in Africa, of one hundred thousand inhabitants, that one white woman can be left alone, in perfect safety, and with no fear' (1872, 110). One particular comment by Hinderer (ibid., 41) summarizes succinctly her opinions, and, it could be argued, those of Slessor, on the issue of race: 'I feel that if I had twenty lives I would gladly give them to be the means of a little good to these poor but affectionate and well-meaning people, who, though black enough their skins may be, have never-dying souls ... their black skin makes no difference to me'.

The wives of colonial administrators had the least contact with west Africans, the very nature of their roles placing limits on their experiences. As Gartrell (1984, 182) argues:

> Women's range of contacts with Africans was often very much narrower than that of their working husbands ... Thus the fear of the unfamiliar remained greater for wives than for their men. Whether through fear or other factors, many women remained profoundly ignorant of, and uninterested in, the life of those beyond the enclave, and even resentful of its penetrations. The very heaviness of the role-demands may have contributed to this narrowness. To be a successful wife, mother, home manager, hostess, mentor and guide to junior wives ... with perhaps a little volunteer work added on, could easily fill one's days.

The domestic responsibilities of these women, therefore, conspired to keep them within the locality of the colonial enclave, and maintained the physical and emotional distance between themselves and the local populations. Unlike the dwellings of the missionaries, these colonial enclaves were not easily accessible to west Africans, and British women had little close contact with the local people. The same fears that prevented Melville from experiencing the landscapes of Sierra Leone to the full – the fear of the unknown – also prevented her from experiencing close contact with African peoples. Once she had moved out of Freetown to the sanctuary of Smith's Hill she was even more isolated. The only close contact that she, Foote and Colvile had with west Africans was through their household servants. Many of their jaundiced opinions of local people were informed by the class snobbery involved in this relationship, and also by the strategies of resistance they encountered to their presence from some of these servants (see Chapter 7).

The differences between the women and their experiences of indigenous peoples point to an expectation of differences in the ways that they portrayed these encounters, and this is certainly the case. However, similarities are also apparent. One common factor amongst these women was that they were all observers from the outside; the fact of their white skin and the unequal power relations in the imperial setting ensured this fact. Even the likes of Mary Slessor, who, to some extent, became assimilated into the Calabar lifestyle, was by virtue of her skin colour an outsider. West Africans, through travel narratives and missionary reports, were to varying degrees objectified and appropriated by women travel writers. However, despite this fact, the distance between the women and the local peoples varied greatly. The residents were only ever able to view west Africans from an objectifying, removed vantagepoint. They very rarely mentioned conversations or close contact with local people. Pratt (1992, 7) suggests that this discursive and geographical distancing was an attempt by such women at 'anti-conquest', in other words 'strategies of representation whereby European bourgeois subjects seek to secure their innocence in the same moment as they assert European hegemony'. Distancing was a form of denial, and denial was innocence. Objective representations, written very often in a disinterested manner, placed the imperial subject outside of their narratives and outside of their own journeys in the theatre of empire. In contrast, the missionaries and travellers established more personal relationships and were able to respond to west Africans on a more intimate, subjective level. Consequently, and as a result of the influence of the prevailing imperialist and racial theories of the various periods in which they travelled, portrayals of west Africans by white women varied greatly. There is no singular 'other' constructed in these narratives, but a multiplicity of 'others'.

Representing west African peoples

The denial of African individuality

The very notion of the 'African' in travel narratives testifies to a cultural bias that blinded the reader to ethnic and individual character. The construction of a mythical 'African' meant the denial of any diversity of individualities within this category. During the nineteenth century all black people were placed in the 'Negro' category, and little distinction was made between the differing populations of Africa, or indeed between Africans and Afro-Americans (Lorimer, 1978, 82–6). To deny the existence of difference was to create a homogeneous mass of people to which the same stereotypes could be applied. It also denied the existence of distinct African cultures and traditions; when stereotypes were applied, they applied to all. This discursive construction within imperial discourse was fundamental to the imperial projects of European powers. Drawing on the writings of Foucault, Butchart (1998) suggests that indigenous peoples were subject to an imperial gaze. As a consequence 'the African' was constructed and analysed, imperial discourse created knowledge about 'the African', and thus subjected African peoples to regimes of power. Generalisations about 'the African' were not innocent, but were deeply implicated in the relationship between power and knowledge.

The predisposition to generalize about Africans was strong during the nineteenth century. As the *Anthropological Review* put it, with reference to both the landscape and the peoples of Africa, 'A sad monotony prevails' (quoted in Bolt,

1972, 142). It was generally believed that all Africans resembled one another physically, and they possessed '... no more individuality than other creatures which live in herds: examine a thousand minds, and you will always find the same cunning, curiosity, sloth, and ... good-natured dishonesty' (ibid., 142). In Victorian discourses on Africa, missionary reports, travel narratives and consular despatches, few Africans emerge as anything other than generic beings, and individual uniqueness is accorded only Europeans 'whose activities are carried out against a background of comparatively indistinguishable Africans' (Cairns, 1965, 115). The only admittance of some African individuality came from those who admired the more war-like ethnic groups, in whom they could recognize some similarities with the presumed British pluck and stoicism. 'Those tribes who enslaved or raided neighbours, though criticized by Britons as a bar to their own influence, were infinitely preferable to those who allowed themselves to be victims' (Bolt, 1971, 146). In general, however, the individual was lost in the 'tribe', and the 'tribe' within the 'race'. All Africans were alike, and all were equally inferior.

As would perhaps be expected, the women residents of this study were those writers most imbued with cultural bias and were thus most likely to deny the individuality of west African peoples. The women who had most contact with west Africans, the missionaries and the travellers, were able to relate to the people they met on an individual level and, for the most part, avoided the construction of a generic west African. The lack of contact by residents with local people, and their observations from a detached position, meant that their assertions were often sweeping and generalizing. This style of observation is most striking in the narrative of Mrs. Foote. Written in the late 1860s, her descriptions were heavily influenced by the developments in racial theory in Britain at this time, particularly the rise of scientific racism and the depictions of Africans as 'bestial savages'.[2] Foote's descriptions were overtly racist, but were not unusual for the time of her writing. For example, she wrote of encountering in Liberia 'real *bona fide* savages, men adorned with feathers stuck in their wool ... with no other clothing worth speaking of ... wild looking men, all grinning and gesticulating like monkeys' (1869, 182). Such descriptions were typical of the 1860s. On several occasions she referred to 'excited gesticulating savages' with 'wild piercing eyes' (ibid., 185, 205, 207, 208) constantly re-emphasising the 'savage' nature of west Africans. Individuals did not feature in the text. She did write that, 'The variety of races to be met with in Lagos, is very interesting to a stranger' (ibid., 209), but then expanded only to draw comparisons between muslims from north Africa, the coastal groups and the peoples of the interior.

The tone of Foote's language contrasts with that used by Elizabeth Melville, but the inability to differentiate between ethnic groups is common to both. Written in the 1840s, Melville's narrative was more in keeping with the philanthropic style of the anti-slavery literature. She did not represent the peoples of Sierra Leone as individuals, but her descriptions were couched in very different terms. She was 'amazed' that her 'waiting-woman' could distinguish people of different ethnic groups visiting the house, 'for, excepting the Jollofs and Mandingoes, all the black people seem alike to me' (1968, 22). This was certainly reductionist; however, through dress and attitude she was able to differentiate the African settlers and the liberated Africans (former slaves), and at the end of her narrative she was able to make some comments on the differences between Maroons, Timmarees and Foulahs (ibid., 275–7). Thus, despite tendencies to objectify local people, sweeping generalizations about west Africans were balanced to some extent by attempts to recognize differences between the many ethnic groups in Sierra Leone, and unlike Foote, Melville avoided framing her descriptions in overtly racist language.

In the course of her travels throughout Nigeria, Constance Larymore encountered many different ethnic groups, including Ashanti, Yoruba, Hausa and Fulani. Although observing from the outside, Larymore commented extensively throughout her narrative on the differences between the various groups, their appearances and cultures. She also remarked upon the universal friendliness of the people she encountered. She wrote (1908, 118) that she felt:

> ... infinitely more alone in Bond Street, where almost every brick and stone is familiar, than I could ever be in the busy streets of Kano, or any other city of Nigeria, which I might enter for the first time, where I should find two hands and one willing tongue all inadequate for the due return of the ceaseless shower of smiling salutations and greetings that would be poured upon me from every side. And this is by no means a tribute to any personal charms of mine. Any traveller, black-skinned or white, receives the same treatment as a matter of course.

However, her only individual contact with west Africans was with her porters, and the emirs to whom she was introduced in Northern Nigeria. Hers was very much a 'habits and customs' type of travelogue. She was unable to make any comments based on individual relationships with west Africans and she repeated the objectification of indigenous peoples found in other travel narratives.

Mary Kingsley was perhaps the most adept at highlighting the complex nature of ethnic groupings in west Africa, and the distinctions between various indigenous peoples, although at times she supported her belief in essential racial difference by referring to 'the African character'. Birkett (1989, 76) has accused Kingsley of reducing the individuality of her guides by giving them names that reflected idiosyncratic physical characteristics or mannerisms. For example, she named her companions on her journey up the Ogowé 'Grey Shirt', 'Silence', 'Pagan' and 'Duke'. This is a fair criticism, but it does illustrate that Kingsley observed and related to west Africans on an individual level, and ascribed to them some individuality that was perhaps lacking in the narratives of other women travellers. Moreover, she adopted the guise of the anthropologist to elucidate the differences between the many racial and ethnic groups in west Africa. In both *Travels in West Africa* and *West African Studies* she outlined the differences between Negroes and Bantus and the sometimes vast, sometimes subtle, differences that existed between ethnic groups in each category. An interviewer for *The London Review* asked Kingsley to explain the difference between Negroes and Bantus, (categories which themselves were older, eurocentric constructions of African ethnicity) to which she replied:

> There is an enormous difference, both racial and cultural, and there are climatic differences to be considered as well. It is too big a question to go into on this occasion but if you think of the difference that obtains between the East European and the West, that will give you some idea of what I mean.[3]

However, on another occasion she challenged even this reduction of Africans to a twofold classification. She wrote (1896a, 70), 'It is entirely unscientific to go on referring to the Africans under even the two great divisions of Negro and Bantu, because there is quite as much difference between tribes in either division as there is between a canny chiel frae Glasgie and a Tipperary boy'. It is perhaps an interesting irony, however, that despite these attempts to disrupt European classifications of Africans, Kingsley chose to illustrate her argument by drawing a parallel between Africans and Britain's own 'others' on the Celtic fringe.

Kingsley was particularly knowledgeable about the religious beliefs of west Africans, and wrote (1899a, 115), 'When travelling from district to district you cannot fail to be struck by the difference in character of the native religion you are studying'. She was able to gain an insight into the complexities of west African religions in an area where numerous different languages were spoken, and where local people were often suspicious of any outsiders. Her knowledge of German anthropological studies, her contacts with the likes of missionary Dr Nassau, who had intimate knowledge of indigenous religions, and the results of her own research allowed her to develop a detailed picture of local indigenous religions.[4] In these ways, therefore, Kingsley challenged hegemonic representations of Africans, and west Africans in particular, as a homogeneous mass of people to which stereotypes could be applied. Mills argues that elements such as these in women's writing may act as a critique of the colonialist enterprise, 'since there is a stress on personal involvement and investment on the part of the narrator' (1991, 106). She argues:

> The stress on people from other countries as individuals is in marked contrast to much Orientalist work, where the divide between 'us' and 'them' is carefully policed. It is this lack of demarcation in women's writing which constitutes

the point at which colonial discourse is most unstable, and which women's writing helps to expose.

Though Mills' contentions cannot be applied to all the women of this study, particularly the residents in west Africa, they can certainly be applied to a certain extent to the narratives of Kingsley, Hinderer and Slessor. Their roles in west Africa facilitated an enjoyment of interpersonal relationships with individual west Africans, and they rarely denied the individuality of west African peoples.

The denial of African history

Of fundamental importance to the notion of African inferiority, and the right of Britain to colonize or exploit Africa, was the denial within British imperial discourse of an African history. It was also a further means of emphasising the supposed primitive nature of African societies. As the explorer Samuel Baker argued (in Cairns, 1965, 86):

> Central Africa ... is without history. In that savage country ... we find no vestiges of the past – no ancient architecture, neither sculpture, nor even chiselled stone to prove that the Negro of this day is inferior to a remote ancestor. We find primeval races existing upon primitive rock formation ... We must therefore conclude that the races of man which now inhabit [this region] are unchanged from the prehistoric tribes who were the original inhabitants.

Many nineteenth-century authorities maintained that Africans had not invented an alphabet and were unable to grasp the letters of other nations. It was believed that Aryan Europeans had invented writing that Africans held in reverence, thus Europeans were far superior. The lack of a written history attested to the barbarity of the African; the absence of numerals and abstract terms in those African languages that were understood by Britons was widely held to prove their inferiority. A lack of a complex language structure was further evidence of this. Since the histories of African peoples were not written down, British imperialists could deny that they had a history, or that this was insignificant. Therefore, Britain could justifiably colonize Africa and write its own history of the continent.

Mary Kingsley's opinions contradicted these ideas. Although she believed African languages to be inferior to European languages, she did not doubt the intelligence of African people. She wrote, 'West African languages are not difficult to pick up; nevertheless, there are an awful lot of them and they are at best most imperfect mediums of communication. No one who has been on the Coast can fail to recognize how inferior the native language is to the native mind behind it ...' (1982, 431). She also wrote, 'the African's intelligence is far ahead of his language'

(1982, 504). Kingsley did not believe that the lack of a written language, and the (according to her) lack of complexity of spoken languages, made the African intelligence in any way inferior to that of the European. Neither did she believe that an absence of a written language meant the absence of African history. She cited the Spanish geographer, El Bekri, who wrote a book on Africa in 1067, to demonstrate that African history had been written down for centuries. Kingsley believed that there was a possibility that Africa was affected by a Dark Age similar to that which afflicted Europe, and that the resulting slavery and Arab invasions plunged the continent into darkness and put an end to the writing of books.[5] This is, of course, a rather romantic version of African history, and remains part of a western orthodoxy that privileges the written word over other forms of narrating histories. However, it is clear that Kingsley was sensitive to the denial of African history and made efforts to counter dominant imperial discourses that perpetuated these ideas.

Kingsley herself had a profound knowledge of the history of ethnic migrations across the continent, and not only did she argue the case for a unique African history, she also envisaged its future. She wrote (1900a, 19):

> Not only do the negroes not die off in the face of white civilisation in Africa, but they have increased in America whereto they were taken by the slave trade. This fact urges upon us the belief that these negroes are a great world-race – a race not passing off the stage of human affairs, but one that has an immense amount of history before it.

Such passages illustrate Kingsley's admiration of west Africans, and she was adamant that Africa had a rich and varied history before its 'discovery' by Europeans. Her attitude is captured in the following:

> We English are not stepping on to Africa out of Noah's ark. We have been in touch with it since 1553. West Africa has not just been blown up from the bed of the ocean by a submarine volcano. It is a very old bit of the world with well-established ways of its own, ways it is not going to alter in five minutes, ways that must be understood before they can be properly altered. It is a grand region, and its natives are an uncommonly fine kind of human being (1899b, 65).

It is clear, however, that despite her admiration Kingsley believed that the destiny of Africa would be determined by a technologically superior Europe; it is significant that she did not question the right of Europeans to alter what had existed for centuries.

Infantilizing west Africans

A particularly prevalent negative image of west Africans during the nineteenth century was their representation as indolent children. As Russett (1989, 51–2) argues, this infantilizing of non-Europeans formed part of the process of defining the Other. She states:

> Anthropologists taught that primitive societies represented cultural stages that fell short of the complete civilization exemplified by the societies of western Europe. In the phylogeny of the human race the nineteenth-century savage, together with his pre-historic forebear, was assigned the role of child.[6]

The implications of this are clear. If west Africans were perceived as permanently childlike, then it could be argued that it was natural and just that the more 'advanced' nations (especially Britain) should become permanent guardians. If Africans were incapable of exploiting their own resources, then surely Britain was justified in governing and developing Africa itself. As Blaut (1993, 96) argues, 'Non-Europeans ... were seen as psychically undeveloped, as more or less childlike. But given the psychic unity of mankind, non-Europeans could of course be brought to adulthood, to rationality, to modernity, through a set of learning experiences, mainly colonial'. The image of infantilism was thus, to a certain extent, used to legitimate colonialism and imperialism under the guise of paternalism. If the perceived responsibilities of the European powers were strongly paternal, however, they also had implications for unequal power relations. The preference for strong rule in the latter half of the nineteenth century sprang not only from notions about savagery, but also from the myth of infantilism, and the general incompetence of the non-white inhabitants of Africa. In the process of 'othering' Africans, an association was made between blackness and madness. It was intimated that the 'simple nature' of Africans, their 'child-like essence' did not 'permit them to function well in the complexities of the modern world and predisposed them insanity' (Gilman, 1985, 140). The extension of empire and 'civilisation' was perceived as a duty for Britain: it was the 'White Man's Burden' to control and enlighten. As Cairns (1965, 95) argues:

> The child analogy was useful to whites for it denied to Africans the privileges reserved for adults. It both reflected and strengthened the idea that African cultures did not represent worthwhile achievements and were too loosely formed and inchoate to offer any significant resistance to an inrush of westernisation. Most important, the analogy acted as a sanction and preparation for white control, for its main implication was paternalism which denied the African the right of deciding on his own future.

The main exponents of this image were not only the explorers and the missionaries; the infantilizing of west Africans also had its roots in scientific racism, which insinuated that Africans had advanced in evolutionary terms no further than a European child. As Broks (1990, 149) argues:

> Evolutionism brought a new dimension and a new scientific authority to racial distinctions and hence to racial stereotyping. It provided a new language to express old prejudices. A timescale was added to racial descriptions where the black man was now seen not simply as 'savage', but as 'primitive' and 'less evolved' than the civilised white man.

On occasions the infantilizing of west Africans is evident in the narratives of the women residents of this study. For example, references were made to the 'simplicity' of west Africans (Foote, 1896, 175; Colvile, 1893, 341), and Larymore referred to the people of Bida as 'light-hearted children' (1908, 29). However, these references were rare, and their descriptions, for the most part, avoided reference to these particular stereotypes. In her writings, Melville adopted a sympathetic attitude towards the causes of the behaviour that Europeans found frustrating in west Africa. She argued throughout her narrative that any flaws in the character of west Africans in Sierra Leone was a result of their oppression, first as slaves and then as forced settlers in the colony of Sierra Leone. Thus, although she confessed to being 'totally ignorant of the national usages and habits of the negroes', Melville displayed a willingness to understand – and not stereotype – the people among whom she lived (Barnes Stevenson, 1982, 18).

Kingsley's narratives, however, went further in that they deliberately opposed the 'established wisdom' about west Africans. She disagreed strongly with those who depicted Africans as innocent children, and condemned forcefully the missionary influence in expounding the infantilism of Africans:

> The portrait painted of the African by the majority, not all, but the majority of West African mission reports, has been that of a child, naturally innocent, led away and cheated by white traders and grievously oppressed by his own rulers. I grant you, the African taken as a whole is the gentlest kind of real human being that is made. I do not however class him with the races who carry gentleness to a morbid extent ... (1899a, 273–4)

In her first article written upon her return to England, Kingsley penned an ironic parable attacking the infantilizing of west Africans:

> There was once upon a time a certain country, and in this country lived birds called Dodos. Many excellent ladies and gentlemen heard of them, and from what they

heard they feared the birds were not in a satisfactory spiritual state ... When they came to the Dodos and found how patient and cheerful ... the birds were, they called this state of mind 'child-like', and said, 'My dear Dodos, you are very sweet, you are our Brethren, and all you have got to do is to learn to sing hymns, and put on some Hubbards and trousers, and then you will be perfect gems quite as good as we are' (1896a, 66).

Here, Kingsley ridiculed the notions of African infantilism and backwardness that were prevalent in Victorian Britain. Her statement was also an attack on the missionaries; she was derisive of their attempts of convert Africans to Christianity in the belief that this would advance them up the ladder of civilization. Kingsley perceived such efforts to be destroying African cultures, in the same way that Europeans destroyed the Dodos. She remarked sardonically that Africans and their cultures, unlike Dodos, did not become extinct because 'the whole flock have not strictly attended to all they have been told' by the missionaries (ibid., 66). She was determined to challenge the image of west Africans as helpless victims of savagery, who required the 'civilizing and Christianizing' influence of British rule. She thus advised, '... you must recognize that these Africans have often a remarkable mental acuteness and a large share of common sense; that there is nothing really 'child-like' in their form at all. Observe them further and you find they are not a flighty-minded, mystical set of people in the least' (1982, 439).

The notion of African drunkenness was a common theme during the nineteenth century that was linked intimately to the perceptions of Africans as infantile. As Birkett (1987a, 156) argues, from mid-century onwards the stereotype of African manhood 'had been successfully conquered by an image of the African as a drunk and weakened child, unable to stand up to the ravages of slavery and alcohol'. The missionaries, in particular, portrayed west Africans as the innocent victims of unscrupulous traders and as unable to resist the evils of drink. Kingsley, however, challenged this image, bringing her into conflict with both the anti-liquor lobby and the missionaries. She did not deny that some west Africans enjoyed a drink. She wrote of the Bubi peoples of Fernando Po, 'Rum is held in high esteem, but used in a general way in moderation as a cordial and a treat, for the Bubi is, like the rest of West African natives, by no means an habitual drunkard. Gin he dislikes'. She argued that the missionaries, on the whole, 'gravely exaggerated both the evil and the extent of the liquor traffic in West Africa' (1982, 62–3). They used alcohol as an excuse for their failure to convert more Africans to Christianity, realizing that public opinion was being swayed by anti-liquor sentiments (1896a, 71). She opposed the missionary depiction of the African as 'an innocent creature who is led away by bad white men', and challenged the picture of the extent of drunkenness in west Africa propagated by the missionaries. She argued (1982, 663–4):

I have no hesitation in saying that in the whole of West Africa, in one week, there is not one quarter of the amount of drunkenness you can see any Saturday night you chose in a couple of hours in the Vauxhall Road; and you will not find in a whole year's investigation on the Coast, one seventieth part of the evil, degradation, and premature decay you can see any afternoon you chose to take a walk in the more densely-populated parts of any of our towns ...[7]

Kingsley, therefore, adopted a pro-liquor stance[8] in order to defend west Africans against the charge of infantilism, and to challenge some of the popular stereotypes of the 1890s.

Mary Slessor was one of the few missionaries whose opinions were not attacked by Kingsley. The two had met on several occasions at the time of Kingsley's travels and they established a firm friendship based on a common understanding of west Africa. Slessor was unusual among nineteenth-century missionaries in that she rarely depicted west Africans as infantile in her publications. On occasions she referred to west Africans as 'simple and affectionate',[9] but she referred to the people of Calabar as her 'true and intelligent friends', at a time when British perceptions of Africans were generally extreme and crudely racist (Buchan, 1980, xii). She also repudiated the view within the Church of Scotland that the people of Calabar were 'not ready' to be taught carpentry and other crafts to allow them to develop local industries. A letter from Slessor to the *Missionary Record* expressing these opinions led to the Church of Scotland founding the Hope Waddell Institute in Calabar, where these very skills were imparted to the local population (Oliver, 1982, 118–19). By challenging notions of African infantilism Slessor thus had an impact on Church missionary policy.

Although Slessor rarely represented west Africans as infantile, the relationship between herself and the people of Calabar was clearly one of inequality. As discussed in Chapter 2, Slessor was a 'benevolent maternal imperialist' (Ramusack, 1990, 319). She was known as 'Ma', and her adoption of abandoned local children was symbolic of her wider adoption of the people of Calabar (McEwan, 1995). On occasions she adopted a 'mother-knows-best' attitude, rebuking chiefs and elders as a mother would a child. This mother-child relationship thus involved elements of inequality – she was British, her 'children' were African, and Slessor believed in the superiority of British morality. Although Hunt (1990, 397) argues that women missionaries 'mediated [their] ethnocentrism through the use of maternal idiom',[10] this 'maternal imperialism' involved disparities in power. Slessor's sense of her own superiority was deflected only slightly by the fact that this was based on a sense of moral superiority as opposed to racial superiority.

Feminizing west Africans

Along with people designated as backward, degenerate, uncivilized and retarded, Africans were often viewed by racial theorists within a framework constructed out of biological determinism; as with elements of British society – delinquents, the insane, the poor, women – Africans had to be controlled and managed by British men. The depiction of Africa as 'feminine' was a potent tool of imperialism, and was used to support the notion of its domination by a superior Britain coded as 'masculine'.[11]

Although she did not portray the landscapes of west Africa as 'feminine', Mary Kingsley did render indigenous people as 'feminine', and the ideas that informed these representations were linked intimately to her opinions on sexual equality. As discussed in Chapter 2, Kingsley was staunchly anti-suffrage, and believed women to be ultimately inferior to men. She also believed that Africans were inferior to Europeans. This belief led her to designate Africans as a 'feminine' race, but in so doing she allied herself to them. As a woman she felt akin to Africans. She wrote, '... the mental difference between the two races is very similar to that between men and women among ourselves. A great woman, either mentally or physically, will excel an indifferent man, but no woman ever equals a really great man' (1982, 659). She wrote to a friend (in Nathan, 1907, 30):

> I will impart to you in strict confidence my opinion on the African. He is not half devil and half child any more than he is our benighted brother ... He is a woman. I am certain that old Herodotus' division of the human race has more in it than meets the eye. Take the white races. Your Hebrew and Teuton are masculine ... Take your coloured races ... Your Negro and Melanesian are feminine.

However, despite believing that Africa was (in her words) a 'female nation', she also believed that Africans were a great world 'race'. She refused to accept that west Africans were passive victims of circumstance. By feminizing Africans she could identify with them, in identifying with them she was able to fight their cause in Britain. Thus, although she accepted and promoted images of Africans as feminine, she used these to argue passionately on their behalf (see Chapter 2).

West Africans as labourers/servants

A change in attitude towards Africans occurred after mid-century. Previously, missionaries and philanthropists had sermonized on the 'noble savage' and 'poor slave', and evinced their belief in the capacity of Africans to fulfil positions of leadership and responsibility. After mid-century, and the growing importance that was placed within British culture on gentility, the assumption was made that Africans could only perform labouring tasks and could never approach gentlemanly status.

'Respectable Victorians simply applied to all men with black skins the same judgements, manners and bearing that they adopted towards their social inferiors within English society' (Lorimer, 1978, 60). When these attitudes concerning social status were combined with racist and xenophobic attitudes, racist portrayals became more rigid and more emotive. However, as with other images of Africans (and racist doctrines more widely), the depiction of Africans as labourers or servants was problematic and deeply contradictory. The portrayal of west Africans as workers controverted those discourses, inspired by imperialist theories of environmental determinism during the latter half of the nineteenth century, which constructed Africans as indolent (Bushong, (1984), Peet, (1985), Semple, (1911)). As Cairns (1965, 75–6) argues, 'The tropics evoked stereotypes of sensuality and indolence in contrast to cold climates which signified puritanism in morals and diligence in work'.[12] Thus the representation of Africans as productive labourers contradicted presumptions of indolence supposedly induced by climatic conditions. Contradictions such as these, of course, were a marked feature of colonial and imperial discourse.

The opinions of Elizabeth Melville illustrate the tensions of writing in mid-century when this shift in attitude was beginning to take place. For example, she wrote (1968, 253):

> They are undoubtedly a lazy and indolent race naturally, yet it must be borne in mind that the same degree of exertion can never be expected from them, as from the inhabitants of more temperate climates, for under the fiercely burning sun of these latitudes, the strength even of the black man flags.

Here, she suggested that Africans were, on the one hand, strong and fit for manual labour, yet, on the other hand, she argued that they were naturally indolent. Her connection of this supposed indolence with the climatic conditions pre-empted the rise of environmental determinism as an established science later in the century. Many of her opinions on west African peoples were formed from her experience of them as domestic servants, combining both her ethnocentric prejudices and her upper-class prejudices towards the working classes. She wrote (ibid., 251):

> However philanthropically disposed you may be towards the negro on taking up your residence at Sierra Leone, so soon as the first novelty of the situation wears off, the indolence, stupidity and want of tidiness (to say nothing the graver faults) of the only persons you have to depend upon as domestic servants, throw you into a sort of actual despair. You teach, persuade, remonstrate, lecture, by turns; your words are listened to with a good-humoured apathy, but neither your rhetoric nor example effecting the slightest improvement, you begin to doubt whether the negro be gifted with any good quality or mental capacity whatever,

and feel irresistibly led to include the whole race in a most sweeping kind of condemnation.[13]

Melville was imbued with a certain cultural arrogance and a sense of her own superiority (undoubtedly a product of her aristocratic background as well as contemporaneous attitudes about race), but despite this she retained a sense of maternalism towards west Africans. Although her ethnocentric comments often seemed rooted in class prejudice, she resisted overt comparisons of west Africans with the working classes of England. For example, she wrote (ibid., 251):

> As a people they have been enslaved and oppressed for upwards of four hundred years and even this solitary consideration tells us, that to form an unbiased judgement of the liberated Africans, we must not institute comparisons between them and the lower classes of our own free England.

She also challenged unfavourable comparisons between west Africans and the English working classes, writing (and revealing her own 'classist' prejudices), 'The younger people and children whether liberated or colony-born, show a much greater aptitude and fondness for learning than you commonly find amongst the lower classes at home' (ibid., 253). Despite her understanding of the legacy of slavery, however, Melville failed to recognize the possible association in the minds of West Africans between work and slavery. This is particularly pertinent when one bears in mind that Melville based her opinions on her experience of African domestic servants. Strobel (1991, 23) argues that *A Residence in Sierra Leone* 'communicates a common attitude toward African servants, found with little variation everywhere'. One could argue that this was simply an attitude towards all servants, black or white.

Melville's attitude was certainly common to other women travelling in west Africa throughout the nineteenth century. In 1860, Anna Hinderer wrote in her journal, 'the natural idleness of Africans in general is trying' (1872, 251–2). Mrs. Foote (1869, 195) argued that, 'an unusual number of servants are required in the family household, however small the family, on account of their incorrigible laziness, which exceeds anything I ever saw in other countries'. Constance Larymore referred to her servants as 'all lazy and stupid ... ignorant of the first principles of order and cleanliness, and, unmistakenly, considering Missus rather a bore when she insists on trying to inculcate these ...' (1908, 207). Zélie Colvile's class snobbery was more in evidence in her narrative than those of the other women. Her aloofness and desire to maintain a distance between herself and indigenous peoples no doubt exacerbated this. She described a Syrian she met on board a steamer as 'a sly, thin, cringing, despicable piece of humanity, like most of his class' (1893, 279). Henry Colvile suggested that his wife substitute the term 'Gentleman of Colour' for 'Black Man' in the title of her book. She 'objected that she could not describe as a gentleman a person who was in the habit of hanging his relations, by hooks through his heels, over a pit full of snakes, as someone she met at Bonny did'.[14] In this sense, therefore, the responses of these women to west Africans were predicated more on attitudes towards social class than they were on attitudes towards race. The maternalistic, philanthropic attitude towards west Africans apparent in the narratives of Melville, Foote and Hinderer, and the prejudices associated with this, were based more on a sense of class superiority than they were on racial superiority, although the two were invariably conflated.

Visual representations of race

Although this study is primarily concerned with written representations of west Africans, some mention must be made of visual representations in the travel narratives of white women. As Ryan (1994, 157) argues, geographers have only recently begun to 'consider the role of visual imagery in the making of cultural landscapes and identities. They have hardly begun to explore the complex relations between practices of visual representation and geographical knowledge, particularly in the context of British imperialism'. Ryan has demonstrated that visual images, particularly photographic lantern slides, were considered by pre-eminent geographers (among them Halford Mackinder) to have important educational potential; 'Mackinder saw in photography the opportunity to capture the scenes and sights of empire for a mass audience' (Driver, 1995, 124). These images were disseminated in a variety of forms, including lantern-slides, post-cards, displays at museums, exhibitions and expositions and, of course, through academic publications (Alloula, (1986), Greenhaugh, (1988), Edwards (1992)). Within the European empirical tradition to visualize a culture was to understand it; the camera provided the objectivism to view the world as a spectacle (McClintock, 1995, 122–6, Corbey, 1995, 71–6). As Rothenberg (1994, 160) points out, photography gave visual images of empire a 'distinctive realism' that other forms of visual representation (sketches, paintings) could not produce. The camera never lied. When included in popular narrative forms, such as travel literature, photographs could be extremely suggestive modes of representation.

Using Alloula's (1988, xiv) terminology, women travellers did not represent west Africans through visual imagery, but rather their own 'phantasms' of west Africans. Only two women, Colvile and Kingsley, used visual representations of west African people, and these are in the form of photographs. None of the women used sketches, and photography was not available to the women travelling in the early part of the century. However, the differences between the images presented by Kingsley and Colvile are revealing. Travelling at roughly the same time, and encountering the same groups of indigenous people, their methods of representation were in stark contrast. Although images in both narratives effectively appropriated west Africans, this appropriation was far more explicit in Colvile's photographs.

While Colvile's few landscape photographs were taken in Africa, her portrayals of (supposedly) west African peoples were taken in Britain, using backcloths and models. The exotic backdrops reproduced west Africa as frozen in time, its primeval landscapes located in a different temporal zone to the modern imperial Britain. In Colvile's narrative (1993, facing 292), a photograph of an African woman and child, entitled 'Negress, Accra' (Plate 5) shows a model, naked to the waist and holding a calabash on her head, posing in front of a backdrop of a forest scene. The child is seated on the ground slightly behind the woman, who, with her heavy breasts and protruding stomach, may be pregnant. A similar depiction (ibid., facing 314) of a 'Ju-ju Priest' (Plate 6) pictures a semi-naked man, dressed in a grass skirt, holding what appears to be a bone in one hand and African medicinal plants in the other, against a similar backdrop. The likelihood of either model originating from such a specific a location as Accra, or even west Africa, is highly dubious. As McClintock (1995, 126) argues, 'The immobility of the sitter conceals behind the surface of the photograph the violence of the colonial encounter'. Colvile is unlikely to have taken these photographs, and it may be that the publishers selected these particular images to illustrate her book, but the effect is to reiterate the epistemic violence of imperialism.

The power of appropriation and the authority to name are apparent in these photographs. For example, the term 'negress' is at once vague, uninformative and suggestive. It attempts to classify the model, but gives no indication of the ethnic group or sub-group to which she is supposed to belong. West Africa and, in particular, large ports such as Accra, were dynamic and complex in terms of the ethnic composition of their populations. However, this image reduces this complexity in a racial epithet. The model is simply a 'negress', part of an undifferentiated, homogenized 'Other' to which all stereotypes and assumptions can be applied. Similarly, the 'Ju-ju priest' is not attached to any particular place. This is an image that is meant to be highly symbolic of the state of societies in west Africa. The 'Ju-ju priest' is a universal feature of these societies, the implication being that the associated cultural characteristics of witchcraft, fetishism, barbarism and cannibalism are also universal. By referring to the model as a 'priest', the image evokes unsubtle but powerful contrasts between British and west African religious structures and authorities. In nineteenth century Britain, the priest was a revered, respected and ultimately authoritative figure, and a supposed guardian of morality. In west Africa, the 'Ju-ju priest' was a 'witch-doctor', who secured his authority through primitive and barbaric witchcraft, and pagan and violent practices. In these images the model is 'essentially a *vagrant* and *unformed* individual' (Alloula, 1986, 64) whom Colvile alone can attach to a site (Accra) and endow with an identity ('Negress', 'Ju-ju Priest').

The phantasms in these images are increased by the semi-nakedness of the models, and are meant to appeal to the voyeurism of the reader. There is little doubt that many women in west Africa wore very little clothing, but the depiction of semi-nudity was often taken by British observers as suggestive of lasciviousness[15], and it was a common feature of most representations of African women in nineteenth century travel narratives. The comparative nudity of west African women was considered indicative of their unrestrained sexuality (Gilman, 1985). The 'Ju-ju priest' is also semi-naked, clothed only in a grass-skirt, the latter itself an anachronistic and inaccurate representation. These images draw on powerful stereotypes of west Africans: the barbaric witch doctor with his tools of witchcraft, the bone in his hand suggestive of cannibalism and primitivism (see Chapter 5), the lascivious, fecund, yet alluring African women. The presence of the child in the image reinforces the image of fecundity. As Alloula (1985, 40) argues, the addition of children evokes the idea of a 'birthrate perceived as being out of control, which the colonial ideology attributes to 'cultural belatedness' and to stagnation'. This woman, supposedly of west African origin, is represented as simultaneously sexual, fecund and more primitive than her European counterparts. The latter is also hinted at by the allusion to work in this photograph. The model carries a calabash, which hints at the relatively hard lives of African women in contrast to the supposedly more respectable lives of their middle-class counterparts in Britain. The relationship between the photographer/observer and the semi-nude model is also of significance. The woman does not engage with the camera/observer but is objectified and gazed upon. The relationship is based on desire, and can also be read as a desire for conquest and possession. It is thus symbolic of Britain's relationship with west Africa during the late nineteenth century. As Rothenberg (1994, 157–8) argues, the model becomes 'emblematic of the mystery and potential riches of remote lands. The reader's eyes perceive a young African woman, clothed in little more than beads ... ; the mind interprets: Africa'. The tension in imperial depictions of African women as simultaneously threatening/repulsive and alluring/desirous is apparent in this image; the sexuality and semi-nakedness of the model is an affront to Victorian morality but the desire to gaze and possess is also an acknowledgement of physical beauty. The beauty of an African woman, however, was never to be confused with the 'real' beauty of the white woman. These photographs, therefore, were 'studio-fantasies' (Graham-Brown, 1988, 40) that say more about Britain in the nineteenth century than they do about the parts of west Africa that Colvile visited and the peoples she encountered. The photographic images speak for the silences in the text; they convey powerful images to Colvile's audience. Neither is referred to in the narrative. They are included for decorative purposes only and to add colour to already spicy descriptions of west Africa in the text.

Kingsley's use of photographs was very different. All were taken in west Africa and were selected by the author. While some of the photographs were synthesized, with groups of west Africans posing for the camera (Plates 7 to 10)[16] others showed scenes of activity, such as craftsmaking, fishing and trading (Plate 11).[17] These images also appropriated west Africans, depicting semi-nudity and encapsulating the desire of the objectified by the imperial gaze. However, they were not heavily overlain with symbolism in the same way as those reproduced in Colvile's narrative. However, Kingsley's representations were no more authentic than those of Colvile. They were portrayals that Kingsley (not unproblematically) perceived to be representative of west Africans and their lifestyles. As Ryan (1994, 166) argues, images of exotic 'others' functioned ultimately to distinguish the 'typically native' from the 'super-added' (and superior) European civilization.

Mary Kingsley's philosophy on 'race'

Although the women of this study both challenged, and confirmed many of the images of 'race' manifest in popular and scientific Victorian literatures on empire, many of the views they expressed were influenced by the prevalent attitudes at the time of their travels. However, Mary Kingsley stood alone in that she flew in the face of established 'wisdom' on racial theories. Kingsley's was very much a backward-looking philosophy, out of sync with attitudes at the time of her travels. For this reason, her views on race merit further exploration.

The context for Kingsley's views is important. The depiction of Africans as 'noble savages' in missionary literature, travel narratives and colonial fiction gradually lost credence during the nineteenth century, and was replaced by more explicitly racist images of barbarism and savagery. Furthermore, social Darwinism and scientific racism eclipsed both monogenist and polygenist theories of the origins of races. While Kingsley's views were very different from prevailing scientific theories during the 1890s, they were not new. Rather than expounding progressive and radical concepts relating to racial theory, Kingsley's philosophy had as its roots the humanitarian, romantic theories of the early nineteenth century. Throughout Kingsley's narratives on west Africa there was a constant evocation of the image of the 'noble savage'. This was most apparent in those chapters of *Travels in West Africa* that recounted her experiences of the Fang[18] peoples of Gabon. Her response to the Fang was a profoundly aesthetic and sensual one. She wrote (1982, 328–9):

They are on the whole a fine race, particularly those in the mountain districts of the Sierra del Cristal, where one continually sees magnificent specimens of human beings, both male and female. Their colour is light bronze, many of the men have beards, and albinos are rare among them. The average height in the mountain

districts is five feet six to five feet eight, the difference in stature between men
and women not being great. Their countenances are very bright and expressive,
and if once you have been among them, you can never mistake a Fan.

Kingsley's admiring descriptions concentrated on the physiques of people she met,
the muscular shoulders and chests of her bearers and canoe paddlers, and the beauty
of young girls on the brink of marriage. Such beauty appealed to Kingsley's romantic
nature. She believed that west Africans were inferior to Europeans, but she
subscribed to the view that 'unadulterated' west Africans were thriving without the
influence of Europe, and were even resisting Europeanization and preserving their
own rich cultures. Kingsley's descriptions evoked the image of the 'noble savage'
living healthily and peaceably in Arcadia, and thus had more in common with the
images expounded by late eighteenth and early nineteenth-century anti-slavers than
with the dominant images of the 1890s. Kingsley's views were, therefore, ultimately
unoriginal and outdated.

Kingsley's unorthodox ideology was a product both of her early education and
her early experiences in west Africa. As a young woman, desperate to educate herself,
her sole reading material was that contained in her father's library. She was, therefore,
imbued with the scientific beliefs of an earlier generation. She referred to herself as a
Darwinist but subscribed to polygenist theory, accepting the supposed superiority of
the white races. She believed in the separate origins of the races, that because of
technological inferiority Africans could only advance up the ladder of 'civilisation'
with the aid of Europe, but that Africans were inferior 'in kind, not degree'. She
wrote (1897b, 66), 'I have *never* said I believe the African to be a low form of human
being ... so when I say the African is different from the European and Asiatic forms
of humanity, I mean *different*'. She reserved most of her criticism for those partially
westernized Africans, who no longer fitted into her image of the 'noble savage' and
who were, to her, a parody of civilized people. She believed that technology,
particularly the steam engine, was a 'manifestation of the superiority of my race', and
accused Africans of mechanical ineptitude. She wrote (1899a, 330 and 670) that
African peoples had never made an even fourteenth-rate piece of cloth or pottery, or
machine tool, picture, sculpture, and had never even risen to the level of picture
writing. Kingsley was therefore unaware that some of the world's greatest sculpture
was either stored or buried within a hundred miles of the Oil Rivers Protectorate
(Oliver, 1982, 89).

Despite these pronouncements, Kingsley's views seemed to mellow over time.
When she first travelled to west Africa her desire was to be identified with the great
explorers, but she soon began to challenge their views and break down popular
images that she believed to be erroneous. She postulated that these fictitious images
of west Africa were based upon the opinions of people who had never been there.
Moreover, she argued that too many travellers and ethnologists took their neat

theories to Africa and looked for confirming instances.[19] Shortly before she died she wrote a letter to the Liberian editor of *The New Africa* pleading for mutual understanding between British and African peoples. She regretted that:

> The stay-at-home statesmen think that Africans are all awful savages or silly children – people who can only be dealt with on a reformatory penitentiary line. This view you know is not mine, nor that of the very small party – the scientific ethnologists – who deal with Africa; but it is the view of the statesmen and the general public and the mission public, in African affairs.[20]

Yet Kingsley's philosophy was one of enlightened colonialism rather than altruism. She was eager for colonial administrators, once they became aware of African values, to permit west Africans to develop along their 'own lines', according to their own racial destiny. 'Her primary fear as a racial determinist was that colonial policy, failing to observe that races evolve very differently from each other, would destroy aspects of African culture that should be preserved' (Steen, 1980, 12). The correlation of Kingsley's philosophy with the ideas of the likes of Livingstone and Stanley, and with the opinions of the racial theorists such as Knox, presented a static, frozen image of west Africans by the end of the nineteenth century. As Birkett (1987b, 11) argues, 'Although questioning many of the popular images of Africa, Mary Kingsley was steeped in the racial theories used to justify and support the expansion of British interests in West Africa'.

There were, therefore, elements of Kingsley's philosophy which today would be considered both distasteful and contradictory, and they bring to light both the complexity of her views and her own confusion and ambivalence. For example, she confessed to a friend that tales of inter-racial marriage in west Africa made her 'mentally sick', and yet she was supportive of Nassau, who had a long-term relationship with an African woman.[21] She had inherited the common Victorian assumption that white skin meant racial superiority. She did not seek to challenge differences constructed on the basis of race, and instead she sought to emphasize these differences. In her plans for encouraging more British nurses in west Africa, she argued that there should be 'white hospital orderlies for the white patients, black for the native wards' (1900c, 370). Paradoxically, while she was undoubtedly racist, her adherence to polygenist theory allowed her to slough off the 'evolutionary straitjacket' (Porter, 147) and challenge the notion that Africans were suffering from some state of arrested development. Erroneous theories of polygenesis allowed her to 'look at Africa on its own terms, without comparison and judgement' (Pearce, 1990, 77). The irony lies in the fact that while she exaggerated and relied on the construction of racial difference, she was also a staunch defender of west African peoples and their cultures.

Conclusion

It is apparent from this study that great differences existed in the ways in which white women related to, and portrayed, the peoples of west Africa. The views of these women were often influenced by powerful racial theories in Britain, and as these theories evolved and changed, so the views of women travelling at different times varied and contrasted. However, on a few occasions, white women travellers challenged some of the prevailing views pertaining to race and racial theory. Kingsley was the prime example of this. Her adherence to the racial tenets of an earlier generation may have made her portrayal of west African peoples less radical than would at first appear. Her views on the 'inferiority' of Africans would today be regarded as racist; however, they were less extreme than the views of many of her contemporaries. She challenged many of the opinions apparent in other popular discourses on west Africa. She was one of the few writers to acknowledge the existence of an African history, and to study Africans from the 'inside'. In this way she was able to relate to west Africans on an individual basis. This, in turn, had profound effects on her representation of the cultures of west Africa.

Individual circumstances, class and gender relations all influenced the representations by white women. Barnes Stevenson (1987, 143–5) argues that women travellers often displayed a sympathy for, and understanding of, peoples whose skin colour distinguished them, as these women often found themselves distinguished as 'other' in Britain on the basis of gender. This was certainly true for Kingsley who became a staunch defender of west Africans, and for Slessor, who wrote, 'What a strange thing is sympathy. Undefinable ... [sic] yet the greatest power in human life'. This encapsulates Slessor's relationship with west Africans; it was based on maternalism and philanthropism, and had as its roots the evangelical belief in racial equality that gained popularity throughout the Victorian period (Bradley, 1976, 88). This attitude of sympathy was also a pervasive one in the narratives of those women travelling around mid-century, particularly those involved in the anti-slavery enterprise. Many of the jaundiced views expressed about west Africans by women travellers were based, to a large extent, on class prejudices rather than racial prejudices. This is particularly true of those women from aristocratic backgrounds and those women residents whose opinions of west Africans were based solely on their relations with their African servants. This is not however, to deny the existence of ethnocentrism, and what today would be referred to as racism, among white women travellers in west Africa. These women all represented and appropriated west Africans in their narratives so that the voices of the latter remained silent, and all had preconceived notions about the peoples they encountered. An understanding of the different ways in which these women mediated and expressed their opinions is of particular importance to critiques of women and imperialism. This is expanded further in the following chapter, which explores the portrayal of west African customs by white women travellers.

Notes

1. The relationships between white women and the women they encountered in west Africa are discussed in Chapter 6, and in McEwan (1994).
2. The transition from depictions of Africans as 'noble savages' to 'bestial savages' during the nineteenth century is examined fully in Chapter 5, since this transition is intimately connected to depictions of African cultures and customs.
3. Kingsley, *The London Review*, May 21, 1898.
4. For example, she identified four different 'schools' of 'fetish', the Tshi and Ewe, the Calabar, the M'pongwe, and the Nkissism or Fjort schools (1899a, 115). She also wrote extensive chapters in both her books on the differences between ethnic groups such as M'pongwe, Igalwa, Ajumba, Fang and Bubi.
5. Kingsley to Edward Blyden, Bay of Biscay, 14/3/1900; see also Hayford (1901, 7–8).
6. Russett draws out the connection between the process of othering non-Europeans, women and children through science: 'That women, children and savages shared many traits in common was a finding that appeared to emerge from the evidence of physical anthropologists and psychologists' (p. 51).
7. The fact that Kingsley lived in London during the 1890s is of importance to her perception of the state of British urban areas. *Travels* was written shortly after the Ripper murders in Whitechapel, which Kingsley would have been familiar with, not least because her father had been a close friend of Sir William Gull, who today remains one of the most likely suspects (see Kingsley, 1900b, 205).
8. Kingsley's pro-liquor stance is analysed in greater detail in the Conclusion.
9. Letter from Mary Slessor to the Church in Scotland, Ikot Okpu, 20/5/1908 (Dundee Museum).
10. See also Ramusack (1990, 309–21). These inequalities existed between all these women and the peoples they encountered, and are explored in greater detail in Chapter 2.
11. The depiction of African landscapes as feminine is well documented; see, for example, Russell (1998, 213); Stott (1989).
12. For a comparative study of colonial depictions of Malays, Filipinos and Javanese, see Alatas (1977).

13. As is discussed in Chapter 7, passages such as these can also be read as evidence of the resistance to the presence of Europeans by west Africans.
14. Colvile, H. (in Z. Colvile, 1893, preface, viii–ix). I suspect this comment is meant to inspire some mirth in the reader.
15. Compare this, however, with Kingsley's descriptions of west African women, or Slessor's haughty dismissal of the missionary-introduced hubbard, which she considered highly impractical in the heat of the tropics (Chapter 6).
16. Kingsley (1982, plates between 358 and 359); there are several more examples of these kinds of synthesized images in *Travels*. Many of these photographs were not taken by Kingsley, but were reproduced in her publication with permission from the Mission Evangelique of Paris.
17. Other such photographs not reproduced here include, 'An Angola Fisherman at Home' and 'A Typical West African River Bank', (ibid., plates between 358 and 359).
18. Kingsley preferred to refer to the Fang peoples as Fans, possibly to reduce the sensationalism that could arise in association with their reputation as cannibals (see Chapter 5).
19. She was a particularly fierce critic of anthropologist James Fraser and his influential book, *The Golden Bough*. She wrote to Edward Tylor, 'When I come across those fairy palaces of theory like the Golden Bough [sic] ... I yearn to heave half a brick through their snowy window', 27/10/96. See also letters to Anna Tylor, 1/10/96, 23/6/98, Rhodes House, Oxford.
20. Letter from Kingsley to Edward Blyden 14/3/1900, reproduced in Kingsley (1899a, xvii–xviii).
21. Kingsley to Violet Roy, S.S. Lagos, off Liberia, 17/8/93. For an account of Robert Nassau's relationship with his nurse, Anyentyuwa, which brought him into conflict with the Church, and of Kingsley's support, see Alexander (1989, 36–142).

Plate 1 Mary Kingsley in 1897

Plate 2 Mary Slessor on furlough in Scotland
with her adopted children

Plate 3 Zélie Colvile: Frontispiece from *Round the Black Man's Garden*

Plate 4 Constance Larymore : Frontispiece of the book to her husband from
A Resident's Wife in Nigeria

Plate 5 'Negress – Accra' (from Colvile, 1893)

Plate 6 'Ju-ju Priest' (from Colvile, 1893)

Plate 7 'Igalwa Women' (from Kingsley, 1982)

Plate 8 'Fan Chief and Family' (from Kingsley, 1982)

Plate 9 'Fans' (from Kingsley, 1982)

Plate 10 'Death Dance Costumes, Old Calabar' (from Kingsley, 1982)

Plate 11 'Caravan for Stanley Pool, Pallaballa Mountains, Congo' (from Kingsley, 1982)

CHAPTER 5

Slavery, witchcraft and cannibalism

Although it is an open question whether the West African negro has yet arrived at
a stage which fits him for the reception of our religion and civilisation, ... there
can be no doubt that the world at large can no longer tolerate the cruelties and
abominations attendant on ancestral and devil worship ... (Colvile, 1893, 305).

The Lagos Travelling Commissioner, who we met at Aiede, seemed to have grave
suspicions of the people there in the matter of twin-murder and human sacrifices
– they certainly looked capable of both (Larymore, 1908, 20–21).

I subsequently learnt that although the Fans will eat their fellow friendly
tribesfolk, yet they like to keep a little something belonging to them as a memento
... [T]hough its [sic] to their credit ... still its an unpleasant practice when they hang
the remains in the bedroom you occupy ... (Kingsley, 1982, 57).

Introduction: objectives of description

As has been argued throughout this book, knowledge, imperialism and power were
intimately related. One of the fundamentals of imperial discourse was its claim to
create 'knowledge' about 'other' peoples. As discussed in Chapter 2, the women of
this study were all empowered by their ability to claim 'knowledge' and 'authority'
about west Africa, and to construct images of west African peoples and cultures in
the imaginations of their readers. However, the images they constructed were by no
means monolithic, and their narratives cannot be read as imperialist in a uniform
manner. This chapter explores some of the nuances apparent in these narratives,
specifically in the ways in which white women travellers wrote about the cultures and
customs of west African peoples. Despite always being problematically located
within hegemonic imperialist discourse, the representations of some of these women
contain strategies which can be read as counter-imperialist.

Profound differences existed in the writings of those women who travelled to
west Africa with open minds, with an expressed desire to learn and understand, and
those who travelled merely to confirm their preconceptions. Mary Kingsley, for
example, would certainly have agreed with the statement that 'the darkest thing about
Africa has always been our ignorance of it' (Kimble, in Birkett, 1992, 57). She
placed great importance on understanding aspects of west African cultures. She
wrote, 'Africa might well become another Ireland if it was left to the kind of men
sent out by the Colonial Office, for they knew little or nothing of the people they

ruled and their main preoccupation was to gain promotion to another, healthier, colony' (in Howard, 1957, 183). Kingsley emphasized her desire to paint an accurate picture of west African customs when she wrote, 'I have tried to honestly and fairly understand the West Africans by studying them in their native homes' (1898c, 267). On another occasion she wrote, 'all I am concerned in is that I should give you as clear and unbiassed [sic] an idea as lies in my power of the spirit world as an African sees it'. She believed that she could do this because her 'mind was carefully kept swept of preconceived notions' (1897c, 332 and 342). Of course, Kingsley could never completely remove herself from her own cultural context, but her intention to attempt to do so was both admirable and unique for the time of her journeys. While travelling in west Africa she attempted to learn a few African languages. She wrote (1898a, vi):

> I feel sure that we cannot thoroughly understand the inner working of the African mind until this department of the study of it has been efficiently worked up; for the languages contain, and are founded on, a very peculiar basis of figurative thought, and until that is thoroughly understood we cannot really judge the true meaning of native statements on what is called totemism, and other sundry subjects.

Kingsley, perhaps in deference to the masculinist scientific community with which she was often at odds, did not make any claims to know the 'truth'. She wrote, 'I do not set myself up to tell the truth. I can only say, look at my series of pictures of things which I faithfully give you, and I hope you will get from them the impression which is the truth' (in Tabor, 1930, 89). She was also aware of the subjectivity of her responses, but she highlighted this to demonstrate the fact that she was observing west Africa from the inside, and thus to add validity to her descriptions. Unlike many women travellers she claimed not to rely upon hearsay and tales that she heard in west Africa. She wrote (1982, xx–xxi):

> I have written only on things that I know from personal experience and very careful observation. I have never accepted an explanation of a native custom from one person alone, nor have I set down things as being prevalent customs from having seen a single instance. I have endeavoured to give you an honest account of the general state and manner of life in Lower Guinea ... In reading this you must make allowances for my love of this sort of country ... and for my ability to be more comfortable there than in England.

Slessor also shared the attitude of abandoning pre-conceptions and attempting to learn African languages in order to facilitate a greater understanding of local cultures in west Africa. This may seem surprising when one considers the nature of the missionary propaganda to which she had been exposed during her formative years, and the particular images associated with Calabar in this body of literature. The survival of the missions on the coast depended upon the flow of funds from Britain, and for this they relied upon powerful images of west Africa and their peoples. The Church of Scotland mission at Calabar was no exception. Conditions in Calabar were undeniably harsh; it had been at the heart of both European and indigenous slave trading and its effects had permeated the whole society. The Efik peoples of the coast had split into Houses that quarrelled with each other over greater shares of the slave trade, and had created a feared secret society, Ekpe. They had forbidden European missionaries to travel up the Cross River, and the Okoyong and other warring peoples of the interior closed the forest to them (Buchan, 1984, 5–6). The Mission was restricted to the coast. Such conditions provided ample scope for revelations in the *Missionary Record*, the mouthpiece and propaganda tool of the Church of Scotland. It was such revelations that helped form the picture of Calabar in the imagination of Mary Slessor, and these were all the more important as at this time the missionaries were amongst the few residents in west Africa. Their knowledge was gained in situ, rather than by fleeting visits in the course of travel or trade. This added greater weight to their claims and validity to their observations. The images they created made a lasting impression on Slessor, and it was the image of the brave missionary, surrounded by peril and adventure, which first encouraged her to become a missionary.

The reputation of the people of Calabar was the poorest in Nigeria. The British considered them to be intractable, their societies unorganized, and their customs barbarous (Nwabughuogu, 1981, 75). Cannibalism and human sacrifice were believed to be widespread, associated with indigenous slavery and the burial rites of kings and chiefs. Widows were subjected to trial-by-ordeal on the death of their husband, twins were murdered and twin-mothers persecuted. These were the customs that were portrayed in graphic terms in the *Missionary Record*, and which informed Slessor's opinions before she travelled to west Africa. However, once she had seen west Africa for herself, Slessor made a point of challenging some of the assumptions about the peoples of the interior. On first going inland into the Okoyong territory she wrote, 'I am going to a new tribe up country, a fierce and cruel people, and everyone tells me that they will kill me. But I don't fear any hurt'.[1] Slessor's insight into the customs of the peoples of Calabar was facilitated by her attempt to adopt an African lifestyle, and also, as with Kingsley, by her knowledge of local languages. Commentators at the time suggested that not only did she speak Efik, but she also understood its every shade of inflection and accompanying gestures (Chappell, 1927, 16).

The efforts made by Kingsley and Slessor to acquire knowledge of local languages provide an important context for their descriptions of the customs of west African peoples. Their attitudes were in direct contrast with those of many other women travelling in west Africa who took with them their preconceived notions about the customs of the area, and looked for confirming instances. What they found often confirmed their prejudices.

Slavery: an African problem?

Accounts of indigenous slavery in west Africa completed the picture of savagery in many imaginations in Victorian Britain. The image of slavery was a powerful facet of the myth of the 'dark continent' (Said, 1978, 208; Ferguson, 1992, 303–7). The first abolitionists had placed the blame for the slave trade mostly on Europeans, but by mid-century, the blame had largely been displaced onto Africans themselves. 'When the taint of slavery fused with sensational reports about cannibalism, witchcraft, and apparently shameless sexual customs, Victorian Africa emerged draped in that pall of darkness that the Victorians themselves accepted as reality' (Brantlinger, 1985, 198). As Ferguson (1992, 303) argues, images of Africans as slaves or ex-slaves helped propagate the 'energizing myth' of British imperialism. Slavery figured quite prominently in the accounts of those women travelling around mid-century.

By the middle of the nineteenth century, slavery was such a fundamental aspect of Yoruba society that Anna Hinderer could remark that, 'there are no riches in Africa; slaves and wives make a man great in this country' (1872, 245). As Agiri (1981, 126) argues, various statements of observers suggest that she was correct in her assessment of the importance of slavery. At the time of the travels of both Foote and Hinderer in west Africa, the British Government was more concerned with trade, both in suppressing the slave trade and encouraging the export of other products, than it was in spreading Christianity. As a consequence, military forces sometimes protected Christian communities, though not always. Against this background, Mrs Foote made a passionate plea at the end of her narrative in support of the missionary effort, a plea that was couched in the rhetoric of Victorian anti-slavery discourse. She wrote (1869, 220–21):

The whole land rings with tales of bloodshed, oppression and wickedness of every kind, and as long as the native rulers are uncivilised and unchristianised, slavery will never cease. The natives consider exchanging men for goods a perfectly fair sort of barter, and in war the victorious party makes slaves of their prisoners as a legitimate part of their success. The love of enslaving his fellow beings is also so innate in man, that even freed slaves, if they get on in this world, spend their first spare money in buying a slave ... [S]lavery will, I fear, still exist in Africa ... until the civilising influence of Christianity has extended itself over those melancholy tracts of land ...

Foote defined her *raison d'être* in west Africa in terms of the anti-slavery effort. Thus she defined her presence there in terms of an accepted feminine pursuit, for, as Midgley (1992) argues, from the end of the eighteenth to the middle of the nineteenth centuries, middle-class women in Britain were very much involved in the anti-slavery effort. Foote was concerned not only with eradicating what remained of the European slave trade, but also in eliminating indigenous slavery. Therefore, the same rhetoric that had been applied to the European trade was now applied to social systems in west Africa, but the blame for slavery lay with the west Africans themselves. Only through the 'civilizing' influence of Britain could slavery be eliminated. This fact suggests that Foote and Hinderer were unaware of the fundamental differences between European slavery and slavery in west African societies. As Northrup (1981, 103) suggests, much of the slavery in pre-colonial Nigeria was based on a kinship idiom, where slaves were treated almost as family members, and could hold the same positions of status as free-born people. Many of the slaves in sub-Saharan Africa were women, and were quickly assimilated into these kinship units (Martin and Klein, 1983, 3). Thus slavery was an essential part of the structure of pre-colonial Nigerian societies. It was only during the colonial period that the misconception about the subordinate status levels of slaves was perpetuated, and it was only with the penetration of market economies during the colonial period that the notion of slaves as subordinated status objects began to increase.[2] The descriptions of the legacy of indigenous slavery in the narratives of Foote and Hinderer, therefore, did not reflect accurately the ideological framework of this slavery. Instead, they used the same emotive and sensationalist terms of reference that had been in used in the anti-slavery propaganda of the late eighteenth and early nineteenth centuries.

The descriptions of slavery by Foote and Hinderer differed from those of Elizabeth Melville, who, writing a generation earlier in the 1840s, was more concerned about the effects of European slavery than she was about indigenous slavery. Rather than condemning west Africans, Melville concentrated her attacks on the European slave trade and exhorted sympathy for indigenous peoples among her readers. In a journal entry of 1843 she wrote (1969, 136):

> A feeling of patriotic pride always mingles with my pity on seeing a slaver brought in, to think that – thanks to Britain above all the other kingdoms on the face of the globe – how soon these, our so unjustifiably oppressed fellow-mortals, will be blessed with a happier freedom than they ever knew in their heathen homes of the far interior ...

Melville insisted that indigenous slave raiding only occurred as a consequence of the demand for slaves in Brazil and the Caribbean. If the trans-Atlantic slave trade was abolished, indigenous slavery would also diminish. However, despite her philanthropic concerns, Melville's anti-slavery tracts formed part of a wider discourse that subsumed the voices of African peoples, and her belief in Britain's role as the guardian of freedom in Africa encoded the continent as one to be controlled and aided by conquest and rule.

Portrayals of west African spiritual beliefs

As contact with west Africa increased after mid-century, more knowledge was acquired about indigenous spiritual beliefs. Much of this, however, was comparative knowledge and viewed from the standpoint of European religions. There was little effort to understand these beliefs from the point of view of those Africans who practised them. Indeed, there was little real interest in understanding or recording the spiritual beliefs of Africans until the turn of the century. Paradoxically, although there was little concern for understanding African spiritual beliefs, the cultural practices that emanated from them provided people in Victorian Britain with a rich source of fascination.

West African spiritual beliefs were termed 'fetishism' by Victorian commentators. Comte had identified fetishism as the first stage of religious development; Lubbock dismissed it as 'mere witchcraft' (in Mermin, 1982, 224). This fetishism was testimony, according to commentators in nineteenth century Britain, to the inferiority of Africans:

> The inhabitants of that world were backward and inferior. This was not an aspersion, it was a fact – for if they had not been backward and inferior, would they have chosen to live in a world governed by fear and magic? They had fashioned their bondage by themselves, long before any European arrived to discover, exploit and increase it. They were bound not only to the past, but in some cases ... actually to the dead, to ancestors who still conditioned their thought and action (Thornton, 1965, 154–5).

These attitudes were often apparent in the narratives of women travellers. Mrs Foote was dismissive of west African spiritual customs. She described offerings to a fetish idol at Lagos as 'all sorts of rubbish, bits of bone, old beads, shells, scraps of crockery and coloured rags, the poor men believing that the fetish will be pleased by such delicate attentions, and preserve their lives from the fury of the waves' (1869, 198). Foote expressed her opinion that west Africans would soon be converted to Christianity and so be rid of such 'superstitions'. Zélie Colvile, writing later in the century was more pejorative in her comments about west African customs. She wrote (1893, 305):

Although it is an open question whether the West African negro has yet arrived at a stage which fits him for the reception of our religion and civilisation, with their attendant liberties in the matter of gin, gunpowder, and forms of worship, and restrictions as to sexual relationship, there can be no doubt that the world at large can no longer tolerate the cruelties and abominations attendant on ancestral and devil worship, nor live cheek-by-jowl – as it must be nowadays with all seaboard populations – with a people which practises them.

Colvile adopted the typical late-nineteenth century attitude that the fault for the failure to convert west Africans to Christianity lay not with the missionaries, but with the inferiority of west Africans themselves; they were simply not advanced enough to understand Christianity and forsake their superstitions. Indeed she argued that the missionaries should be thanked for having 'stamped out the outward and more objectionable forms of West African superstition' (ibid., 305). In the narratives of both Foote and Colvile there were no attempts to understand and relate to the local spiritual practices of indigenous peoples.

Constance Larymore was more sympathetic. She argued that although she was interested in fetish, she never ventured to discover which 'schools' the various peoples belonged to, for she held the 'belief in treating any man's religion with as much reverence and reticence as he himself does' (1908, 122). Unlike Foote and Colvile, Larymore recognized that African spiritual beliefs approximated to religious beliefs, they were not merely superstition, and she expressed a certain amount of respect for these beliefs. She also expressed her amusement at the lack of understanding of west African religious customs amongst colonialists. She repeated a story that she had heard of an English soldier in Northern Nigeria (ibid., 18–9). On seeing a red ant hill, he, 'took it to be a 'heathen fetish', and, plunging his sword through and through the imaginary idol, exclaimed to the astonished villagers and his troops, 'Thus does the Great White Queen destroy the Black Man's Ju-ju!' The villagers, of course, thought him mad ...' This ridiculing of an incident of misunderstanding by a British colonialist undermines imperialist discourse on west African spiritual beliefs. The figure of fun is not the African steeped in superstition, but the Englishman ignorant of both the landscapes of Northern Nigeria and the spiritual beliefs of the people who lived there.

Mary Kingsley's portrayal of 'fetish-worship' also challenged, to some extent, the images constructed in imperialist discourse, in that she attempted to negate the image of barbarism in west Africa. She contended that 'fetish-worship' was as viable a religion as any practised in the west, and she also attempted to familiarize it by writing:

... you white men will say, 'Why go on believing in him then?' but that is an idea that does not enter the African mind. I might just as well say 'Why do you go on

135

believing in the existence of hansom cabs,' because one hansom cab driver malignantly fails to take you where you want to go, or fails to arrive in time to catch a train you wished to catch (1982, 506).

Kingsley explained that the word 'fetish' originated among Portuguese explorers, who named the objects worshipped by west Africans *Feitico* after the images of saints that they themselves worshipped (ibid., 429). Thus Kingsley drew a parallel between an interpretation of European Christianity and spiritual beliefs in west Africa, undermining any claims to the superiority of Christian belief. She argued (1899a, 95):

> The final object of all human desire is a knowledge of the nature of God. The human methods, or religions, employed to gain this object are divisible into three main classes:
> *Firstly*, the submission to and acceptance of a direct divine message;
> *Secondly*, the attempt by human intellectual power to separate the conception of God from material phenomena, and regard Him as a thing apart and unconditioned;
> *Thirdly*, the attempt to understand Him as manifest in natural phenomena.
> I personally am constrained to follow this last and humblest method ...

As was discussed in Chapter 3, Kingsley equated her own beliefs with those of Spinoza, but she also recognized that the beliefs of Africans fitted into this third category, and further identified her belief in animism with that of west Africans. Fundamental to her understanding of west African spiritual beliefs was her comprehension of their worship of spirits. This comprehension led to Kingsley's defence of African beliefs. She wrote (1897c, 342):

> You will often hear this religion of fetish called a religion of terror and painted black with crimson patches. Well, facts are facts; find me a more cheerful set of human beings ... than the West Africans, and then, and not till then, will I say fetish is a horrible thing. I will grant you there is human sacrifice under it from Sierra Leone to the Niger; I will grant you there is sending down with the dead of their wives, slaves, and friends; I will grant you it kills witches, that it produces cannibalism in this region; but before you write down the men who do these things as fiends, I ask you to read any respectable book on European history, to face the Inquisition and the fires of Smithfield, and then to go and read your London Sunday newspapers. West Africa could not keep a Sunday newspaper going in crimes between man and man; its crimes are those arriving from a simple direct absolute belief in a religion. From no region that I know can so truly go up the sad cry to God, *Doch, alles was dazu mich trieb, Gott, war so gut! ach! war so lieb!* as in West Africa. The mere fact of the Bantu doing little or nothing in the way of

human sacrifice or sending-down killing, does not make me prefer him to the Negro.

Kingsley, therefore, argued that west African spiritual practices were no more barbaric than those that had taken place in Europe, and that there was, in fact, less crime in west Africa than in Britain. 'Fetish-worship' and 'witchcraft', with all their attendant brutality, were not violence for the sake of violence, but arose from deep-seated spiritual beliefs. Kingsley understood that everyday life for people in west Africa was dominated by their belief in the spirit world, and, consequently, they held a profound belief in witchcraft and its effects. She elucidated the African belief that witchcraft could act in two ways, 'witching something out of a person', or 'witching something into a person' (1982, 462–3; 518). Some indigenous peoples believed that they were born with four souls: the soul that survives death, the shadow on the path, the dream-soul, and the bush-soul (1897a, 144). Witches, who could be hired by any member of a village, continually set traps for the soul that wandered from the body during sleep, and if this were caught the owner would sicken as the soul withered. Many west Africans took great care not to offend their bush-souls that lived in some plant or animal in the forest. They also believed in other spirits, such as disembodied human spirits, ghosts, spirits resident in inanimate objects and spirits causing sickness. These spirits could be 'witched' into charms that would provide protection for the wearer. Kingsley emphasized that such a proliferation of spirits meant that every event in a person's life was controlled by some form of spirit; the belief in witchcraft was thus a fundamental aspect of social control in west African societies (1899c).[3] From her knowledge of indigenous spiritual beliefs, Kingsley attempted to understand, and thus portray objectively, the fact that at almost every death the suspicion of witchcraft arose, which meant trial-by-ordeal for unpopular men, or the wives and slaves of the deceased (1897a, 145).

For Kingsley it was such a profound belief in the spirit-world, and the fear that witchcraft inspired, that produced what the west regarded as a savage blood lust and a delight in gore. She argued that Africans did not take pleasure in violence, but that this violence was a manifestation of the terrible burden of fear that they carried around with them. She wrote (1899a, 127–8), 'An African cannot say, as so many Europeans evidently easily can, 'Oh, that is alright from a religious point of view, but one must be practical, you know', and it is this factor that makes me respect the African deeply and sympathize with him'. Kingsley tried to remain dispassionate about the violence that seemed inherent in west African societies; she withheld any opinions that she had on the matter, and neither condoned nor condemned it, except to say that there was a 'strange element of common-sense in apparently rank superstitious folly' (1896a, 69). However, she went beyond the usual ethnocentric response of shock and abhorrence, and attempted to avoid sensationalising these aspects of life in west Africa. She attempted to delve deeply into the minds of the people she met in an effort to understand their customs. For her, those customs that were inherently violent were not a product of the barbarity of west Africans, but a manifestation of their profound spiritual beliefs. Kingsley attempted to persuade her readers to avoid condemning west Africans as barbaric on the basis of their spiritual practices. Although these practices could be considered violent, they were no different to the witch-hunts, persecution and mass-murders which had taken place in Europe in the name of religion.

Kingsley went further in attempting to defend west Africans from the charge of barbarism, and undermined images of the 'bestial savage' by portraying west Africans as affectionate and noble. She wrote (1899a, 142):

> That the Africans are affectionate I am fully convinced. This affection does not lie precisely on the same lines as those of Europeans, I allow. It is not with them so deeply linked with sex; but the love between mother and child, man and man, brother and sister, woman and woman, is deep, true, and pure, and it must be taken into account in observing their institutions and ideas, particularly as to this witchcraft, where it shows violently and externally in hatred only to the superficial observer.

The idea of an affectionate African was a contradiction in terms to many Europeans who expounded their views on the barbarism of Africa; for others, as discussed in the preceding chapter, this affection was a manifestation of infantilism. Kingsley, however, represented the affection of west African people as testament to their nobility. Thus she challenged the image of the 'bestial savage' by re-invoking images of the 'noble savage'. Constance Larymore also alluded to similar images. On arriving in Hadeija, she and her husband were greeted by a cavalry of African soldiers, whose 'military precision would not have disgraced any regiment of British cavalry'. Larymore wrote (1908, 100):

> I was myself [interested] at seeing this spectacle of truly barbaric African splendour ... amid so much brilliance and colour! It seemed to take one back centuries in the world's civilisation, and, with a gasp, came the realisation that we had stepped into a world where time had stood still, and the ages passed over without leaving a mark!

These representations by Kingsley and Larymore were, of course, deeply ethnocentric and still represented west Africans as Other. The least 'noble' people of west Africa for both women were those who had been influenced by Europe; those who had adopted aspects of what Kingsley termed 'second hand rubbishy white culture – a culture far lower and less dignified than that of either the stately Mandingo or the bush chief' (1982, 20). As has been pointed out throughout this study, women travellers were often influenced by nineteenth-century romanticism. The late nineteenth-century romantic movement in Britain and its emphasis on spiritualism influenced Kingsley, in particular. However, her depictions of west Africans owed less to the ideas of atavism and primitivism (as expressed in the works of Haggard, Conrad, Wells, and Bram Stoker) than they did to late eighteenth-century portrayals. For Kingsley, the noblest of west Africans were the 'unadulterated' groups such as the Fang peoples. Unlike the late nineteenth-century romantics, Kingsley did not wish to see west Africans 'civilized' and Christianized but wished to see their customs protected from Europeanization. She admired the Fang because they had resisted and rejected completely any missionary influence, preserving their ancestor cults, witchcraft and secret societies that were fundamental to the nature of their society. It was these qualities of resistance in the Fang that appealed to Kingsley's vision of the 'noble savage'. They had fought back successfully against the invasion of European cultures, and continued to mint their own currency (in the form of miniature axe-heads or *bikei*) in order to maintain the independence of their trade networks. According to Kingsley, they were 'full of fire, temper, intelligence, and go, very teachable, rather difficult to manage, quick to take offence'; they epitomized Kingsley's 'noble savage'. She wrote, 'I like him better than any African' (1896b, 121–2).

Despite drawing on earlier, ethnocentric images, Kingsley's depictions of west African spiritual beliefs challenged the image of the 'bestial savage' apparent in many other imperial literatures. The missionaries were among the major contributors to this image, and their reports in the missionary magazines were full of graphic images of violence. In the *Missionary Record*, fetish rites were of 'the most sanguinary character'; the priests were 'frightful monsters, whose weapons of rule [we]re terror and the knife'; 'the mangled limbs of the victims [we]re hung on the branches of the horrid fetish tree'; and the skulls of the dead were 'seen scattered in all directions'.[4] Mary Slessor's descriptions, however, avoided these graphic images. Although she was often depressed and appalled by incidents of violence that she witnessed in Calabar,[5] she did not see anything fundamentally wrong in the nature of Calabar societies. Her obvious mission was to spread the Gospel and to eradicate many of the violent customs inherent in indigenous religious beliefs. However, Slessor believed that it was important not to destroy indigenous cultures. Like Kingsley, she had a profound understanding of religious beliefs in west Africa, and recognized that they were fundamental to the maintenance of social order. She believed that the marriage of west African customs, without their attendant violence, with a belief in Christian morality would improve the quality of life in west Africa. As suggested in Chapter 2, Slessor actually devoted more effort to the protection of Calabar customs from British encroachment, and to the peaceful settlement of local disputes, than she did to spreading Christianity. Her respect for the spiritual beliefs of the peoples of Calabar, and her adaptation of Christianity to a form more suited to accommodate west African customs, was a visionary idea for its time, and one which became a policy of British missions in the 1920s, five years after Slessor's death.

The mystique of west African cultural practices: cannibals, killings and secret societies

Of all the perceived atrocities in west Africa, cannibalism was the most sensational. Imaginations in Victorian Britain were titillated constantly by tales of anthropophagy in far-off regions of the world, particularly west Africa and New Guinea. Exaggerated claims of cannibalism were used to elucidate the supposed debasement of 'bestial' west Africans, and cannibalism was a much-exploited theme from mid-century onwards. The apparently disparate traits of paganism, nakedness, and cannibalism formed a syndrome. Nakedness often implied cannibalism and fetish-worship; a clothed cannibal was a contradiction in terms. Images such as these were favourites with travellers in west Africa.[6] However, as Arens argues, people in Victorian Britain were probably far more obsessed with cannibalism than west Africans ever were.[7] Modern anthropology casts considerable doubt on the existence of cannibalism in Africa, and suggests that any instances were linked to witchcraft rather than to the gustatory cannibalism of Victorian imperial discourse. Arens argues that while there was a vast amount of literature alluding to the existence of cannibalism, there is no satisfactory first-hand account of it as a socially approved custom ritually practised anywhere in the world. He writes (1979, 20–21), 'the widespread African belief that Europeans are cannibals or use human blood for evil intent is interpreted as an indication of African ignorance. As a correlate, the 'fact' of African cannibalism is thought to be the result of African ignorance of civilized standards'. Few writers have analyzed the possibility that west Africans may have spread rumours of their own cannibalism, either to maintain social order, to prevent attacks from other ethnic groups, or to discourage the European powers from penetrating further into the forests of west Africa (this is discussed in more detail in Chapter 7). However, the theme of African cannibalism remained an extremely popular one during the Victorian period, and one that was guaranteed to attract an audience.

Despite this, few women travellers mentioned cannibalism in their narratives, and only Mary Kingsley discussed it at any length. Despite ascribing the image of the 'noble savage' to west Africans, Kingsley did not deny the existence cannibalism in west Africa. This may seem an anomaly, but it appears that initially she did not wish make an issue of cannibalism. She subscribed to the views of explorers such as Burton, de Brazza and du Chaillu in considering that certain groups in west Africa were cannibals.[8] Blunt (1994, 82) argues that Kingsley used the notoriety of the Fang 'to establish herself within the masculine tradition of exploration', and this certainly fitted with her identification of herself with her heroes. However, she attempted to play down the subject rather than to sensationalize it. It was mentioned in Chapter 4 that, unlike her predecessors, she referred to the forest peoples of Gabon as Fans rather than Fangs. In the index to *Travels in West Africa* there are only two page references to cannibalism. She wrote of the Fang, 'He has no slaves, no prisoners of war, no cemeteries, so you must draw your own conclusions. No, my friend, I will not tell you any cannibal stories' (1982, 330).

Kingsley wanted to avoid the sensational but, in defending west Africans in the face of scientific racism of late-Victorian England, she was forced to defend cannibalism, to argue that although it did exist it was practised for nutritional purposes only and was not a threat to white people.[9] She expressed an indifference to cannibalism when questioned about it, and consequently her critics accused her of flippancy.[10] What these critics failed to appreciate was that by instilling a little humour, Kingsley was attempting to forestall any immediate ethnocentric response to west African customs. She attempted to encourage her reader towards a more sympathetic response rather than one that was culturally conditioned. She wrote (1982, 330), 'The Fan is not a cannibal from sacrificial motives ... He does it in his commonsense way. Man's flesh, he says, is good to eat, very good, and he wishes you would try it. Oh dear no, he never eats it himself, but the next door town does'. This amused objectivity pervaded Kingsley's work. For example, when she found a bag in her hut filled with various parts of human bodies, she commented that though it is 'touching' that cannibals kept such 'mementoes', 'its [sic] an unpleasant practice when they hang the remains in the bedroom you occupy' (ibid., 273). Kingsley could be accused of a certain amount of unfounded presumption in her depiction of Fang cannibalism. These 'mementoes' were not necessarily evidence of cannibal feasts. She never saw a Fang eat human flesh, yet she accepted that they were cannibals without any hard evidence. She took the Fang's filed teeth as evidence of cannibalism without analysing the cultural significance of this custom (Hogg, 1958,115). She interpreted the lack of burial places as possible evidence for cannibalism, but did not consider that the Fang might bury their dead beneath their huts, which she knew to be the practice of other indigenous groups. However, she did not seek to sensationalize the issue of cannibalism and it featured hardly at all in any of her publications. She even challenged the picture of the supposed violence of west Africans in British imaginations. She wrote (1898b, 538–9):

> ... the English public mind has a sort of tired feeling about the African. A feeling that it is really impossible to understand the creature that turns up in mission literature as a Simple Child of Nature, our Unsophisticated Brother, &c. [sic], and in newspapers as an Incarnate Fiend wallowing in blood, in Benin, Ashantee, and Dahomey, given to cannibalising round corners whenever the white eye is off him, and a lazy brute when the white eye is on.

When she was forced to defend cannibalism she portrayed it in a humorous light designed to elicit a sympathetic response. Thus, while not dispelling the myth of cannibalism, she went some way towards challenging the image of African savagery that prevailed at the time of her travels.

Of the other women travellers, only Zélie Colvile mentioned cannibalism. In a chapter entitled *The Land of Death* it could be expected that Colvile would sensationalize the supposed violence inherent in west Africa. However, she wrote (1893, 306), 'Many were the stories told to us of cannibalism ..., I fancy mostly exaggerated; for, as far as I know, cannibalism has never been practised in this region except as part of a religious ceremony'. Colvile, therefore, refused to believe any of the rumours that she heard while travelling in west Africa without first-hand evidence.

The notion of cannibalism was intimately connected to ideas about secret societies, especially in Sierra Leone and what was to become southern Nigeria. As Kingsley wrote (1896b, 122):

> It is needless to say that cannibalism is not allowed nor practised, in districts close to the Government stations. I myself doubt whether there is half as much cannibalism near a station of the Congo Français as there is in the stations in the Oil Rivers. Of course it is more difficult to suppress in the Rivers, because it is connected to the secret societies ...

Secret societies were viewed with suspicion by both the British and by Africans themselves. However, what had been a local annoyance was transformed by imperialist discourse into an international threat aimed at the very roots of British imperialism. As Johnson (1991, 174) argues, 'European perceptions of African 'secret societies' were partly moulded by the history of European response to their own secret societies, but there were parallels to the European situation in the African experience'. The suspicions of African rulers about subversion and uncontrolled meetings, even when they themselves were members of the societies, combined with the paranoia of the colonial powers, often led to exaggerated reports about the activities of the 'secret societies'. That little was known about these societies heightened their mystique, making them 'harder to fathom and easier to shudder at' (Kiernan, 205). Kingsley, however, attempted to separate west African secret societies from the notion of witchcraft. She argued that they were 'not essentially religious, their action is mainly judicial' (1982, 526); in other words, secret societies existed to maintain law and order, and to ensure that justice was preserved. This was true, for example, of the Egbo (or Ekpe) in Nigeria, which existed to settle trade disputes and debt palavers. Kingsley believed that without the existence of a police force, law courts and prisons, the methods of the secret societies were perfectly logical in the context of west Africa. Some of these societies, she argued, practised cannibalism and human sacrifice, particularly the various leopard and alligator societies, but again, these were mainly for judicial purposes rather than being linked to witchcraft (ibid., 526–43). For this reason she exclaimed her support for their existence; she wrote, 'I am absolutely for Secret Societies' (in Howard, 1957, 225). On another occasion she complained to Joseph Chamberlain at the Colonial Office about the images associated with secret societies and what she believed to be the fallacious accounts of these by people who knew little about them. She wrote that reports of the secret societies of Sierra Leone were:

> ... a piece of madness we have I fancy to thank the Bishop of S.L. [sic] for who I am informed is the *only* person out there that the Govt. [sic] will listen to. I am not speaking on this matter merely as an ethnologist but as one influenced greatly by Sir Claude MacDonald ... a private friend of mine. He regarded the great ... law keeping society of Egbo as a valuable aid in keeping internal law and order – a thing requiring regulation not suppression. There are Secret Societies and Secret Societies – some are law keepers like Purroh – others law breakers. When you next see a Sierra Leone official or trader – you ask them the difference between Purroh and Kufong and if he does not know, do not listen to him on Secret Societies – its not his line.[11]

Here, Kingsley not only presented herself as an expert on the subject of secret societies in west Africa, but also attacked the Government for drawing information about such matters from people who were not experts and who were often misinformed. Furthermore, she censured the sweeping condemnation of all secret societies by those who did not understand the critical differences between the functions, constitutions and activities of the many secret societies in west Africa. Kingsley believed that British administrators should suspend judgement on such cultural practices until they had a deeper understanding of them. This was very much in line with her attitude towards west African customs in general, and which has led to her being acclaimed as one of the pioneers in cultural relativist approaches to anthropology (see Chapter 2).

Tales of ritual sacrifice were also bound up with stories about cannibalism and secret societies, and European travellers in west Africa had long expressed their horror of human sacrifices and public executions (Hammond and Jablow, 1977, 65). Women travellers were not exempt from alluding to ritual sacrifice. Colvile, for example, while dismissing the existence of cannibalism in Bonny, accepted that human sacrifice was widespread. She wrote (1893, 306–7):

> Only a few weeks before our arrival ... thirty slaves were killed at a place not fifty miles from Bonny, in order that their late master might not be unattended in the land of the spirits; while the relations of another deceased chief, also in the

immediate neighbourhood, had buried alive two of his slaves in his, and had hung up two more, head downwards, by hooks passed through their heels; in which position they remained until the flesh rotted away, and the poor wretches, still alive, fell into a pit full of spikes, on which they were impaled.

These were images of seemingly gratuitous violence based on hearsay and exaggeration. However, other comments by Colvile suggest that she believed there was a political function underlying the practice of human sacrifice:

> Horrible as this religion is, it has the advantage of putting enormous power into the hands of the rulers, and thus enabling them to maintain a degree of order which our milder methods fail to effect. Men who had travelled in the interior told me that, in point of honesty, the civilised compared most unfavourably with the uncivilised parts (ibid., 307).

It is apparent from Colvile's comments that she perceived west African societies to be inherently barbaric, requiring equally barbaric methods of punishment in order to maintain some semblance of order. The milder, more 'humane' methods of the British were ineffectual in the face of this barbarity. Thus, while Colvile believed that human sacrifice was unacceptable violence in the eyes of the British, it was an acceptable, if not inevitable, means of maintaining social order in west Africa. In other words, it was symptomatic of the violent nature of west African societies.

Mary Slessor perhaps had most first-hand encounters with incidents of violence related to customs in west African societies, and she attempted to prevent such incidents as far as she could. She may have learned from the failed attempts of her predecessors to eradicate such customs through proselytizing, and instead attempted to prevent individual episodes by reasoning and pleading with the protagonists, and by establishing close relationships with village leaders over whom she hoped to exercise some influence. An example of this occurred in 1888, when she intervened at the burial of an Okoyong chief's son to prevent trials-by-ordeal. After two weeks of pleading, arguing and belligerence by Slessor he was buried without a single attendant death; this was previously unheard of in Okoyong.[12] Such interventions by Slessor were commonplace. She avoided condemning African practices outright in her publications, and on one occasion reconciled African fears of offending the spirits with Old Testament fears of a vengeful God as a motive for believing, honouring and obeying 'all the tabus [sic] and sacrifices and ceremonies of his native god'. According to Slessor, therefore, 'fear for the vengeance of the offended deity' was usually the motive for the persistence of customs such as human sacrifice, 'the same as runs through the history of the Old Testament' (in MacGregor, 1917, 162). Thus, although Slessor wanted to see these customs eradicated, she understood why they prevailed, and attempted to explain them to others by drawing parallels with European beliefs.

The fear of the spirit world among many west Africans to which both Colvile and Slessor alluded was, for Kingsley, fundamental to understanding indigenous customs. Kingsley argued that human sacrifice was only comprehensible if the fear that pervaded African society and dominated everyday life was properly understood. However, it was one of the few customs that Kingsley wished to see eradicated in west Africa. She wrote (1896a, 68):

> This killing at funerals is a custom that, from every civilised point of view, must be stamped out, although at present the stamping-out process merely means adding another to the escort accompanying the original deceased, but it is not fair to the Government to expect the immediate and wholesale eradication of the custom, because of the deep root it has in the Negro mind.

Kingsley, therefore, did not condone the custom of ritual sacrifice, but she attempted to communicate to her readers why it occurred, to persuade them to suspend judgement and to refrain from condemning west Africans on the basis of their beliefs. Larymore went a step further in undermining the images of violence associated with west African customs. While in Kabba she wrote (1908, 126):

> There are many minor ceremonies and festivals, connected with matters agricultural, the ultimate success of the crops, the coming of the new yams, etc., but there is little variety in the proceedings, the main point being apparently, the making of a 'cheerful noise' and the sacrifice of nothing more dreadful than a few fouls!

Here Larymore questioned nineteenth-century British assumptions about west African customs; she was aware of the depiction of west Africa as a place of extreme violence in other colonialist discourse and attempted to undermine this image with this description of local customs in Kabba. Both Larymore and Kingsley used these occasional, seemingly frivolous remarks to disrupt stereotypical images of west African customs in the minds of their readers, and, in this way, presented a significant challenge to 'Orientalist' discourses about west Africa.

One aspect of local customs that was particularly appalling to people in Britain was the killing of twins. Travellers and missionaries alike used its existence as evidence of the wanton cruelty and barbarity of west Africans.[13] Some west African peoples believed that the birth of twins meant that the mother had committed adultery with an evil spirit, and this spirit manifested itself in the form of one of the twins. Since there was no way of telling which child was the evil spirit, both were killed, often along with the mother. Kingsley understood that for the African, 'Twins are a *sin* not a *crime*, hence the horror of them – sin as ... [you know] in our own parts is an offence against a spirit – twins are an adultery – wherever you find adultery worked up with a very serious affair, you find him [the African] killing'. As with human sacrifice, Kingsley maintained that it was the profound fear inspired by the belief in spirits that provoked such extreme actions, and again she avoided judging the custom in terms of nineteenth century British morality.

Slessor also understood the source of the fear of twins in west Africa, and committed herself to dispelling this fear. She walked miles to rescue twin babies from the bush, adopted them as her own, and raised them to adulthood. The communities in which she lived could see that these babies grew into normal adults, and in this way Slessor made some inroads into the superstition. By the time of her death in 1915 the killing of twins was considerably reduced in the Calabar area.[14] It was this humanitarian work in saving the lives of twins that evoked uncharacteristic praise from Kingsley, who normally had very few positive comments to make about missionaries. As Russell (1988, 43) argues, the two struck up an immediate friendship and an unlikely partnership, for they were both intent on promoting a better understanding of west African customs. Slessor's renown was increased in Britain as a consequence of Kingsley's description of her deeds in *Travels in West Africa*.

The preservation of West African customs

Several women travellers expressed their desire to see customs in west Africa remain, for the most part, intact. Kingsley, in particular, campaigned amongst British imperialists for the respect for and understanding of these customs. Although the following letter, written to Liberian Edward Blyden, highlights the ethnocentrism contained in Kingsley's polygenism, it also illustrates her concern for the preservation of west African cultures:

> I believe that no race can, as a race, advance except on its own line of development, and that it is the duty of England, if she intends to really and truly advance the African on the plane of culture and make him [sic] a citizen of the world, to preserve the African nationalism, and not destroy it; but destroy it she will unless you who know it come forward and demonstrate African nationalism is a good thing, and that it is not a welter of barbarism, cannibalism and cruelty ... I beg you, Sir, to do your best and prevent this fate falling on your noble race. I believe you can best do it by stating that there is an African law and an African culture; that the African has institutions and a state form of his own (in Hayford, 1901, 7–8).

146

Kingsley believed that it was erroneous to regard African religions, customs, law society, and political organisations as mere childish groping towards a supposedly higher – European – set of concepts. Instead they were natural expressions of west African personalities. Such institutions had arisen from a process of historical development, and should be intensively researched and understood before any attempt to change them was made. Ideas such as these lay behind Kingsley's intensive, and perhaps unbalanced, dislike of missionaries and educated Africans, whom she believed to be destroying the indigenous cultures of west Africa. A particular hatred of Kingsley's was the imposition of western garments, such as the hubbard, on west African women. These were made in Europe, often did not fit, and were completely unsuited to the climate of west Africa. With her usual Swiftean humour, Kingsley wrote (1982, 221):

> ... what idea the pious ladies in England, Germany, Scotland and France can have of the African figure I cannot think, but evidently part of their opinion is that it is very like a tub ... It is not in nature for people to be made to fit these things. So I suggested that a few stuffed negroes should be sent home for distribution in working-party centres, and then the ladies could try the things on.

Kingsley often used humour to 'force her readers to acknowledge the legitimacy of African cultural institutions and to startle them out of complaisant assumptions of cultural superiority' (Barnes Stevenson, 1982, 132). Thus, when one of her guides, Kiva, was seized by a creditor in a Fang village, who intended to settle the debt that Kiva owed by (according to Kingsley) eating him, Kingsley drew a powerful cultural comparison:

> Evidently this was a trace of an early form of a Bankruptcy Court; the court which clears a man of his debt, being here represented by the knife and the cooking pot; the white-washing, as I believe it is termed with us, also shows, only it is not the debtor who is whitewashed, but the creditors doing themselves over with white clay to celebrate the removal of their enemy from his sphere of meretricious activity. This inversion may arise from the fact that whitewashing a ... [person] who was about to be cooked would be unwise, as the stuff would boil off the bits and spoil the gravy. There is always some fragment of sound sense underlying African institutions (1982, 285).

Kingsley's humour and satire disrupted conventional images of west African customs. She drew further cultural parallels when she claimed that the west African was a 'logical, practical man, with feelings that are a credit to him, and are particularly strong in the direction of property ... His make of mind is exceedingly like ... [that] of thousands of Englishmen of the standing-no-nonsense, ... house-is-his-castle type (1899a, 318–19).

Despite her belief in polygenesis, Kingsley was one of a few travellers who were little weighed down with the presumptions of their own culture, and according to Holmes (1949, 145), 'it is unlikely that any other woman ever penetrated so deeply into the savage mind'. She was convinced that the occasionally violent customs that she studied in west Africa were the result of the harsh conditions of African life. All natural forces were the enemy of west Africans; they believed that the spirits must be appeased, and a constant and ruthless war must be waged against those who used the spirits for evil purposes. This fundamentally spiritual outlook appealed to Kingsley's own pantheist beliefs, and she thus exhibited a rare sympathy for indigenous customs. According to Middleton (1973, 151), her travels were:

> A campaign to interpret all things West African and to break through the apathy and ignorance of her countrymen who were faced, at the turn of the century, with the responsibility of administering great tracts of the so-called 'Dark Continent' which the European powers were carving up into 'spheres of influence'.

Kingsley believed that interference by missionaries and administrators, who failed to realise or understand the nature of African beliefs, would upset the delicate balance of societies without seriously affecting indigenous beliefs and practices. As one critic argued:

> Her understanding of the African mind caused her to be firm in her conviction that wise rule must be built up within the framework of African tribal laws and customs, and that it would be nothing short of national murder to attempt to impose on an ancient people an imitation of European government.[15]

Furthermore, she expressed her own fundamental belief that:

> all members of Parliament and officials at the Foreign and Colonial Offices should be compelled to join the Folk-Lore Society; for I am sure that the work it would do in the careful and unprejudiced study of African beliefs and customs would lead to a true knowledge of the Africans (1897a, 138).

Essential differences, therefore, existed in the ways in which women travellers approached west African customs. Clearly, Kingsley wanted to understand these customs in order to preserve them. Although the missionaries wished to contribute to an understanding of African cultures, they wanted to understand in order to change (Mazrui, 1969, 671). This was perhaps less true of Slessor than it was of Hinderer. Slessor was to some degree 'a child of her time'; on first encountering aspects of the more bloody of local customs she wrote, 'it is impossible to love these people for their own sake, one can only do it for it for Christ's sake' (Hudson et al, 1978, 57). However, she quickly gained an understanding and appreciation of the fundamentals of Calabar customs. For example, when she became a magistrate (see Chapter 2) she used the local Mbiam oath rather than a Christian oath, and worked within a framework of African law rather than British law. She believed that a marriage of Christian morality with west African customs would eradicate the worst aspects of Calabar societies while preserving the essence of their cultures and lifestyles. She did not think it desirable to completely destroy indigenous west African cultures. In contrast, the likes of Melville, Colvile and Foote made very little effort to understand west African customs; therefore, their representations tended to be coloured by their own prejudices. Although Melville confessed to knowing nothing at all about west African customs, she was still able to make absolute judgements about the nature of those societies. She argued that the:

> ... impossibility of rooting out the idolatry, superstitions and barbarous practices of those grown up ere they come here, or of teaching humanised habits to any except the mere infants among them, is perfectly beyond comprehension to those who have never tried to tame or teach an ignorant savage (1968, 272).

For the most part, the travels of women residents served only to reinforce their ethnocentrism; they saw only what they were expecting to see. West Africans would only 'advance' through 'westernization' and Christianization. The opinions of these women contrasted greatly with those of Kingsley, who concluded that west Africans could not be 'westernized' and should not have an alien system imposed upon them. Existing cultures were viable ones that should be improved through education rather than be destroyed.[16] For Kingsley, the errors of the earlier government officials (and their wives) arose from the conditions that surrounded them in west Africa, and the nature of their restricted experience and influence. Her evocation of the 'noble savage' may have had its roots in the uncertainty about the value of civilization at the turn of the century, and whether a 'civilized' person was an improvement on a 'primitive' person. It may also have been purely aesthetic; she 'saw the diversity of race and custom spread out in front of [her] like an artist's palette and resented any movement which reduced that picturesqueness' (Ridley, 1983, 93). However, it was also recognition of the uprooting effects of 'westernization' and, from an assumed superior but solicitous standpoint, she regarded the assimilated Africans as objects of pity. In attempting to convince people in Britain that west Africans were not inferior, she found herself having to make a spirited defence of such customs as cannibalism, witchcraft, and even slavery – 'the very things that distorted ideas about Africa and which she would therefore have liked to play down' (Keay, 1985, 122).

As Flint (1963) argues, it is certainly possible to find fault with Kingsley's theories. Her evocation of the 'noble savage' was an essentially backward-looking philosophy, and it would have been impossible for Africa to remain a preserve for indigenous cultures once the forces of modernization (such as trade, of which Kingsley was a great supporter) had been introduced into the continent. As Cline (1980, 17) argues, she was equally naive in her failure to recognize that trade would be just as disruptive to African cultures as Christianity. However, her romantic views of the peoples of west Africa meant that she was the first to espouse the idea of the separate cultural worth of African societies. At a time when west African customs were regarded with condescension in Britain, her 'long, continuous, steady fight for native institutions and native law in West Africa' (Green, 1901, 9) was a valuable challenge to prevailing assumptions.

Conclusion

The images of peoples and customs were of fundamental importance to the popular images of west Africa in Britain. Portrayals of west Africans as 'savages', and of their customs as barbaric and violent, added to and confirmed the metaphor of the 'dark continent'. Apart from Kingsley and Slessor, however, white women travellers did not write in any great detail about the customs of west Africa. This was primarily because of the lack of contact between themselves and indigenous peoples. All of the women studies here tended to avoid the graphic reporting found in other imperial discourses on west Africa. Only Kingsley went into any detail about potentially sensational indigenous customs, and did so only when she was forced to defend west African peoples and their cultures. The absence of graphic imagery may have been due to the fact that constraints controlled the subjects that these women felt able to write about, and this may also explain why landscape descriptions are much more prominent in their narratives than accounts of cultural practices (see Chapter 3). However, this is not to say that when they did describe indigenous customs these women all wrote in the same manner. Kingsley, Slessor and Larymore, to varying degrees and in different ways, challenged the misconceptions about these customs, and thus, on occasion, undermined imperialist images of west Africans as savages. This was, perhaps, because they took an interest in understanding west African cultural practices, rather than in merely having their preconceptions confirmed. Foote and Melville, who travelled earlier in the century, and Colvile, who travelled as a tourist, had less contact with west Africans, and tended to rely on their preconceptions of indigenous customs rather than first-hand experiences when formulating their descriptions. Therefore, the images created by women travellers of west African customs were often very different from those in other imperial discourses, but there were also significant differences amongst the women and the popular images that they created of the peoples and cultures of west Africa. These complexities are also to be found in their representations of the women of west Africa.

Notes

1. Slessor to Hart from Use Ikot Utu, 6/7/12, Slessor Papers, Dundee Museum.
2. As Northrup (1981, 119) explains, nineteenth-century sources stress the relative equality between the freeborn and the slave in certain west African societies before the mid-nineteenth century. This was because the kinship idiom was most prevalent at this time (as opposed to economic and status conceptions of slavery, which assumed greater significance later in the century as the palm oil trade grew. The picture is complicated by the fact that economic conceptions often served to reinforce the kinship idiom).
3. Kingsley argued that west African religion and law were intimately connected. She wrote, 'remember that in those great regions under fetich [sic] rule there are no unemployed, no paupers, no hospitals, workhouses, or prisons, and the African chief keeps order therein' (1899c, 372–3).
4. 'Report on the state of the missions', *Scottish United Presbyterian Church Missionary Record*, January 1846, 4.
5. Letter from Slessor to her sister Maggie 17/4/77, Slessor Papers, Dundee Museum.
6. See, for example, the works of Stanley, Winwood Reade, Ward and Johnston. Cannibalism was also a popular theme in fiction; for example, Conrad's *Heart of Darkness* continually evokes images of cannibalism. On the cannibal syndrome, see Hammond and Jablow (1977, 36–7).
7. For example, the report on John Franklin's disappearance while searching for the North-West Passage was spiced up by stories of the crew resorting to cannibalism (Loomis, 1977). In 1816, the wreck of French vessel *La Meduse* evoked images not of noble suffering, but of murderous, cannibalistic panic. The Dracula stories of the late nineteenth century were based on a renewed interest in the gruesome and cannibalistic exploits of Vlad V the Impaler (Tannahill, 1975).
8. On European fascination with the Fang peoples, see Chamberlin (1978, 429).
9. Many of her comments on cannibalism were in response to an article in the Spectator, probably written by Meredith Townsend and entitled 'Negro Future', detailing in sensational fashion the supposed evil cruelty of Africans.
10. She did tell an interviewer from *The London Review* that cannibals had eaten her Uncle Gerald, but that this had not deterred her from travelling to west Africa

(*The London Review*, May 21, 1898). She repeated this story in her memoir of her father (1900b).

11. Kingsley to Joseph Chamberlain, 5/8/98, Chamberlain Papers, Birmingham University Library

12. For accounts of this incident see Christian and Plummer (1970, 72); Livingstone (1916, 91–9); Oliver (1982, 113–5).

13. For example, Hope Waddell, the founder of the Calabar mission, perceived the killing of twins as 'proof of the darkness and deadness of heart and mind which ignorance of the Gospel and prevailing sin produced, when women and mothers like them could advocate and practise the murder of new-born infants, contrary to natural feelings, and worse than brutes', *Missionary Record*, September, 1852.

14. Chappell (1927, 41) argues that by 1898, seventeen years before her death, Slessor had rescued fifty-one children; the final figure must have been much higher.

15. Anonymous, British Commonwealth Leaflets, 1948; courtesy of the British Commonwealth Society.

16. For an appraisal of Kingsley's views on education in west Africa, see Pearce (1988, 283–94).

CHAPTER 6

Colonized counterparts

King Ja-ja's subjects came to draw water for their households: fat elderly negresses, swathed in two or three particoloured square dusters; slim agile young matrons, looking anything but matronly in half a yard of the same material ... all carrying huge water jars on their shoulders ... and all laughing and talking and splashing to the utmost of their powers (Colvile, 1893, 303).

Women servants are seldom kept unless there are children in the family, and the good ones are few and far between. They are even more lazy than the men, and are careless, dirty, and cold hearted (Foote, 1869, 196).

I requested, and obtained permission to pay a visit to the ladies of the harem ..., I passed through the heavy door and found as great a contrast to the dim quiet scene I had just left as could well be imagined! A crowd of women, some mere girls, others middle-aged, nearly all carrying babies ..., all laughing, clapping their hands, calling greetings and salutations incessantly (Larymore, 1908, 28).

Introduction

The contact between white women and their west African counterparts created the possibility of totally unequal and dependent relationships in which British women helped to define and describe the conditions under which west African women lived, as well as the nature of those women themselves. As Blunt (1994, 29–30) argues, nineteenth-century travel writing 'played an important part in claiming authority in the vivid representation of recurrent motifs constructing the sexuality of the other'. This was particularly important in terms of the representation of non-European women, and British women travellers had a significant role to play in this. As Ware (1992, 163) argues, the grotesque imagery of the suffering Indian female, and the portrait of non-European women whose situation provoked shame and sorrow, are examples of the ways in which British women were instrumental in reinforcing the image of 'Oriental' women. They were often represented as passive, quiescent victims of male power, 'whose subordination was sometimes connected with, but always relative to, that of Western women'. Some, like Slessor, felt morally obliged to help west African women improve their lives and throw off the shackles of male domination, which was perceived to be linked to heathen customs and a lack of Christian morality. The paradox lay in the fact that at the same time in Britain, women were beginning to oppose their own laws and institutions that were also oppressive of women. What is important for the purposes of this chapter, however, are the various ways in which women either reinforced or challenged the images of west African women found in other imperialist discourses. An understanding of their relationships with west African women is fundamental to this.

External observers or internal allies?

Gender, in addition to skin colour, was a significant factor in allowing British women travellers access into west African societies. They presented little threat to the authority of African men, their status as women facilitated easy and frequent access to African women, and they were thus able to consider their lives from within the context of African culture and customs. As Kingsley (1899a, 320) wrote, 'I openly own that if I have a soft spot in my feelings it is towards African women; and the close contact I have lived in with them has given rise to this, and, I venture to think, made me understand them'. Consequently, indigenous women feature extensively in the texts of white women travel writers. However, only Slessor represented women in ways significantly different from her portrayals of indigenous men. She often represented local women as her allies in her fight against what she perceived as the abuses and injustices of polygamy (Jeffrey, 1950, 629). She considered Ma Eme, the sister of a prominent ruler in Okoyong, to be her closest ally in helping her to prevent the ill treatment of women (Livingstone, 1916, 71). The fact of her gender enhanced and facilitated Slessor's relationships with indigenous women. Gender also propitiated access to west African women for other women travellers, especially those like Kingsley and Larymore who took an interest in their west African counterparts. However, they remained observers from without, and their accounts of indigenous women were often no different from their accounts of indigenous men. Geographical and textual 'closeness' to west African women was predicated on the imperial authority they derived from their status as white women. This gave them privileged access to west African women, a privilege often denied to British men.

As discussed in Chapter 5, Kingsley believed that the only way to understand west Africa and its peoples was to observe from the inside, to see 'things as they are, with all the go and glory and beauty in them as well as the mechanism and the microbes'.[1] Therefore, although she spent much time at mission stations and colonial offices, she also spent time alone in west African villages. In this way she fostered relationships with local women during her travels in the French Congo. In her publications, lectures and articles, these relationships with west African women are evident. Kingsley witnessed the customs of women in different west African societies, and described in detail their roles within village life and local economies. Like other women travellers she paid particular attention to the different practices of dressing, ornamentation and hairdressing.[2] In such descriptions, Kingsley's position seemed to be one of a detached, objective observer. This has led some commentators to doubt Kingsley's proximity to the Africans whom she described, and a paradox existed between her self-proclaimed 'closeness' to west African women, and the distance she maintained as a scientific observer. Birkett (1992, 148) suggests that much of her knowledge was in fact second-hand, based on the work of other anthropologists (R.E. Dennett, Edward Tylor), missionaries (particularly Robert Nassau), and explorers (De Brazza, Du Chaillu, and Richard Burton). Although it is true that she drew heavily on the works of such experts, Kingsley's own comments suggested that she developed real relationships with west African women. She wrote (1899a, 387–8), 'I own I like African women; we have always got on together. True, they have made some spiteful remarks on my complexion, but I must ignore these in the face of the thousand kindnesses for which I am their debtor'. On another occasion she wrote:

> I cannot understand the view against the African woman, held ... so commonly. They in their womanhood seem to me to quite hold their own morally with white women. Yet when one says this, as I often do, you see the white lady gaze at you aghast ... I dare say it may be some defect in my character, but I always think just the same of Ayentyuwa [Nassau's African nurse] as I do of Lady Pembroke or Mrs Green, or any other white woman (in Alexander, 1989, 136–7).

Here, Kingsley's identification and formation of close friendships with African women is clear. Dennett supported Kingsley's contention when he wrote, 'no one can be more sensible to kind treatment or even looks than a Fjort woman and the names of certain whitewomen [sic] live for years in their thoughts and songs. Miss Kingsley's name is one of these'.[3]

Constance Larymore also shared an unusual proximity with west African women; she was unique in that she was allowed to enter the harems of the emir of Bida, becoming the first white woman to do so. This was perhaps a reflection of Larymore's powerful status in west Africa. As the wife of a major in a region that had been conquered by the British military forces she had considerable influence, but her white skin gave her authority independent of that of her husband. Therefore, she gained a privileged insight into a facet of Nigerian life that remained murky and mysterious in the imaginations of many in Victorian Britain. As already suggested in this book, Larymore's role as the wife of an active agent of British imperialism tended to keep her separate from local populations, as it did with Melville, Foote and Colvile. In their travelogues their position as observers from without was apparent, and there seemed to be little interaction between themselves and the women they observed. Their status and social class forced them to maintain a 'respectable' distance between themselves and African people. As in the case of Kingsley, there is thus a paradox between their (geographical) 'closeness' to west African women, and the distance that existed between themselves as observers and the women they observed.

Mary Slessor perhaps took the greatest interest in the women of west Africa.[4] In 1878, Salisbury drew up a treaty with the rulers of Duke Town, the administrative centre of Calabar, banning twin-murder, human sacrifices, trial-by-ordeal, and the enforced mourning of widows. However, this treaty was practically impossible to implement outside Duke Town. Slessor took it upon herself to enforce the treaty. In her opinion, the lives of west African women could only be improved by raising the women's own low view of their status within society. As discussed in preceding chapters, she quickly integrated into west African societies, and this integration allowed Slessor to intervene actively on behalf of women. The wives of missionaries had sometimes attempted pioneering work with west African women, but family life, although intended to set a Christian example, was inclined to keep the missionaries aloof and apart from local populations.[5] However, the presence of a single woman operating independently and living in close proximity with the people had a much more immediate impact. As her familiarity with the women of Calabar grew, Slessor devoted increasing energy to fighting their cause. Thus her relationships with indigenous women were often much more intense than those of other women travellers.

Anna Hinderer may have had more contact with west African women than other missionary wives because of the peculiarity of her situation. This was particularly so when her husband was cut off from their base in Ibadan by the Abeokuta wars, and she was left dependent on the local population for survival. When she first arrived in Ibadan, the local women were eager to visit the first white woman to enter their town. Hinderer wrote (1872, 65):

> I have had many visitors this week, particularly women. Their tenderness over me
> is touching; if they see me hot, they will fan me; if I look tired, they want me to lie
> down. I have had much talk with them, through my little maid Susanna ... They
> are kind and respectful and [have] really polite ways of speaking, and ... their
> tender and affectionate feeling towards me ... must be seen to be fully known.

Unlike Slessor, Hinderer's intimacy with Ibadani women was restricted by her inability to speak the local languages. However, when she began to take Ibadani children into her house as boarders she had greater contact with their mothers, who would often visit their children. In reference to these visits, Hinderer drew a striking parallel between British and African parental relations with their children. She wrote that the visiting mothers would often bring their children 'something they like to eat; they think here as we do at home, 'mother's cake is very sweet" (ibid., 173). Unlike many missionaries, Hinderer disrupts standard images of the brutality of life in west

Africa that were found in other imperialist discourses, and in this instance she normalizes the relations between west African mothers and their children.

Physical descriptions

The different relationships that white women formed with their west African counterparts led to considerable differences in the ways in which they represented the lives of these women, but also in how they represented the women themselves. Those women that had the least contact with indigenous women tended to restrict themselves to physical descriptions, in keeping with the 'manners and customs' approach apparent in many nineteenth-century travel narratives by white women. These descriptions were based on the women's position as external observers. For example, Colvile (1893, 292, 303) and Foote (1869, 177, 196) were restricted to describing the patterns of dress of the women they observed, and to making a few comments on the physical attractiveness of these women. Foote (ibid., 210) wrote:

> The only African women that I admired were some from Tripoli, who had accompanied their lords and masters right across the interior. They had beautifully soft dark eyes, with a timid pleading expression, sad to see; they were dressed *a l'Arabe*, and the lower part of their faces was quite concealed by the usual band of white linen.

Several conventions are apparent in this description. Firstly, Foote's comments revealed her own attitude towards the role of women in that she admired only those African women with whom she could identify. Her own travels were defined by her husband's role, wherever he went she was honour-bound to follow, and she admired the women from Tripoli for undertaking their journeys with grace. Secondly, she intimated by reference to their 'pleading expression' that these women were oppressed and unhappy at their plight, thus evoking the stereotype of downtrodden African women. Thirdly, her observance of the women from a distance, and her focus on their physical features and detailed descriptions of clothing, which were also a feature of other women travellers, was a form of appropriation typical in many imperialist discourses. Local women were looked at and could offer no resistance to the imperial gaze. Finally, the reference to veiling evoked a further image of exoticism, mysticism and eroticism. These conventions are typical of imperialist discourse, and suggest that constraints may have influenced the production of the text, compelling Foote to write in a conventional manner.

These constraints were also apparent in Kingsley's narratives. As Mills (1991, 153–74) points out, the external constraints concerning the reception of the text led Kingsley to adopt a multiplicity of conflicting voices, both masculine and feminine, objective and subjective, in her struggle to create an image of a scientifically accurate explorer while maintaining her 'femininity'. Throughout *Travels* Kingsley assumed multiple identities; she was at once an ichthyologist and an ethnologist, identities which she maintained in other publications.[6] She deliberately adopted a scientific, objective, detached, masculine voice to lend credence to her text; she did not wish to be seen as another 'globetrotteress'. The masculine voice is particularly evident in Kingsley's descriptions of West African women. Both *Travels* and *West African Studies* abound with descriptions of the dress of west African women, and emphasis is placed particularly on their physical beauty. She was struck by how 'picturesque' and 'very pretty' the women of Freetown were; this was her first glimpse of African women. On another occasion she wrote (1982, 72):

> The 'Fanny Po' ladies are celebrated for their beauty all along the West Coast, and very justly. They are not however, ... the most beautiful women in this part of the world ... I prefer an Elmina, or an Igalwa, or a M'Pongwe, or – but I had better stop and own that my affections have got very scattered among the black ladies of the West Coast, and I no longer remember one lovely creature whose soft eyes, perfect form, and winning pretty ways have captivated me than I think of another.

Blunt (1994, 84) points out that this naming and listing served to 'depersonalize and objectify the women being described and reflected imperialist strategies of control through categorization'. Not only are west African women objectified, however, they are also appropriated by Kingsley's adoption of a masculine voice to describe them. For example, of the M'Pongwe and Igalwa women she wrote (1982, 223):

> They are quite the comeliest ladies I have ever seen on the Coast. Very black they are, blacker than many of their neighbours, always blacker than the Fans, and although their skin lacks the velvety pile of the true negro, it is not too shiny, but it is fine and usually unblemished, and their figures are charmingly rounded, their hands and feet small ... and their eyes large, lustrous, soft and brown, and their teeth as white as the sea surf ...

It is clear from these descriptions that Kingsley's responses were of a personal and sensual nature, but textual constraints and notions of femininity made it difficult for her to express this reality. Consequently, her sensual response to indigenous women could only be expressed through the adoption of a masculine, objective voice, suggestive of a sexual attraction and addressed to a masculine audience (Mills, 1991, 157–8). She was also constrained by the inescapable fact of her gender to deny the scientific nature of her travels, arguing that she was merely 'skylarking' or 'puddling about' (Kingsley, 1982, 8), and that she in fact had very little knowledge of scientific methodology (ibid., 101, 141). Nonetheless, Kingsley made positive claims for the role of women in anthropological fieldwork, arguing that her gender was an important factor in allowing her access to west African women. Personal relationships and subjective inquiry gave her a privileged insight into the lives of African women that was denied to male travellers. However, as a single woman travelling in west Africa, she repeatedly felt the need to emphasize her own femininity, particularly with regard to her appearance and clothing. In this way she countered the masculine voices she was forced to adopt to describe her adventures, but the tensions between objective/masculine and subjective/feminine voices are apparent throughout her narratives.

Portrayals of the lives of west African women

Many indigenous customs within west African societies were used by Europeans to portray African women as oppressed and downtrodden, particularly polygamy, human sacrifice, and the violence perpetrated by secret societies. However, the access British women had to west African women meant that they sometimes challenged the ethnocentric assumptions concerning the lives of the latter.

Polygamy

The reverence in nineteenth-century Britain for the virtuous wife meant that polygamy was perceived as an immoral means of maintaining the subservience of African women. According to the prevailing view, African women in polygamous marriages were treated as chattels. Kingsley's understanding of polygamy was considerably different, though it was also revealing of her own prejudices. When asked in an interview, 'I suppose, Miss Kingsley, that the African woman is a very degraded specimen of humanity?' Kingsley replied:

> Not altogether; her position has been greatly exaggerated by travellers and as most
> of them were men they had small opportunity for judging. As a woman I could
> mix freely with them and study their domestic life, and I used to have long talks ...
> and gleaned a lot of information. I believe, on the whole, that the African married
> woman is happier than the majority of English wives (in Frank, 1986a, 219).

Although presenting polygamy in a favourable light, and undermining unfavourable comparisons between the lives of African women and those of British women, Kingsley's response to the question of African women being in a state of degradation was suggestive of her underlying racist beliefs. She challenged the notion that polygamy was a repressive institution for women, arguing that from her experience in west Africa, she was:

[C]ompelled to think polygamy for the African is not an unmixed evil; and that at the present culture-level of the African it is not to be eradicated ... It is perfectly impossible for one African woman to do the work of the house, prepare the food, fetch water, cultivate the plantations, and look after the children attributive to one man (1899a, 662).

In other words, although polygamy was unacceptable for 'civilized' Europeans, it was quite acceptable, and perhaps inevitable for 'uncivilized' Africans. An attitude such as this was deeply patrician and indicative of Kingsley's belief in polygenesis and European superiority. It is also interesting that she did not draw on the parallel between the domestic duties of both colonized women and British women. Thus her ideas about racial difference were not transcended by any sensitivity to a shared female experience (see Blunt, 1994, 85). Class difference was fundamental to this. Kingsley was in a position as a middle-class woman to employ an Irish woman to undertake her own domestic work (Kingsley, 1982, 211), and this prevented her from identifying with west African women on a profound level with regard to their domestic duties. In her view, polygamy was of benefit to African women when placed in the context of the state of African society, which she saw as inferior to that of Europe. It reduced the burden of labour, allowing women time to become involved in domestic economies and trade. Furthermore, Kingsley argued that although African societies granted sexual freedom to men while denying it to women, the burden of coping with the sexual demands of one man was shared in a polygamous household, as was the burden of childbearing. In many societies a husband was not allowed sexual contact with a wife who was breastfeeding a child (Hyam, 1990, 183–4). According to Kingsley, therefore, African women had considerable rights and freedom within marriage. For her, the image of the downtrodden African wife was an erroneous one when placed in the overall context of African societies.

Kingsley understood that polygamy was a fundamental aspect of the structure of west African societies, and that the attempts by the missionaries to eradicate the custom were causing distress and disruption within these societies. On many occasions Kingsley vented her wrath against this interference by missionaries. She cited a case of a chief with three wives who had converted to Christianity and 'profoundly and vividly believed that exclusion from the Holy Communion meant eternal damnation'. The missionaries would not allow him into the congregation unless he abandoned two of his wives and married the other in a Christian service. However, he did not want to lose any of his wives, and the three women were united in their opposition to their separation. The situation caused immense distress; as Kingsley (1896a, 72–3) argued, 'The poor old man smelt hell fire, and cried 'yo yo yo', and beat his hands upon the ground. It was a moral mess of the first water all round'. For Kingsley, 'the missionary-made man is a curse to the Coast', and the missionary attacks on the custom of polygamy did more harm than good.

Mary Slessor's position on polygamy was unclear, since she rarely mentioned it in her reports. This may be an indication of the constraints on the production of travel narratives that existed at the time of her writing. She had spent many hours in the women's compounds, and yet did not describe her experiences there in her reports. Her male predecessors had written lengthy reports about polygamy and the 'debasing' effect that it had on society,[7] but it may have been unacceptable for a woman to allude to such descriptions. Despite this, she wrote of polygamy in her private correspondence and was sympathetic to Kingsley's defence of the custom.[8] However, she also wrote, 'God help these poor downtrodden women! The constant cause of palaver and bloodshed here is marriage. It is a dreadful state of society'.[9] Slessor perceived marriage and, therefore, polygamy, to be oppressive, but she realized that it was such a fundamental part of west African cultures that there was very little that she could do to eradicate it. It seems that Slessor's primary concerns lay in eradicating what she saw as the more barbaric aspects of west African customs, such as the killing of twins and human sacrifice. However, she adhered to the demands of her Church in allowing only men with a single wife to become members of her congregations in Calabar, Okoyong and Enyong; this was the standard policy of the missions in attempting to undermine the custom. She also supported wives who fled from their polygamous marriages to become Christians. In this way, Slessor took a small but significant stand against polygamy.

Slessor adhered to ethnocentric attitudes towards polygamy, but attempted to provide practical alternatives. She was appalled at the treatment of women in Calabar, and wrote of one of her court sessions, 'What a crowd of people I have had here today, and how debased. They are just like brutes in regard to women' (in Jeffreys, 1950, 629). There was no place for women outside the women's compounds, but Slessor was convinced that they could govern their own lives given the opportunity. They did most of the work on the farms and most of the selling in the markets. She believed that if they had their own land they could be self-supporting. They had no rights as citizens and were the property of their husbands. If they were rejected as wives they often starved. The scenes that most aroused Slessor's indignation were those that she witnessed in the compounds of the coastal towns and villages. In her first year in Calabar she wrote, 'The women are the great drawback to our success. To visit these yards, and to see so many women going, or rather *lolling*, about almost naken [sic], – to know their habits and their deceit, – one only wonders that the men are as they are'.[10] Gradually, Slessor's attitude changed and she attached the blame for the state of women's lives not on the women themselves, but on the patriarchal structure of Calabar society. It was this she believed to be responsible for the confining of women to these hovels, where they were poverty stricken and often close to starvation.[11]

As a consequence of these deprivations, Slessor fostered an intense dislike of the institution of marriage, particularly the pressure placed on women to marry in order to survive. This resentment was not only directed towards the institution of marriage in west Africa, but also towards the teachings of her own religion. In one of her Bibles, against the passage where St Paul lays down the rules for the subjection of wives to husbands, she scribbled in the margin: 'Na! Na! Paul, laddie! This will no do!' (in Buchan, 1980, 195). As discussed subsequently, much of Slessor's energy was directed towards removing the necessity of marriage for west African women, and providing opportunities for them to live independently of men.

Constance Larymore lent her support to Mary Kingsley's rebuttal of the myth of the oppressed African wife; she wrote of the trading women in the market at Kabba (1908, 116):

> The tender-hearted philanthropist would have to seek far and long in this merry crowd for the 'downtrodden women of Africa' and the 'black sister of slavery', of whom one seems to have heard. There is not much that indicates subjection or fear about these ladies, sitting at graceful ease among their loads, or strolling about in the hot sunshine.

Like Kingsley, Larymore believed that African women were the driving force behind indigenous trade and economies, exercised great power within the villages, and contributed to the maintenance of public order.[12] She wrote (1908, 286), 'I have a strong conviction that (in spite of the laments indulged in by good people at home, over the sad position of the downtrodden woman of Africa) the ladies rule the villages and set the public tone'. However, she did have some preconceptions about the state of the women in the harems. This is reflected in her complete surprise at what she found, after having obtained permission to enter the harems of the emir of Bida. Her portrayals of the harems of Northern Nigeria are very different from Slessor's depictions of the compounds in Calabar. Larymore found the harem to be a community of women and children of all ages, and was amazed to find them 'all laughing, clapping their hands, calling greetings and salutations incessantly'. This was not the scene of lasciviousness that she had expected. The women did not mob her in their excitement at seeing their first white woman. Instead, 'their perfect courtesy, that fine characteristic of the African people, prevailed to restrain them. There was no ... pushing, or crowding' (ibid., 28–9). Larymore's descriptions of the harems were, therefore, quite different from many contemporary portrayals.[13] Melman (1992, 1) argues that this was a separate, feminine experience of the harems, but Larymore's experiences as a white woman make her descriptions all the more relevant.

As several writers have discussed, the very notion of the 'harem' was linked implicitly with images of exoticism, and particularly with the exoticizing of Islam.

(In this respect it is perhaps of interest that the women's yards of Southern Nigeria were referred to as compounds, whereas the women's quarters in Northern Nigeria were referred to as harems.) Only recently have critics of imperialism recognized that women were not only the objects of the 'Orientalist' gaze, but were actively involved in producing 'Orientalism' (Lewis, 1996). As Larymore's descriptions illustrate, this imperialist gaze was not hegemonic in a monolithic way, but was itself riven with complexities and contradictions. Much of the fascination with the harem emanated not only from 'Orientalist' authority, but also from the ideology and aesthetics of the concept of separate spheres for men and women. However, as Melman argues, descriptions of harems by women such as Larymore, drawing on experience rather than external textual authority, were often thinly veiled critiques of western patriarchy and the position of women in the west. Furthermore, travel writing by women subverted gender ideology and the ethos of domesticity, 'Writing a travelogue involved a redefinition of the feminine space and sphere of action. And the new genre anatomizes the tension between the emancipating effects of travel in what had been literally and metaphorically man's land and culturally dominant notions of femininity' (ibid., 17–18). Not only did Larymore transcend the boundaries of the 'feminine' sphere by travelling and writing, she also challenged 'Orientalist' depictions of the harem. Race and class defined her as an outsider, but the fact of her gender ensured her access to those 'feminine' spaces within the harem that were denied to men. Her representations cannot be read as counter-hegemonic simply because they were informed by gender. She may have challenged dominant patriarchies by her presence in the harems. She may have written differently about the harems to her male counterparts. However, her narrative is still rooted within imperialist discourse. It could be argued that she had the same desire to penetrate to the interior of the harem found in 'Orientalist' writing. However, despite being located within the nexus of power, knowledge and imperial discourse, Larymore's descriptions were a challenge to those external, masculinist observations which depicted the harem as the locus of an exotic and abnormal sexuality, and which had fascinated Europeans for decades.

Physical violence and west African women

Women of west Africa were not only perceived to be downtrodden in the minds of many Victorians, they were also considered the victims of cruel and barbarous practices. As with polygamy, the secret societies of west Africa (discussed in Chapter 5) were sometimes portrayed in a negative light in respect of the part they played in the lives of west African women. Many European travellers believed that much of the perceived oppression of these women emanated from the secret societies and the fear that they brought. The societies were considered the sole domain of men, and inherently linked to witchcraft and cannibalism through which villages, and in particular, women were terrorized. Kingsley, whilst recognising the fear that the secret societies inspired, did not believe that they were completely disadvantageous to west African women. She argued that secret societies were not religious but judicial. Men's societies existed to keep the women in check, and arose 'from the undoubted fact that women are notably deficient in any real reverence for authority, as is demonstrated by the way that they continually treat that of their husbands' (Kinglsey, 1982, 526). (Whether Kingsley saw this as a positive attribute is somewhat unclear, but one can detect as certain irony in Kingsley's writings.) She cited the existence of women's secret societies, and suggested they were equally as powerful and exclusive as those of the men: 'a man who attempts to penetrate the female mysteries would be as surely killed as a woman who might attempt to investigate the male mysteries' (1899a, 527). As discussed previously, for Kingsley, the secret societies were a means of maintaining social harmony, and they were, therefore, of benefit to women rather than a means of terrorizing them.

Mary Slessor's attitude towards the secret societies and their treatment of women was rather different and often contemptuous. The most feared society in west Africa was perhaps the Egbo of Nigeria, whose members were believed to have the power to transform themselves into wild animals to attack people. The Egbo 'runners' brought fear upon the villages, and any woman found on the streets as they passed through was attacked or molested. Slessor's way of dealing with the Egbo was to confront them, exercising the power arrogated to her by her white skin. One of her adopted children, Daniel, described how she frequently attacked the Egbo runners. He wrote that the Egbo 'tremble because she a woman, of what power they cannot say, can dare to even come near, let alone attack without the fear of instant death'.[14] Slessor wanted to break the spell of fear that the Egbo held over the women of Calabar, and she made every effort to dispel the superstitions concerning the powers of the Egbo runners, ignoring the charms that they left to obstruct her path and confronting them wherever possible.

Apart from the secret societies, the treatment of widows was perhaps the most difficult aspect of the lives of African women for British women to confront. In some west African societies, women were often required by indigenous laws to undergo trials-by-ordeal, ritual sacrifice, or enforced mourning at the death of their husbands. Such customs were alien to the sensibilities of nineteenth-century British women. However, Kingsley, for the most part, was able to suspend judgement in order to explain these customs from the point of view of west African cultures. She argued that 'cruelty' towards widows emanated from the fear of witchcraft and was, therefore, an understandable part of African law, rather than an expression of misogyny. The fear of witchcraft meant that the first people suspected of a man's death were his wives, who were then tried. Kingsley explained that for Africans, the confining of widows was a means of protecting the soul of the dead man, which remained around the house until the burial. She also downplayed the length of confinement, writing that, contrary to the impression given by missionary reports, the period of mourning ended with the burial of the husband. The widow was then free to marry again (Kingsley, 1982, 483–4; 487–91; 526).

The 'sacrifice' of widows at funerals by some indigenous groups was in order that they should accompany the husband to the spirit world, ensuring that he did not arrive as a pauper (a man's wealth was measured by the number of wives he had). According to Kingsley, a Calabar chief had explained to her that the British Government's rigorous suppression of this custom meant that men went into the next world as paupers. This also 'added an additional chance of his going there prematurely, for his wives and slaves, no longer restrained by the prospect of being killed at his death and sent off with him would, on very slight aggravation, put 'bash in his chop" (Kingsley, 1899a, 489). In other words he would be poisoned. Kingsley suggested that the threat of ritual sacrifice thus helped to maintain social order. For other tribes that believed in reincarnation, such as those around the Niger Delta, women were 'sent down' with their husbands to determine the class of the reincarnated soul. There was a great fear that a person would be reincarnated as a slave if he were sent down without his wives. Kingsley adopted the mantle of the anthropologist in attempting to rationalize such customs by referring to local customary beliefs. However, as Mani (1992, 395) argues 'When reading Kingsley's accounts of the sacrifice of widows, there is no understanding of why the women allowed such violence to be perpetrated on them. Possible reasons are lack of property and safeguards for the future, ostracism, and ostracism of children'. Therefore, Kingsley probably placed too much emphasis on witchcraft and indigenous spiritual beliefs, and ignored other social and cultural influences on the practice of the sacrificing of widows. For this reason she was unable to explain why the women themselves allowed the practice to continue. The paradox between distance and 'closeness' is again apparent in Kingsley's descriptions, with Kingsley becoming the detached scientific observer, but claiming that her knowledge was based on her 'intimate' relationships with west Africans. The tensions of being both inside and outside imperial discourses are also apparent. Kingsley attempted to challenge some of the ethnocentric assumptions about west African customs, but she was forced to adopt the voice of the external observer, gazing from a position of authority upon the subjects of British imperialism to give credence to her observations and opinions.

The societal role of west African women

Several white women travellers contradicted the image of west African women as downtrodden victims. As discussed previously, Kingsley and Larymore offered direct challenges to the prevailing images of indigenous women, and Slessor insisted that it was only the dependency of these women upon marriage that maintained their subservience. Kingsley, in particular, wrote a great deal about the virtues of women in west Africa. For example, she described a liaison with a Cabendan woman on a beach. The woman was a young mother, carrying with her a baby and a basket of fish, and Kingsley was struck by how miserable the woman appeared. She tried to speak to the woman in a local language but she did not understand. Kingsley then noticed that the woman was staring at a large crab-hole, and realized that her sadness emanated from the fact that it would take two people to catch such a crab. Kingsley helped to catch the crab, to the delight of the woman, who then reluctantly offered it to her. Kingsley refused it, but the next day at market the woman seized her and introduced her to everyone present. Kingsley was not only a heroine in this village, but the Cabendan woman ensured that her reputation preceded her into the surrounding villages, guaranteeing that she was able to gather much more information about the local peoples than would otherwise have been possible. Kingsley (1899a, 390) wrote, 'From these things and many like them I can say nothing against the African woman, but yet it is an undoubted fact that she imposed on the male explorer, and caused him to give the idea that the African woman is the down-trodden fool of Creation who is treated anyhow'.

It was this image of the African woman, purported by missionaries as well as explorers, which Kingsley sought to challenge and counteract throughout her narratives. She had a detailed knowledge of the societal roles of African women, and thus came to more objective conclusions on their position and status in these societies. She argued that African women could at times be hostile to western 'civilization' because they felt that it would remove the constraints of their own cultures from their children. The law of *mütterecht* made the tie between the mother and the children closer than between the father and the children; British culture and law would reverse this system and was, therefore, alien to African women. Furthermore, between husband and wife there was no community of goods under African law – each had a separate estate. Again this was very different from Victorian law, which ceded all possessions to the husband on marriage. For these reasons, African women were often more forceful in their rejection of Europeanization than African men. It is apparent in her narratives that Kingsley believed African women to have real power. For example, when she entered a Fang village the guards, on seeing this strange white woman, consulted their mother before acting. Kingsley was able to settle her intentions with the woman, and together the two of them established peaceful relationships between this village and its rival, from which Kingsley had recently travelled. The Fang woman obviously had a great deal influence in the local vicinity. Kingsley, therefore, told this story to contest images of west African women as downtrodden and oppressed.

Kingsley was also aware of the fundamental role played by African women in trading. Most west African markets – the mainstay of indigenous economies – were run by women. This fact was often completely ignored by missionaries and travellers. Furthermore, Kingsley demonstrated that African women were adept businesswomen. In Fang villages, the men collected the rubber and the women manipulated it for market. Kingsley (ibid., 293) described how the women adulterated the rubber with clay or yam to add to its weight:

> So great is the adulteration, that most of the traders have to cut each ball open. Even the Kinsembo rubber, which is ... shaped like little thimbles formed by rolling pinches of rubber between the thumb and finger, and which one would think difficult to put anything inside of, has to be cut, because the 'simple children of nature' who collect it and bring it to that 'swindling white trader' struck upon the ingenious notion that little pieces of wood shaped like the thimbles and coated by a dip in rubber were excellent additions to a cluster.[15]

The African woman that Kingsley encountered was, therefore, much more intelligent, and more involved in local trading activities, than the stereotype often envisaged by her contemporaries. The women were also much more involved in the rituals of daily life and, therefore, had much more influence than the downtrodden woman in imperialist discourse. For example, Kingsley pointed out that on the island of Corisco it was customary for women only to catch the fish in the inland lakes; men were prohibited. Women representatives from each village were expected to attend any fishing to observe that the catch was properly divided. The responsibility of food provision, therefore, lay with the women of Corisco. This also ensured that good relations were maintained between the villages and that quarrels were avoided. The women were, therefore, the peacekeepers of the island.

Both Slessor and Kingsley recognized the power of the local matriarch in west African societies. Slessor, in particular, forged links with the most influential women in the villages of Calabar in order that they could influence the elders and obtain support for her policies. Hinderer also recognized the authority that women could exercise in Ibadan. She wrote (1872, 110–11):

> The Yoruba people have some very nice arrangements about their form of government. I found out that there is an 'Iyalode' or mother of the town, to whom all the women's palavers are brought before they are taken to the king. She is, in fact, a sort of queen, a person of much influence, and looked up to with much respect. I sent my messenger to her to tell her I would like to meet her, to tell her I should like to visit her. She sent word she should be delighted ... [I] found a most respectable motherly looking person, surrounded by her attendants and people, in great order, and some measure of state ... We two Iyas made strong friendship, ... and the lady settled that we were to be the two mothers of the town, she the Iyalode still, and I the 'Iyalode fun fun', the white Iyalode.

Hinderer recognized the authority that the Iyalode could exercise in Ibadan, and immediately sought to ally herself with her in the same way that Slessor sought to ally herself with Ma Eme. Friendship with the Iyalode was a means through which Hinderer could establish her own status in the town and exercise her own authority as a white 'mother'. She used this authority in much the same way as Slessor. She provided refuge for those women who had left their husbands to join the congregation. She also supported those women who were beaten by their husbands for attending church. She described an incident of a husband attempting to prevent his wife from attending church; 'she was ... cruelly beaten with sticks and cutlasses and stoned, till her body swelled all over' (ibid., 131–2). Such beatings were apparently common occurrences in Ibadan, and although Hinderer did not actively intervene in the same manner as Slessor to prevent such attacks, she did provide shelter for these women, and encouraged them to stand up to their husbands. Rather than depicting Ibadani women as downtrodden, Hinderer paid testament to their bravery, and cited many incidents of their belligerence (ibid., 132).

Active intervention: Slessor's settlement for women at Use

As stated previously, of the women studied here, Slessor was most closely involved in the lives of west African women. The longer she spent in Calabar the more she moved away from attempts to Christianize the population, and the more time and effort she dedicated towards improving the lives of local women. The ultimate aim of Slessor's work was to establish a woman's settlement, where women who were confined to the compounds, and if unmarried were apparently vulnerable to rape, torture, assault or injury (Miller, 1946, 113), could find refuge. Such a settlement, she believed, would free women from the need to marry. She wrote (1908, 4):

> The kind of advance, which concerns the women of the Church more especially, lies in the direction of some development of our work which will make the native women something more than a mere cipher in the community; something more than a mere creature to be exploited and degraded by man ... Not only must we provide some way of protecting and sheltering women, but in order to meet this end we must create some industry by which these women may earn their living, and thus become independent of the polygamous marriage and the open insult.

Over time her ideas began to assume greater clarity. The women of the settlement would not only be independent, but would also contribute to the local economy, producing food and goods with which to trade with neighbouring villages. She also advocated training schools for women where they could achieve independence and self-confidence. As discussed previously, she gained the trust of the people among whom she lived by forging friendships with women close to the chiefs and elders, in the hope that they would use their influence and enable her to pursue her policies and ideas. Slessor apparently repaid this closeness of west African women for, when she became a magistrate, it was widely rumoured that no woman ever lost a case in her court (Jeffreys, 1950, 629).

Slessor's dream of creating a woman's settlement was realized in 1908 when a site near Use on the Cross River became available. She purchased the land in the name of her adopted daughters and built a refuge for widows, orphans, the mothers of twins and their children, and refugees fleeing the harems. Her financial independence from the Church of Scotland, which was based on her trading with the people of Calabar to generate an income, meant that she could build this refuge without the consent of the Church. For the first time women had a place to go outside the societies that had rejected them. Furthermore, a training centre was established to educate women and girls in traditional industries, crafts, and farming. Slessor disagreed with the quasi-religious education promoted by the Mission, and believed that training in traditional methods was best suited to west Africa (Oliver, 1982, 118–9; Hewat, 1960, 203). Again, she pursued her own policies independent of advice from the Mission. Slessor ensured that the settlement was located near large potential markets; the goods produced were thus exchanged for materials such as medical supplies, books and writing equipment, and the community became self-sufficient (Jubilee Booklet, 1948, 13). The settlement was known as the Mary Slessor Mission Hospital until it was destroyed in the wars for independence in the late 1950s.[16] Slessor thus provided a safe-haven for orphans, twins and their mothers, and refugees from the harems, who would otherwise have been driven out of their villages to starve. The establishment of the women's settlement was typical of Slessor's efforts to improve the lives of west African women, she did not attempt to attack overtly existing customs, but provided an alternative, both to these customs and to the official solutions offered by the Church of Scotland.

Conclusion

West African women featured prominently in the narratives of white women travellers, and in the case of Slessor, Kingsley, Larymore and Hinderer, particular emphasis was placed on their experiences of, and with, west African women. Gender, as well as race, was a significant factor in this, allowing these women closer contact with west African women, and especially access to the harems and women's compounds. By describing the lives of women in west Africa and the day-to-day activities in the domestic spheres of local towns and villages, British women travellers reaffirmed their own femininity, locating their own interests firmly within the domestic sphere. This was, to a certain extent, a result of the textual constraints that partially shaped their descriptions. As discussed in Chapter 1, women tended to be excluded from political and scientific discourse, and their texts were thus directed more towards descriptions of landscapes and peoples. It is, therefore, not entirely unexpected that women travel writers should have chosen to devote extensive passages to their west African counterparts, and thus have a greater concern for the subject of their enquiry. Nevertheless, the descriptions by white women travellers revealed their own interest in the lives of west African women. Moreover, the information that they imparted about the role of women within west African societies and economies, particularly in the case of Slessor and Kingsley, was invaluable to subsequent policies in colonial education and administration (see Chapter 2). However, there were also constraints governing the content of their narratives, and the distinction between public and private writings is an important one in this respect. The textual constraints that may have controlled published narratives were not present in private correspondence, where women were often freer to express their opinions regarding even the most taboo of subjects in Victorian society. That textual constraints controlled published narratives becomes clear when one compares the opinions expressed in print to those communicated in private correspondence. For example, Kingsley excluded descriptions of the practice of female circumcision from her published narratives. This custom was a fundamental ceremonial rite in many parts of west Africa, but none of the women discussed here referred to it. Kingsley was aware of its existence, but did not allude to it in any of her anthropological studies. Neither could she bring herself to describe the practice to the anthropologist E.B. Tylor; instead she hinted at the custom in letters to his wife, in the hope that she could communicate the information back to Tylor.[17] Constraints such as these meant that several of the women could not comment upon such customs as the killing of twins and the persecution of widows, and the likes of Melville, Foote and Colvile were restricted to describing the dress patterns of various ethnic groups.

However, for some white women travelling in west Africa it soon became clear that despite the perceived horrors of polygamy, infant marriage, secret societies, and cruelty towards twin-mothers and widows, in some ways west African women had many more rights, freedoms, and much more influence in everyday life than certain imperialist discourses suggested. In the opinion of Kingsley, west African women had more freedom than British women themselves had in Victorian society. As Melman (1992, 307–8) argues, 'Observation of women's life in another culture brought on a re-evaluation by the western women, of their own position as individuals *and* as a marginalized group in a patriarchal culture'. There was certainly a hint of envy in Kingsley's descriptions of the lives of west African women. Therefore, in many ways, the narratives of white women travellers challenged the images of their west African counterparts that are often found in other imperialist discourses. Kingsley's work is particularly notable for the attention she devoted to describing west African women and their roles in society. She wrote (1899a, 387), 'The subject of women is one I habitually avoid except when it comes to dress', but an analysis of her work proves otherwise. Although she painted detailed pictures of African dress and the hairdressing customs of women in west Africa, the real motive behind her detailed descriptions lay in her determination to challenge the image of the downtrodden African woman in imperialist discourses. Both Kingsley and Larymore were convinced that African women had more influence and independence than was suggested by existing literature on west Africa. West African women had a fundamental role to play in ensuring that economies functioned properly, that discipline was maintained, and that the indigenous culture of the society was retained. They believed that African women were not anonymous entities incidental to their travels, nor victims of barbarism perpetrated by 'savages', but functioning members of society with certain rights that accorded them status within this society. Slessor recognized that certain women within west African cultures held positions of authority, and despite her perception that the marriage customs of Calabar were oppressive of women, she believed that every woman could be independent if given the right opportunity.

Not only did these portrayals by white women travellers disrupt imperialist images of non-European women, but they were also founded, in some cases, on completely different relationships with these women. As Melman (1992, 7–8) argues:

> Travel and the encounter with systems of behaviour, manners and morals, most notably with the systems of polygamy, concubinage and the sequestration of females, resulted in analogy between the polygamous Orient and the travelling women's own monogamous society. And analogy led to self criticism rather than cultural smugness and sometimes resulted in an identification with the other that cut across barriers of religion, culture and ethnicity. Western women's writing on 'other' women then substitutes a sense of solidarity of gender for sexual and racial superiority.

This was evident in the narratives of Slessor, and apparent to a lesser degree in the work of Larymore and Kingsley. Furthermore, the exploration of the negotiation by these women of racial, gender and, to a lesser extent, class differences within the theatre of empire raises important questions about the construction of a singular 'other'. In Victorian Britain, white women were othered on the grounds of their sex in the same ways that different groups were othered on the basis of their social class, race, mentality, wealth, sexuality, and so on. However, with the possible exception of Slessor, although certain women travellers may have felt some affinity towards their west African counterparts, the recognition of racial difference was not transcended by the sense of a common female experience. White women travellers perceived themselves in west Africa more in terms of their skin colour rather than their femininity and, therefore, retained a sense of racial superiority in their relationships with, and representations of, west African women.

Notes

1. Kingsley to George Macmillan, n.d., Macmillan Papers, British Library.
2. See, for example, Kingsley (1982), 21, 46–8, 72, 222–4, 341, 531.
3. R.E. Dennett, 'Miss M.H. Kingsley's visit to Cabinda, 1893', original hand-written manuscript, Highgate Literary and Scientific Institute.
4. Slessor was particularly concerned with the quality of life for west African women. She herself had been accustomed to hardship. Her father was a violent man who eventually drank himself to death. The streets of Dundee were often places of crime and violence, fuelled by massive unemployment. On a number of occasions in her youth, she had been threatened with violence on her way to church. Slessor's upbringing in the slums of Dundee may have provided the impetus to improve the lives of west African women.
5. See *Sunday Mail Story of Scotland*, 3, 39 (1988), 1091–2, in Slessor Papers, Dundee Museum.
6. Kingsley referred to herself as an ethnologist in 1897a; 1897b; 1897c; 1898a; 1898c; 1900d. She referred to herself as an ichthyologist in 1896b and 1896c.
7. For example, see Hope Waddell, report in *Missionary Record* (1848, 169), and a report on the state of the missions, *Missionary Record* (1851, 88).
8. Slessor to Irvine, 12/12/03, St Andrew's Hall Missionary College Library, Selly Oak, Birmingham.
9. Letter from Slessor, 7/10/05, *Women's Missionary Magazine*, January 1906, 20.
10. Letter from Slessor on her first impressions of Calabar, *Missionary Record*, February 1877, 371, British Library.
11. Letter from Slessor, *Missionary Record*, November, 1879.
12. There is a long tradition in Africanist travel literature of describing (and often misrepresenting) the roles that women played within local economies and societies. For example, the French explorer Duveyrier (1864) expounded the matriarchal nature of the Touareg society, see Heffernan (1989).
13. For analyses of accounts of harems by European male travellers, see Alloula (1986); Kabbani (1986); Melman (1992); Said (1978).
14. Daniel Slessor to Thomas Hart, 30/11/1948, Slessor Papers, Macmanus Galleries, Dundee Museum.
15. This account of the adulteration of rubber as evidence of forms of resistance to European imperialism by west Africans is discussed in Chapter 7.

16. Kathleen Goldie Papers (1949), Dundee Public Library, p. 13.
17. Kingsley to Mrs Tylor, 7/12/96, E.B. Tylor Papers, Rhodes House, Oxford. Kingsley wrote: 'Now if <u>you</u> would turn ethnologist I could tell you a lot of queer things that have very important bearings on what we will call the external skeleton of the ceremonials'. She also wrote to Keltie: 'I can go and tell ... Mrs T. [sic], who can tell him why they kill twins in West Africa and such like things', suggesting that she and other women travellers had access to information about Africans denied to men (Kingsley to Keltie, 1/12/99, Kingsley Papers, Royal Geographical Society).

CHAPTER 7

Retrieving subaltern histories?

[H]istory is mostly about power. It is the story of the powerful and how they became powerful, and then how they use their power to keep them in positions in which they can continue to dominate others. It is because of this relationship with power that we have been excluded, marginalized and 'Othered' (Tuhiwai Smith, 1999, 34).

Introduction

The preceding chapters have focused on women travellers and the knowledges that they constructed of west Africa and west African peoples through their printed narratives. However, as this chapter seeks to elucidate, there are perhaps other stories that can be recovered from these same narratives. A primary aim of the discussion throughout this book has been to counter the erasure of women and women's voices from histories of geography and imperialism, and to explore the potential for the recovery of the agency of women in these histories (Domosh, 1991a and b; Rose, 1993 and 1995). It has been demonstrated in the preceding chapters that the narratives of white women travellers provide a rich source around which more inclusive versions of history might be constructed, and through which histories of geography and imperialism might be deterritorialized. Building upon this argument, this chapter seeks to respond to the contentions of critical theorists that exclusion is not merely determined along the lines of gender. As Hall (1996, 70) points out:

> Feminist historians have been too preoccupied with rewriting histories through gender or recovering women's worlds and have been very slow to respond to the black feminist critique which has insisted on the interconnections between the power relations of 'race' and gender and the implications of imperial history.

The preceding chapters have attempted to remain mindful of the power relations of 'race' and class. They have attempted not to create proto-feminist heroines, but to write critical accounts of white women's representations of west Africa. As has been suggested, the writings of white women travellers are already ambivalently positioned vis-à-vis imperial discourse; they are of the 'centre' but also of the 'margins'; they are part of dominant discourses but simultaneously excluded from them. However, I am also interested in the ways in which these texts might be used to further deterritorialize histories of geography and imperialism. There are a number of important questions that need to be asked with regard to this project. For example, what other agencies, in addition to that of white women, might be apparent within these texts and in the construction of geographical and imperial knowledges? Is it possible to recover the agency of white women without simultaneously erasing the agency of colonized peoples? Can the agency of colonized peoples in histories of geography and imperialism be recovered from those same narratives that have been used to construct inclusivity along the lines of gender? These questions frame the discussion throughout this chapter.

Postcolonial scholars have argued that the structuration of western academic knowledge was itself complicit with colonialism and, indeed, remains neo-imperialist today. As Chakrabarty (1994) argues, historiographical knowledge, however indirectly, always refers back to Europe. It can be argued that the denial of the historical agency of the colonized remains a problem even in many postcolonial studies, from Said (1978) to the most recent explorations. Despite critiquing eurocentrism, little has been achieved by postcolonial theorists in recovering the historical agency of colonized peoples or their role in the production of knowledge. Thus, in the light of critiques such as Hall's, this chapter explores two dimensions which have yet to figure in any large measure in debates concerning critical histories of geography. Firstly, I interrogate the question of the place of Europe's 'others' (especially colonized 'others') in histories of a putatively western discipline. In particular, the question of the agency of the colonized in the construction of imperial geographical knowledges of west Africa is explored. Secondly, I attempt to disrupt eurocentric accounts of British imperialism in west Africa by recounting and analysing incidents of resistance. The premise here is that evidence of this resistance can be found within the dominant narratives of imperial discourse, in this case the published texts of white women travellers. Moreover, it is recognized that even critical accounts of imperialism might still be complicit in the erasure of the agency of colonized peoples. For example, recovering the agency of white women in the construction of histories of geography and imperialism, as the preceding chapters have attempted to do, does not necessarily counter the erasure of the agency of indigenous peoples. Indeed, it could be argued that such a project merely 're-centres' these histories in the west. However, it might be that those very same narratives also contain evidence of the agency of the colonized in knowledge construction, and also of their resistance to the presence of European colonizers. Thus, in addition to reading the narratives of women travellers in west Africa with the aim of recovering their agency in histories of geography and imperialism, one can also find traces of other agencies within these metropolitan discourses. This chapter, therefore, attempts to combine a postcolonial reading with a critical feminist reading of women's travel writings about west Africa, whilst simultaneously acknowledging the paradoxes and contradictions in this reading strategy.

According to Childs and Williams (1997, 26):

> It has been one of the staples of Western historiography to emphasize the imperial process as one focused exclusively on Western activity... The possibility that indigenous people might be active agents in the making (if not the writing) of their own histories was something which was rarely if ever entertained by Western writers, and then usually in highly negative terms.

A major reason for this was that the principal mode of indigenous agency was resistance to European imperialism and domination. As Childs and Williams discuss, the typical response by European imperial powers was to pretend that resistance had not happened or was not worth mentioning, that it had failed, or to depict it as treachery. Running parallel to the military approach of literally obliterating resistance, imperial discourse had the effect of discursively erasing evidence of resistance. The simultaneous effect was to obliterate all evidence of the agency of the colonized, both in terms of their part in the making of their histories and in terms of the construction of imperial knowledges about colonized countries.

Following on from these arguments, it can be suggested that much of the recent work on critical histories of geography is problematic in that it continues to privilege the 'west' as the site of the production of geographical knowledge. In so doing, these critical histories continue to deny the possibilities of the historical agency of colonized peoples. As Sidaway (1997, 76) argues, there is still a tendency by historiographers to recount a singular, eurocentric and self-contained disciplinary geography: 'the existence and articulation of different histories enfolded within what is being represented as the western geographical imagination/tradition is not one that is being very much confronted'. The narration of the history of 'western' geography tends to suggest that the origins of these knowledges are located solely in the west, and thus ignores the contribution of 'non-western' geographical knowledges in their formulation. The writing of histories of geography, therefore, tends to re-privilege the west as the site of the production of knowledge. Here, as with masculinist renderings of the history of the discipline, the problem lies with the ways in which boundaries are drawn to determine what does and does not constitute geographical knowledge. As has been intimated, attempts to uncover the ways in which British women travellers, for example, contributed to the production of geographical knowledges within imperial culture runs the risk of re-privileging the former imperial powers as the producers of this knowledge. Colonial representations by white women might be read critically, as has been attempted throughout this book, but the imperial gaze is still privileged and the voice of the colonized 'other' remains silent. Thus, there is an enduring paradox in that feminist historiographies are critical of power and knowledge in respect of gender, and yet remain complicit in (neo-)colonial relationships of power.

As Sidaway argues, if there is a western geographical 'tradition' it must be treated as an irredeemably hybrid product, and not uniquely the product of Europe. Non-western knowledges are deeply embedded within western geographies, but there are few accounts exploring this. Sidaway himself scrutinizes the Arab and Ottoman role in the production of geographical knowledges previously assumed to be putatively European. Barnett (1998) also attempts to counter hegemonic histories by unsettling notions of the modern geographical enterprise being solely the product of metropolitan energies and initiative. In his discussion of the Africanist discourse produced by explorers in the nineteenth century, Barnett illustrates not only that European knowledge appropriated extensive local knowledges in Africa, but that Eurocentric geographical knowledge was formed through the effacement of these alternative ways of knowing. Thus, explorers such as Burton and Speke constructed their geographies of Africa by appropriating local indigenous knowledges, but in positioning these knowledges as scientific and rational they actively dismissed and erased from their publications those subjective, local knowledges upon which they drew. This simultaneous appropriation and erasure of indigenous knowledges is symptomatic of colonial discourse, and is evidence of the epistemic violence that continues to write out the agency of the colonized in the production of geographical knowledge. As Barnett (ibid., 248–9) argues, 'A critical reading of the production of modern geographical knowledge must account for the historical processes that condemned certain knowledges, meaning and subjects to a place outside the field of what was considered intelligible, rational and disciplined scientific discourse'. While I make no claims to answer fully the questions raised by such a project, I hope in this chapter to begin the task of 'making visible the 'trace of losses' that is constitutive of modern geography' (ibid., 249). In what follows, therefore, I present some suggestions on how discursive spaces might be opened up to reveal multiple agents in the production of imperial geographies, in an attempt to reveal multiple sites for the production of geographical knowledges. The subsequent discussion explores the possibilities for recovering the agency of white women whilst simultaneously allowing for the agency of the colonial subject in the making of their geographies. In attempting the latter, I also confront the dilemmas and contradictions in acknowledging simultaneously the agency of 'first world' women and that of the subaltern in both the production of geographical knowledge and in imperial histories.

Strategies for postcolonial readings

The notion of countering Eurocentrism in histories of geography is obviously inspired by what could loosely be termed a postcolonial critique. A postcolonial approach (referring here to ideological orientations rather than an epochal stage, which presumes a closure of the colonial era),[1] demands an interrogation of the history of geography as it has been constructed not only in hegemonic masculine terms, but also as a putatively 'western' tradition. According to Williams and Chrisman (1993, 16), 'colonial discourse analysis' has concerned itself with, among other things, the ways in which the subaltern native subject is constructed within these discourses. What has been less explored is the extent to which the subaltern may have played a constitutive rather than reflective role in colonial and domestic imperial discourse and subjectivity. Rather than being that onto which the colonizer projects a previously constituted subjectivity and knowledge, native presences, locations, and political resistance need to be further theorized as having a determining or primary role in colonial discourses, and in the attendant domestic versions of these discourses. In other words, the movement may have been as much from 'periphery' to 'centre' as from 'centre' to 'periphery' (Barnett, 1997, 139). However, when almost all available accounts and documents are written by the colonizers, or an indigenous elite, how does the historiographer give a voice or an agency to those sections of the colonized who participated in the construction of geographical knowledges about themselves, and in anti-colonial resistance? As is demonstrated in this chapter, this endeavour is fraught with difficulties, dilemmas and paradoxes. We might consider performing the task of de-centring Eurocentric versions of geographical knowledge either through a reconceptualization of the imperial encounter, or through a deconstruction of those dominant narratives. Both strategies can be considered as a means of adopting a more critical reading of the narratives of British women travellers in nineteenth-century west Africa.

Mary Louise Pratt's (1992, 6–7) concept of the 'contact zone' is useful in attempting to reconceptualize the imperial encounter. The idea of a contact zone in which the imperial encounter takes place allows for the possibility of countering notions of a self-contained European geographical knowledge. It does this by viewing the imperial setting as one in which (at least) two cultures came together, each influencing the other but against a backdrop of inequality. As suggested above, in histories of imperialism the colonized appear as passive, since the west was the subject of this history, and the colonies were the inert object it acted upon. However, as Seth et al. (1998, 7) point out, just as the colonies were subjected to governance, exploitation and transformations, so too the colonizers were transformed by the imperial encounter. Not only did they reap colonial profits, which fuelled further industrialization and urbanization; the administration and exploitation of the colonies also shaped the west's sense of self, and created new forms and regimes of knowledge. It was from this that new disciplines such as geography and anthropology were born. 'In short, the new ways of perceiving, organising, representing and acting upon the world which we designate as 'modern' owed as much to the colonial encounter as they did to the industrial revolution, the Renaissance and the Enlightenment' (ibid., 7). In a similar vein, Pratt's notion of 'transculturation' is an important departure from the European expansionist perspective of imperial history in that it allows for the possibility of agency from within the colonies. Transculturation describes one of the key cultural processes that operate between hitherto sharply differentiated cultures and peoples who are forced (usually by the processes of imperialism or globalization) to interact. This interaction often takes place in profoundly asymmetrical ways in terms of relative power between different groups. However, as with the notion of a 'contact zone', this concept breaks down the 'centre'/'periphery' binary, and facilitates to some extent the notion that the subaltern or the colonized is also an agent of change within the theatre of imperialism (Ashcroft et al., 1989; Pieterse and Parekh, 1995; Tiffin and Lawson, 1994).

Reconceptualizing the imperial encounter in terms of contact zones, where two different cultures collided and influenced each other, albeit in an unequal fashion and often with disastrous consequences for the less powerful, is a particularly useful strategy. It is certainly an improvement on Eurocentric notions of imperial expansion and a unidirectional notion of cultural impact. However, the possibilities of recovering colonized voices and agencies from within the contact zone are still problematic. For example, in the case of west Africa there are very few written accounts of interactions with and responses to Europeans during the nineteenth century. It is not always possible to retrieve subordinated voices from imperial archives because they are not always there to be emancipated. In addition to reconceptualizing the imperial encounter, therefore, there is also a need to deconstruct dominant imperialist narratives. As discussed subsequently, some postcolonial theorists overplay the absence of the colonial voice in the imperial archive. There are a few publications and a few surviving documentary sources that do contain the direct testimony of west African peoples. However, the fact remains most imperial discourses actively erase the voice of the colonized. It is in the light of this that postcolonial theorists call for deconstructive readings of the imperial archive. As Barnett (1998, passim) suggests, a deconstruction of dominant discourses allows for an exploration of the epistemic and real violence that suppressed the colonized voice. It also allows for the retrieval of evidence of this suppression from within the imperial archives, and points to the subsequent denial of the role of the colonized in the production of geographical knowledge about the empire. In addition, it seems that while the voice of the colonized may ultimately be irretrievable from the archives, it is only within these archives and the dominant discourses they contain, that evidence of agency and resistance by colonized peoples in British and European imperialism can be recovered. My concern here is not with finding alternative sources within the imperial archive – that is entirely another research project – but to use the same sources analysed throughout this book to produce rather different accounts of agency and resistance. Deconstructing dominant narratives, such as those of white women travellers, is therefore of some importance in producing deterritorialized histories of geographies and imperialism.

Reflecting on the work of the *Subaltern Studies* group in India, Gayatri Spivak (1985, 338) argues that the relative absence of subaltern testimonials and written histories does not preclude the uncovering of the agency of the colonized subject. Rather, the colonial archive is shaped not only by the will of the colonizer, but also by the will of the colonized: 'it is only the texts of counterinsurgency or elite documentation that give us the news of the consciousness of the subaltern'. Therefore, official documents, diaries, travelogues, missionary reports and such like contain evidence of the will of the colonized,[2] and of the extent to which the subaltern may have played a constitutive rather than reflective role in colonial discourse. Deconstructing the colonial archive also allows for a more subtle analysis of the production of geographical knowledge, and the possibility of de-centring a putatively western tradition by viewing the production of these knowledges as a complex process of cultural exchange and negotiation, in which colonized populations played an active part. Spivak's concern with revealing the ways in which power and knowledge are intimately related and, in particular, the epistemic and actual violence of writing out the agency of the colonized in histories of imperialism, seems to have a great deal of resonance with the concern of feminists in recovering the agency of white women in the production of geographical knowledges. Deconstructing the narratives of women travellers in west Africa allows, to some extent, for recovery of the agency of the colonized subject, both within the theatre of imperial culture and in the production of geographical knowledges. Thus, while it is impossible to avoid privileging the authorial voice in exploring (albeit critically) representations of colonized peoples and landscapes by white women, this does not preclude the exploration of resistance to their presence, nor of subaltern agency in the formulation of their geographies. As discussed subsequently, evidence of both agency and resistance is quite clearly contained in the narratives of white women travellers.

Subaltern agency in geographical knowledges about west Africa

As the preceding chapters have sought to exemplify, exploring issues of ethnicity in colonial discourses allows for critical reflection on the relationships between colonizing women and colonized others. It is the contention here that it should also be possible for a critical feminist approach to de-centre western knowledges, including histories of geography. Deconstructing the texts of women travellers can allow, to some extent and (as is discussed below) not unproblematically, for the recovery of the agency and resistance of colonized others in histories of imperialism and geography. For example, there is evidence within these narratives of local agency in the construction of popular racialized and imperialist myths. This point can be explored more fully using the exemplar of representations of cannibalism in the narratives of British women travellers. There is also evidence of indigenous agency in the geographical knowledges that women travellers were able to impart to their readers.

Cannibal tales

As discussed in Chapter 5, of all the perceived atrocities in west Africa (there were, of course, many in British imperial representations), cannibalism was the most sensational and titillating, and featured in many popular portrayals of the continent. It was a fundamental staple in the construction of nineteenth-century European 'knowledges' about west Africa. Exaggerated claims of cannibalism illustrated the supposed debasement of west African peoples, and anthropophagy was a much-exploited theme from mid-century onwards. Despite the fact that modern anthropology casts considerable doubt on the existence of cannibalism in Africa (Arens 1979), few writers have analysed the possibility that west Africans themselves may have spread rumours of their own cannibalism. There are a number of reasons why indigenous peoples in west Africa should have propagated such rumours, including the need to maintain social order or to prevent attacks from other villages. More importantly, few writers have explored the possibility that maintaining rumours of cannibalism was a deliberate strategy to play on the fears of Europeans and to discourage the imperial powers from progressing further inland. This latter strategy is certainly suggested in Kingsley's narrative. It was mentioned in Chapter 5 that Kingsley wrote of the supposedly cannibalistic Fang: 'Man's flesh, he says, is good to eat, very good, and he wishes you would try it. Oh dear no, he never eats it himself, but the next door town does' (1982, 330). Kingsley confessed to never having witnessed evidence of cannibalism, but the stories that were told to her by Africans were many. Although she did not sensationalize the subject of cannibalism in any of her publications, Kingsley did seem to take these rumours as evidence for its existence in parts of west Africa. She failed to recognize the possibility that the spreading of these rumours, particularly by the coastal peoples, could have been an act of resistance towards the imperial powers. The villagers that she encountered were keen to dispel rumours of their own cannibalism, but at the same time were quite happy to spread rumours about cannibalism in the towns further inland. It must also be remembered that the Fang peoples had migrated from central Africa into the central and coastal areas of western Africa during the nineteenth century, and were no doubt keen to prevent Europeans from incursions into their territories (Chamberlin, 1978). Spreading rumours about cannibalism was one such means of discouraging Europeans from further penetrations from the coastal areas. It might also have encouraged Europeans to continue to use African 'middle-men' (as Kingsley referred to them) in various trading relationships, rather than to take formal control of all aspects of resource exploitation in west Africa. There were considerable benefits for west Africans employed in bringing rubber and palm oil from the interior to the coastal trading stations. Any suggestions that the interior was too dangerous for Europeans helped maintain local involvement in the trading of goods and resources.

In addition to the Fang peoples spreading rumours about cannibalism, it is also significant that other indigenous groups that Kingsley encountered also told stories of Fang cannibalism. On one occasion she was accompanied by both Ajumba and Fang guides. She wrote (1982, 287), 'the Ajumba wanted meat, and the Fans, they said, offered them human. I saw no human meat at Egaja, but the Ajumba seem to think that the Fans eat nothing else... [T]he Ajumba have a horror of cannibalism'. Again, the context of the Fang migrations into western Africa is important here, and it is not surprising that either the Fang themselves, or those ethnic groups threatened by the in-migration of large numbers of Fang peoples, would propagate stories of cannibalism. A further aspect to this debate is that the contrived quality of the words that were allegedly spoken makes it unlikely that they were ever actually spoken by Africans with whom Kingsley met. Neither, of course, is there evidence that these were outright fictions. The point about this is not whether these words were actually spoken by Africans, or whether Kingsley's readers believed in their authenticity. That these words might have been pure fictions on the part of their author underlines the nature of the power relations in operation in the imperial encounter. This was a power that 'required not only the African body as an object, but also a consciousness that could be made visible and monitored through speech' (Butchart 1998, 88). However, of importance here is that it seems from the evidence in Kingsley's narrative that myths about cannibalism in west Africa were not simply a product of European imperialist discourses. The peoples of west Africa themselves probably had some agency in the construction of these representations.

Local knowledges and cultural exchange

Further evidence exists of indigenous agency in the production of Kingsley's knowledges. Recent biographies (Alexander, 1989; Birkett, 1992) have pointed out that although she was considered an expert on west Africa she spent only eighteen months there. Much of her own knowledge was gleaned from the German anthropology texts that she had translated for her father, and from the missionaries in west Africa, with whom she spent the majority of her time. However, there seems little doubt that Kingsley's knowledge was often informed by local knowledges and fashioned through the process of cultural exchange with the various groups of indigenous peoples with whom she travelled. Unlike her male counterparts (see Barnett, 1998), Kingsley did not dismiss local knowledges as hearsay, and used her proximity to west Africans to claim authority for her observations. As Blunt (1994, 51–2) argues, the debate between Kingsley and her publisher, George Macmillan, about the inclusion of a map in *Travels* is revealing of Kingsley's anxiety over the textual authority of her narrative. However, it could be argued that this anxiety about maps is also revealing of her dependence upon African knowledge forms in the construction of her own geographies. Kingsley was keen not to include a map in her first publication because she was anxious that this could undermine her authority. She wrote, 'Its (sic) not a question of where *I* have been – or rather where I say I have been [–] so much as a map to show the geographical facts I have stated. Remember, I have said I will not draw my line on it'.[3] As Blunt argues, Kingsley's reluctance to map her route is symptomatic of her ambiguous identification as similar to, but different from, male explorers. Kingsley preferred to map her journeys in textual and metaphorical ways, rather than in a linear manner. This form of mapping is not only revealing of Kingsley's gendered subjectivity, but it also allows for the presence of indigenous knowledges in her narratives. Her textual and metaphorical mapping did not enable her to construct a linear map, and for this reason she was loath to include one in the first edition of *Travels*.

Reading *Travels* there seems to be another reason why Kingsley did not want to include a map; on many of her journeys she did not always know where she had been! When crossing between the Ogowé and the Rembwé rivers she was in uncharted territory, and completely dependent on her guides. Her account of this journey (Kingsley, 1982, 231–307) is revealing of her deep uncertainty. She was in control of neither the speed nor direction of the journey, and she describes herself stumbling about chaotically in a country 'laid down as an obstacle track for ... Titans' (ibid., 307). Even in charted territory, she found difficulty in locating herself in the forests. Her guides could not help her. She wrote (ibid., 237):

> None of them... seem to recognise a single blessed name on the chart, which is saying nothing against the chart and its makers, who probably got their names up from M'pongwes and Igalwas instead of Ajumba, as I am trying to. Geographical research in this region is fraught with difficulty, I find, owing to different tribes calling one and the same place by different names.

With her usual mirth, Kingsley continued:

> I am sure the Royal Geographical Society ought to insert among their 'Hints' that every traveller in this region should carefully learn every separate native word, or set of words, signifying 'I don't know', – four villages and two rivers I have come

across out here solemnly set down with various forms of this statement, for their native name.

It is clear from these statements that 'geographical research' (i.e., mapping and naming) for European travellers was highly dependent on the knowledges of local peoples. The ways in which those different local knowledges were appropriated by individual European explorers contributed to the differences and confusions in the geographies they produced. It was this dependency on these different local knowledges that led to the very public disagreements about the geography of Africa between the likes of Stanley and Speke. However, unlike the latter, Kingsley freely admitted this dependency rather than erasing it from her narrative. It was difficult for Kingsley to map her journeys in any formal sense because this process was alien to those knowledges upon which she was attempting to draw. Indeed, later in *Travels* she writes, 'I learn that these good people, to make topographical confusion worse confounded, call a river by one name when you are going up it, and by another when you are coming down' (ibid., 245). Again, unlike her male counterparts, Kingsley does not dismiss this local knowledge as unscientific; indeed she presents this as perfectly logical despite being confusing for Europeans. Moreover, this confusion presents Kingsley with opportunities for moments of comic irony. It seems that transculturation within the contact zone was a complex matter, but Kingsley made no attempts to deny that this process was taking place in the formulation of her descriptions and understandings of west Africa.

It is apparent, therefore, that more subjective responses to west African environments were fashioned through a process of knowledge exchange. Kingsley warned that unless the traveller learns how to understand the forests of west Africa, 'It is like being shut up in a library whose books you cannot read, all the while tormented, terrified, and bored' (ibid., 102). She wrote 'The Fans ... did their best to educate me in every way: they told me their names for things ... they also showed me many things' (ibid., 266). She also recounts an occasion in *Travels* when one of the Fang chiefs she met drew her a map with leaves (in Kearns, 1997, 459). Clearly, Kingsley's understanding of west Africa was based to a large extent on what her guides had communicated to her. The fact that that she was taught how to 'read' the forests through which she travelled enabled her to relate to her surroundings, and influenced the ways in which she represented the physical environment. Her representations of the forests are not the dry, factual accounts found in other exploration narratives, nor was she able to map her journeys in classic, linear, European exploration tradition. Rather, her account is poetic and metaphorical, with references to animism and pantheism and occasional details on the practicalities of living and surviving in such an environment. Thus, in addition to being gendered, her accounts are also deeply inscribed with indigenous knowledges, which is, in turn, reflective of the agency of her west African companions in the production of her geographies. This is most clearly seen through Kingsley's spiritual responses to the physical environment, which, as was discussed in Chapter 3, she herself identified as 'pure African'. As Kearns (1997) argues, Kingsley was producing a different kind of geographical knowledge to traditional imperial geography. Hers was more ethnology than scientific geography. Kingsley herself claimed that she belonged to a group who 'are not explorers of Africa – because we never exactly know where we go, and we never exactly care' (1899a, 379). She bemoaned the preference for plans over people in imperial policies and the lack of knowledge of indigenous inhabitants compared with landscapes in imperial discourses. Although still part of imperial endeavour and possessive of the will to knowledge, Kingsley's approach makes the agency of west African peoples in the production of her geographies more visible than in other imperial discourses.

It seems, therefore, that the narratives of some women travellers may facilitate the recovery of the agency of colonized peoples in the production of knowledge more than other colonial discourses. Women such as Kingsley were products of a culture that defined womanhood in very prescribed ways, and being more open to 'hearing' indigenous knowledges fits into the set of dominant ideas that defined femininities at the time. The textual authority of women travellers was much more ambiguous than that of their male counterparts. It was acceptable and desirable for male explorers to position themselves as 'men of science' and 'experts', which demanded they simultaneously and necessarily write out the local, subjective, 'unscientific' knowledges upon which many of their own suppositions were based. However, it was much more problematic for women to claim objectivity and authority or to engage scientific and political discourses. Kingsley and Slessor claimed a subjective authority, which they did not deny was based largely upon local knowledges. Indeed, Kingsley claimed that her observations were more reliable than the opinions of 'aged blind armchair geographers'[4] and anthropologists. It was acceptable for women to 'hear' indigenous knowledges and to recount these subsequently in their publications. This was undoubtedly influenced by the presumed relationship between spiritualism, subjectivity and femininity in the late nineteenth century (Walkowitz, 1986). Thus, it is important to understand the presence of subaltern agency in women's travel accounts as part of the sphere of knowledge considered socially acceptable for Victorian women.

Evidence of subaltern resistance

Direct resistance

In addition to going some way towards revealing subaltern agency in the production of geographical knowledges by white women travellers, a deconstruction of their narratives can also reveal subaltern resistance to European imperialism and the presence of Europeans in west Africa. There is no more obvious example of this resistance than that presented in the writings of Anna Hinderer. As was mentioned in Chapter 2, the Hinderers were caught up in the Abeokutan Wars. These wars were a product of growing antagonisms between various branches of the Yoruba peoples over their relationship with British imperial powers. There existed an intense rivalry between the new town of Abeokuta, with its contingent of British missionaries, and the older power of Dahomey to the west. Dahomey had invaded Abeokuta in 1851, and the British government came under increasing pressure from the missionaries to intervene, culminating in the British annexation of Lagos in 1861 (Crowder, 1981, 51). The wars themselves are a clear example of violent resistance to British imperialism, and the ill feeling created by British involvement in disputes between the various Yoruba peoples lasted throughout the 1860s and 1870s. This was to have enormous consequences for Anna and David Hinderer.

The antagonisms in his part of southern Nigeria rumbled on throughout the 1850s, and in 1860 the disputes flared up again in response to increasing interference by Britain. The Hinderers were based in Ibadan at this time. The Ijebus and the Egbas allied against the Ibadanis and blockaded the road to Lagos, creating extreme isolation for the Hinderers over the next five years, during which time they both almost starved to death. In 1867, war was threatened again as the people of Abeokuta rebelled against the British presence. They resented the policies (formulated and operated by Glover, a captain with the Third Niger Expedition) of keeping open roads to the coast, and the attempts by the British colonial administration, aided by the missions, at suppressing the slave trade. In response, the local population forced the missionaries out of Abeokuta. The Egba and Ijebu peoples closed the road once more to Lagos, and the Hinderers were again marooned in Yoruba. Both suffered declining health. Written within this context, Anna Hinderer's published letters are revealing not only of her own privations, but also of the level of localized and widespread resistance to the British presence in west Africa. The precarious nature of the Christian mission in this part of west Africa is at the forefront of many of these letters. It is clear from her narrative that during the seventeen years she and her husband spent in Yoruba there was almost constant and simmering tension between local peoples, the British imperial government and British missionaries stationed in the area. This constant tension regularly erupted into violent resistance by west Africans against the British and anyone seen to be in sympathy with the British presence in Yoruba. Hinderer's narrative, therefore, can quite clearly be read not only as an example of how white women discursively constructed west Africa, but also as evidence that British imperialism in west Africa was met with sustained and, in some cases, violent resistance.

Intransigence

Evidence of resistance to the presence of white individuals can be read in most exploration narratives, even where direct confrontations with indigenous populations are not apparent. However, the imperial archive is also revealing of resistance to British imperialism in a wider sense. For example, Mary Slessor's communiqués with colonial officials in Calabar are revealing not only of her own extraordinary influence, but also of indigenous resistance to the colonization of southern Nigeria from the 1890s onwards.[5] Slessor's warning to the Consul-General of the Oil Rivers Protectorate that the Okoyong people were not ready to tolerate a government official in their midst, nor to accept without bloodshed the sudden introduction of new laws[6] can be read in two ways. On the one hand, Slessor's warning, together with her knowledge of local laws, prompted the colonial government to appoint her as the first female Vice-Consul in the British empire in 1892, granting her the powers of a magistrate. Thus Slessor may have exaggerated the dangers of imposing British institutions and neglecting local customs in order to increase her own authority in the Okoyong area. On the other hand, Slessor's warning is evidence of the potential for local disturbances against the British. Unlike many of her predecessors, Slessor was not prone to exaggeration in representing west Africa and the peoples of Calabar in her reports, and her cautionary remarks to the Consul-General suggest that there was widespread resistance to the imposition of British colonial institutions. Indeed, this is borne out by the difficulties that the colonial administration had in taking a census in Calabar. Slessor's refusal to take the census to the local rulers can be read as an act of resistance on her part against British colonialism (McEwan, 1995, 134), but her complaints are also evidence of her awareness of localized resistance to the British presence. She maintained that the people were too suspicious of the British government to complete it, and were too busy working on the land during the day and in the markets in the evening to comply.

It seems clear that in many of Slessor's locations during her forty years in the Calabar area the local populations not only tolerated her presence, but also encouraged her to use her influence with the colonial administrative bodies to their advantage. It was discussed in Chapter 2, for example, that in 1910 the people of Akpap complained to her that they were being compelled to build a road through a sacred grove of yams. Slessor's furious response in the form of a letter of complaint to the Assistant District Commissioner was evidence of her own considerable belligerence towards colonial officials, but it also highlighted how quickly were the peoples with whom she lived to recognize and utilize her maverick qualities. Slessor's belligerence, then, is itself reflective of indigenous resistance to elements of British imperialism, which operated at the local level in southern Nigeria. The various peoples of Calabar with whom Slessor came into contact certainly used her position of authority with the colonial powers at times to their own advantage, and particularly in strengthening their own acts of resistance.

Examples of various levels of intransigence by west Africans are also apparent in Kingsley's narrative. Kingsley, unlike many of her male predecessors, tended on the whole to enjoy good relations with her west African guides. However, there is also evidence in *Travels in West Africa* of resistances to her presence. Kingsley's ascent of Mount Cameroon, which was frustrated by the intransigence and subsequent desertion of her African guides, highlights one example of this. The guides were supposed to carry enough water to enable Kingsley's party to reach a waterhole on the mountain. However, on reaching the waterhole Kingsley discovered this to be dry, and it seems that the guides deliberately set out with insufficient water supplies in the hope that the trek would be abandoned. Kingsley (1982, 574) wrote 'it is evidently a trick played on me by the boys, who intentionally failed to let me know of this want of water before leaving Buea, where it seems all have learnt it'. Kingsley suspected a deliberate attempt at sabotage by the guides. She wrote (ibid., 574), 'Now they evidently think there is nothing to be done but to return to Buea, and go down to Victoria, and get their pay, and live happily ever after, without having to face the horror of the upper regions of the mountain'. She also knew that other white travellers had fallen for this trick. However, she refused to return to Buea and instead sent one of the guides to fetch further water supplies. On the failure of this attempted sabotage, Kingsley (ibid., 574) described her guides as 'sulky', and it is clear from the rest of the episode that they were far from helpful in her mission to reach the summit of the mountain. In fact, the majority of them attempted to desert and go back down the slopes while she pressed on. When Kingsley caught up with them, they gave her conflicting statements to explain their desertion (ibid., 580), including tiredness, fear of the lack of water, sickness and drunkenness. The following day, the guides refused to ascend to the peak on the grounds that they were too cold and tired (ibid., 593). Kingsley went up alone. Considering that Mount Cameroon was, by the 1890s, a well-trodden tourist site and little more than a stiff walk, the behaviour of Kingsley's guides can be interpreted as deliberate interference and resistance. Therefore, the ambiguity of Kingsley's imperial authority (discussed in Chapter 2) was constituted not merely by her gendered subjectivity, but also by the agency of her guides.

Resistance through 'laziness'

Non-co-operation of the kind that Kingsley experienced was a common feature of encounters between white women and west Africans. As was argued in Chapter 4, the theme of the apparent laziness of west Africans was a common stereotype in imperial discourse. It was a form of racialized othering that was prevalent in the narratives of white women travellers, especially those women who were resident in west Africa and thus reliant upon African domestic servants. This apparent laziness, however, might also be read as evidence of resistance to colonial authority. For example, Mrs Foote (1869, 195–6) wrote:

> An unusual number of servants are required in the African household, however small the family, on account of their incorrigible laziness, which exceeds anything I ever saw in other countries... Women servants are seldom kept unless there are children in the family, and the good ones are few and far between. They are even more lazy than the men, and are careless, dirty, and cold-hearted.

Foote's inability to deal with the local currency (cowrie shells) meant that she had to devolve some control of the household economy to her head servant. She wrote 'For one week or so, I attempted house keeping, but gave it up in despair on account of the cowries, so our head man had everything in his hands again; much to his triumph, no doubt, as he secretly rejoiced at my discomfiture' (ibid., 197). Therefore, not only were Foote's servants actively resisting her authority, they were also at times able to subvert and undermine her authority, at least within the domestic sphere.

There is similar evidence of this level of resistance in Elizabeth Melville's narrative. She wrote (1968, 13), 'The domestics here are all men, and they appear to be very indolent, so that you require eight or nine household servants, where in a similar establishment in England three or four would be found sufficient'. On her second stay in Sierra Leone, she employed a new servant called Natti-barra. Apparently, this servant didn't work very well and preferred to play. Melville wrote: 'She was, besides, as mischievously inclined to pilfer as any magpie...' (ibid., 204). On another occasion, as was discussed in Chapter 4, she wrote:

> [T]he indolence, stupidity and want of tidiness... of the only persons you have to depend upon as domestic servants, throw you into a sort of actual despair. You teach, persuade, remonstrate, lecture, by turns; your words are listened to with a good-humoured apathy, but neither your rhetoric nor example effecting the slightest improvement... (ibid., 251).

This quote is worth repeating here since it highlights very clearly certain strategies of resistance and perhaps even subversion taking place within colonial residences. As discussed previously, Melville, like many other residents in west Africa, neglected to consider the fact that domestic servants in this part of Africa perhaps did not work well because they associated work with slavery. The similarities of inequalities of power relations between white master/mistress and African slave and white master/mistress and African servant were no doubt all too obvious to indigenous peoples in west Africa. The apparent laziness of west Africans working in domestic service, therefore, can be read as evidence of resistance to the presence of British colonizers, and as deliberate acts of transgression towards their employers. Playing 'dumb', pretending not to understand, being untidy, and giving the impression of idleness and sloth were all strategies designed to compromise the authority of the colonizers. Resistances such as these by colonized peoples often led to sweeping condemnations written in racial terms within imperial discourses, but they also demonstrate the agency of west Africans and the inability of British colonizers to exercise complete domination as they would perhaps as wished.

West Africans might have been able to do little in resisting the might of imperial Britain at a grand scale, but they were certainly not inactive in exploring avenues of localized resistance and subversion. West Africans, therefore, were not dispossessed and disempowered in a simplistic manner as is sometimes suggested by histories of imperialism. It is clear from imperial discourses such as travel writings that indigenous peoples were never completely dominated and disempowered. Instead, they were able to subvert imperial authority by adopting various strategies of resistance and intransigence. The tendency to imagine the peoples of west Africa as unwitting victims of economic imperialism is further disrupted by evidence, in Kingsley's narrative particularly, of their attempts to take advantage of trade relations. For example, as discussed in the previous chapter, Kingsley describes the adulteration of rubber by west African peoples in their attempts to deceive white traders and create advantage for themselves from economic relations between Britain and west Africa. She describes how the rubber was often mixed with fine white clay to add to its weight. A piece of smoked Koko plant was often stuffed into the middle of each rubber ball, also to add to the weight. 'In fact, anything is put there, that is hopefully regarded as likely to deceive the white trader' (Kingsley, 1982, 292). Incidents such as those described in Kingsley's travelogue highlight local resistances to British traders and the subversion of existing power relations between traders and west Africans. They also disrupt notions of west Africans as passive victims of imperialism.

Cutting power lines in the palace?

The erasure of the historical agency of the colonized remains a problem in many studies of imperialism, even within some of the more recent explorations purporting to adopt a critical stance. Indeed, Aijaz Ahmad, one of the most fervent critics of postcolonial theory, suggests that the whole theoretical enterprise, with its focus on discourse and roots in French high theory, is a diminution of politics and an ascension to western hegemony (1992, 69). However, as this chapter has attempted to demonstrate, the self-reflexivity of postcolonial theory can be useful in acknowledging and revealing the historical agency of colonized peoples. As Gikandi (1996, 6) argues, one of the most critical interventions has been the recognition that 'colonized space was instrumental in the invention of Europe just as the idea of Europe was the condition for the possibility of the production of the modern colonial and postcolonial society'. One can argue along similar lines that the agency of the colonized was also significant in the creation of geographical knowledges, and of imperial histories during the nineteenth century. In addition, as Barnett (1997, 149) argues, 'Finding traces of subaltern resistance provides oppositional academics with a lever with which to challenge and displace the totalizing, coherent, and linear narratives which characterize hegemonic disciplinary discourses'. This chapter has attempted to demonstrate through a deconstruction of a small number of texts that geographical knowledge was not simply a product of metropolitan theory and enterprise. Instead, it was often produced within the 'contact zones' of empire, where indigenous knowledge informed and partially constituted the geographies of white explorers and writers. Furthermore, it is within these discourses of empire that evidence of resistance to British imperialism is found. However, this kind of re-reading of white women's travel narratives is not without its attendant problems and contradictions.

Gayatri Spivak argues in her famous essay 'Can the Subaltern Speak?' that, in fact, the subaltern cannot speak, because the subaltern is only produced by the subject-effects, the inscriptions, found in colonial historiography (Childs and Williams, 163). Speaking, in this sense, involves speaking and listening, getting a response to speech and the responsibility this entails. For Spivak, this does not happen in the realm of the subaltern because they are not actively listened to; so the subaltern cannot speak. Spivak argues that any subaltern 'voice' that is heard within colonialist texts has already been appropriated and mediated by the dominant discourse. There is also the added problem of silence as an act of resistance; does the colonized voice always wish to be emancipated? As Barnett (1997, 139) argues, there is often a tendency when analysing colonial discourses to appropriate the voice of the colonized in order to speak on their behalf, whilst 'simultaneously appropriating the omnipotent rhetoric of imperial discourse itself in order to provide authoritative counternarratives'. The fundamental problem, then, concerns who performs this emancipation. Pointing to the erasure of subaltern agency and resistance within imperial discourse at least highlights the epistemic violence performed in the imperial moment. Writers in the West, Spivak argues, must be vigilant to see that they are not complicit with the further production of the subaltern and that they learn to critique colonial and post-colonial discourse without offering alternative figures of the colonized. In other words, critics should resist the desire to retrieve the voices silenced by imperialism, first because they are irretrievable and secondly because such a move would subscribe once more to the humanist notion of the voice as the free expression of an 'authentic' individuality. Spivak concludes that there is not an alternative history to be written from the point of view of the subaltern. Postcolonial critics must learn not to seek for the subaltern's voice but to point to the silence and the ways in which this erasure has been brought about. Spivak refers to this process as 'unlearning privilege' as one's loss. In other words, recognising that those privileges ('race', nationality, gender, class, and so on) may have prevented us from gaining certain kinds of other knowledge. She writes:

> In seeking to learn to speak to (rather than listen to or speak for) the historically muted subject of the subaltern woman, the postcolonial intellectual *systematically* 'unlearns' female privilege. This systematic unlearning involves learning to critique postcolonial discourse with the best tools it can provide and not simply substituting the lost figure of the colonized.

Our social positions mean that there are certain knowledges, histories and understandings that are beyond the realm of understanding of the privileged intellectual. Therefore, the recovery of the voice of the colonized in nineteenth century west Africa is difficult and problematic, but this does not mean that evidence of agency and resistance cannot be recovered and included as part of a more critical and inclusive history of geography and imperialism. In addition, it is perhaps pertinent at this juncture to counter again Spivak's claim that the recovery of colonized voices is completely impossible. My concern in this book has been those metropolitan texts produced by white women travellers. In this chapter, I have endeavoured to demonstrate that the trace of subaltern resistance and agency is present within these metropolitan texts and in imperial discourse more widely. Exposing this where previous studies have erased it is an important endeavour. It raises the possibility that there are always other stories that might disrupt linear, hegemonic histories of geography and imperialism. These stories might not be retrievable by the postcolonial critic, but acknowledging the possibilities of their existence provides a means of writing a more critical history. In addition, however, it is important to remember that resistance does not always exist as a mere trace. There are other bodies of narrative where the voice of the colonized has been recorded and is therefore perhaps recoverable. One can think of the texts of the colonial elite. Certainly, the writings of the likes of Reverend Mark Hayford, Bishop Edward Blyden and other nineteenth-century west African intellectuals were shaped by their missionary education. However, whilst often being pro-imperialist, these men were also responsible to their local constituencies. Their writings and opinions, therefore, cannot simply be dismissed by contemporary postcolonial scholars as unproblematically pro-imperialist. Further investigation of their writings and journals would no doubt reveal evidence of their own localized resistances to the presence of Europeans, and it is certainly the case that these colonial elites did have a voice through their publications that exists today as more than a trace. Furthermore, there are other documents still housed in the imperial archives of west African countries where the voices of ordinary west African people are recorded. For example, court records contain the testimonies of west Africans prosecuted for various minor and localized resistances towards the colonial powers. Their voices may have been translated and transcribed by court officials and they were articulated within the spaces of imperial domination, which means that they were always already in some way mediated by dominant discourses, but their testimonies are historical records. Evidence of resistance and of the articulation of the colonial voice in these testimonies surely exists as more than a trace. In this case, the imperial archive can be seen to contain the direct articulation of voices of dissent; to assume that these voices do not exist is perhaps ironically to perpetuate simplistic notions of uncontested western hegemony. There are thus profound implications for any scholar located in the first world metropolitan academy tacitly assuming that the ancestors of contemporary west Africans exist as mere traces in the historical record.[7] The focus of this book has been on metropolitan imperial discourses, where evidence of agency and resistance do exist as mere traces, but there is certainly scope for further investigation of those archival sources where the more direct voices of resistance and intransigence have been preserved.

Turning now to the construction of geographical knowledge, this chapter has endeavoured to counterbalance an attempt to recover the agency of white women in histories of imperialism and geographical thought with recognition that, paradoxically, this project might continue to erase other agencies in the construction of these histories. Thus, in addition to writing a critical account of the role of white women travellers in imperialism in west Africa, and of the geographies that they created within their published narratives, this chapter has also explored the possibilities of exposing evidence of the agency of those west Africans marginalized by the processes of imperialism and within imperial discourse. However, this endeavour is also not without its attendant problems and contradictions. The work of Gayatri Spivak is informative in this respect. Spivak (1985; 1991) points out that there is a problematic and antagonistic relationship between the affirmation of white women's agency in the production of knowledge on the one hand, and the recovery of non-western agency and resistance on the other. The two are not complementary. Indeed, Spivak (1991, 159) argues that the two are incompatible:

> [A] concern with women, *and* men, who have not been written in the *same* cultural inscription, cannot be mobilised *in the same way* as the investigation of gendering in our own ... We understand it more easily when folks of other *gender* inscription wish to join *our* struggle ... Yet when we want to intervene in the heritage of colonialism or the practice of neo-colonialism, we take our own goodwill for guarantee.

She goes on to argue that 'feminism (within 'the same' cultural inscription) and anticolonialism (for or against racial 'others') cannot occupy a continuous narrative space' (168). This is because feminism itself is a product of specific cultural contexts, and is therefore always already implicated in relationships of power. I have attempted to deal with some of the problems and discomfitures that Spivak refers to. As academics working in 'the west' we are situated in a 'theatre of cultural imperialism,' and we are, often without knowing so, complicit in this cultural imperialism. However, from this position on the 'inside' we can begin to reveal the ways that lines of power still operate to re-privilege 'the west(ern male)' as the site of the production of knowledge. In addition to exposing the operation of relationships of power in the production of knowledge, it is imperative that historians of geography construct alternative, critical, and non-exclusive histories, and that the old lines of power and paternalistic remaking of geography are disrupted if not dismantled. If Spivak is correct, then constructing a history of geography that is simultaneously postcolonial and feminist may be impossible. It is certainly not without some difficulties. There is not equivalence between the exclusion of white women and non-western subjects from histories of geographical and imperial knowledges. The recovery of the former does not necessarily enable the recovery of the latter.

These problems are worthy of serious contemplation, but they should not be disabling. In terms of teaching and researching histories of geographical thought vigilance is the most important strategy. Acknowledging that there are always alternative stories to be told, and creating space for these to be heard, is a beginning. As Sidaway (1997, 77) argues, it then becomes possible to see that western geography more widely has relied upon and appropriated many elements of other local ('indigenous') geographical knowledges. As this chapter has suggested, European explorers and travellers could rarely operate without some input or intelligence from local guides. The task of recovering such subaltern knowledges from the texts of explorers and geographers is deeply problematic. Yet, once we stop privileging the west as the sole site of production of geographical knowledges, then a much broader notion of how these have come about comes within grasp. It might be that a complete history of imperial geographies is impossible, and that those subaltern knowledges cannot be recovered. However, as Sidaway (ibid., 77) suggests, 'we might care to think hard about how western geography has been able to get away with claiming that what is the work of many cultures is the product of one'. As this rather limited example has suggested, there is certainly scope for considering imperial geographies as the product of multiple agents, rather than the product of an inherently superior culture.

Notes

1. See Mishra and Hodge (1991), Hall (1995), McClintock (1995) for discussions of the meanings of post(-)colonialism.
2. See also Bhabha (1984) on mimicry and parody as resistance, and McClintock (1995).

3. Kingsley to Macmillan, 25/11/96, Macmillan Archive, British Library, Ms. 54914

4. Kingsley to Macmillan, 2/1/96, Macmillan Archive, British Library, Ms. 54914

5. Slessor's acquisition of autonomy from the Church of Scotland and influence in the colonial politics of Calabar is discussed in greater detail in McEwan (1995b)

6. Slessor to Sir Claude MacDonald, cited in Christian and Plummer (1970, 90). This is discussed in greater detail in Chapter 2.

7. I am grateful to Reg Cline-Cole for enlightening me on this issue, and for pointing out the problems in Spivak's assumption that the voice of the colonized has been completely eradicated from the imperial archive. It is, perhaps, paradoxical that assumptions such as these might repeat the erasure of those colonized voices that are still to be found within the colonial archive.

CHAPTER 8

Conclusions

Examining the differences among women ... in their historical configuration assists us in constructing a genealogy of feminism's reigning exclusions, even though they may not match current differences. I hope by identifying those differences in their historical particulars to contextualise the struggles, and thus to reimagine the future of feminism rather than to celebrate the differences (Nussbaum 1995, 18).

Introduction

The fact that nineteenth-century British women travellers committed their ideas to paper and were published is of importance, since their narratives formed part of a much bigger literature on west Africa. Travel and exploration narratives were exceedingly popular with many sections of British society during this period, and travel narratives by women thus had potentially large readerships. The women of this study, therefore, produced a popular literature on west Africa, and their narratives contributed in some part to imperial culture in Britain between 1840 and 1915. That they actually travelled to west Africa, and that they recounted their experiences as women in this region, added novelty and interest to their accounts. The publication of their travelogues by large publishing companies (Macmillan, Routledge, Blackwood) is also indicative of their potential popularity.

As was suggested in Chapter 2, white women gained authority in various ways as a consequence both of travel and travel writing. Of significance is the fact that they wrote for different audiences; they exercised varying levels of influence upon different groups of people. Several of the women, such as Zélie Colvile and Constance Larymore, produced popular travelogues in which they recounted their experiences and added to popular images of west Africa. Others, such as Elizabeth Melville and Mrs Foote, wrote narratives containing forceful arguments in support of Britain's anti-slavery efforts in west Africa. Anna Hinderer's journals were published posthumously, but contained arguments strongly in favour of the Christian missions. Mary Slessor had access to a large public audience through her publications in the missionary magazines, and used this to express her own opinions about church policy in west Africa. Mary Kingsley had the largest potential audience; her narratives and treatises on the administration of west Africa were very popular, and she used newspaper and journal articles, as well as public lectures, to advance her own opinions on the region and the future of Britain's interests there. In addition to communicating their visions and impressions of west Africa through published travel accounts, several women used other popular media to publicize their travels. Like Kingsley, Slessor and Colvile used public lectures to voice their opinions, and Colvile also published a journal article. Through these media, women travellers acquired a public voice with which to express their attitudes towards British imperialism in general, and to represent specifically the landscapes and peoples of west Africa. Thus to varying degrees (which are difficult to quantify but nevertheless important), British women travellers contributed to the imperial culture of Britain during the nineteenth century, adding to the great mass of material written about territories beyond Europe and subsequently available for public consumption.

In light of the above, it is the contention here that any study of geography, gender and imperialism must take account of the fact that white women were empowered by travel in the imperial context on the basis of 'race' and class. They gained a public voice and an audience for their opinions; they represented and, to some extent, appropriated landscapes and peoples; they conducted inequitable interpersonal relationships with indigenous peoples. The knowledges they produced helped construct nineteenth-century visions of west Africa in Britain. Thus, despite the constraints and restrictions shaping the lives of women travellers, which were related particularly to the patriarchal nature of Victorian society and to the specific form of British femininity that arose at the time of their travels, the opportunity to travel in the empire was ultimately empowering. As we have seen, however, this does not mean that west Africans were completely disempowered by British imperialism, and even within dominant narratives one can find evidence of their resistance and agency. I will return to this idea at the end of this chapter. However, at this point it is necessary to draw together the major themes apparent in the geographical knowledges produced by white women travellers.

Common narrative themes

The absence of women from the traditions of geographical inquiry and exploration, particularly at the time of the establishment of geography as a scientific and academic discipline, does not preclude them in histories of geographical thought in the broader sense. This book has illustrated that white women were not only active within the British empire, and were empowered through unequal imperial power relations that would not have been possible in contemporary patriarchal British society, but they also produced geographical knowledges of the lands through which they travelled. I have focused on four prominent themes that recur throughout the travel narratives of British women in west Africa: landscape, 'race', anthropological description, and west African women. I have attempted to unpack these images and explore British women's visions of Africa. At this juncture I wish to reflect briefly on four key points: the significance of the ways in which images of west Africa changed rapidly in tandem with Britain's interest in the region during the nineteenth century, the extent to which this is reflected in descriptions by women travellers, the ways in which these differing contexts creating differences in the ways in which white women represented west Africa, and the significance of their narratives in relation to broader imperial discourses.

Landscape

Representations of the physical environment played a powerful part in the creation of geographical knowledges about west Africa. Many British travellers at this time held firm views on Britain's role in the fulcrum of European economic and political imperialism. Indeed, Said (1978,156) suggests that there was a powerful partnership between those who travelled in and studied the empires of Europe, and those who governed them, with complex linkages between the financiers of explorations and travellers. The latter reported their findings back in Britain, representing imperial lands in specific ways, and providing the imperialists with the arguments to support extension of the British empire. Depictions of the physical environment were important in establishing enduring images of west Africa in nineteenth-century Britain.

Portrayals of non-European landscapes proved to be powerful tools for both pro- and anti-imperialists in Britain. Positive, favourable renderings of these landscapes were often used to encourage further travel and interest in certain areas, providing an impetus for colonial settlement and subsequent development and exploitation of these environments. These colonies provided an escape from the filthy, unhealthy industrial cities of Britain, and many people resorted to travel, or emigration, as a means of improving their health. Conversely, negative, unfavourable renderings of non-European landscapes were sometimes used to further the cause of the pro-imperialists. Overseas territories were often represented as vast tracts of wilderness that required European domination to establish order and facilitate economic development. In the case of west Africa, images of the physical environment evolved with the changing nature of British imperialism in the region. The anti-slavery supporters fostered an image of an Edenic landscape, but with the failure to convert west Africans to Christianity, and as a result of the high mortality rate among Europeans travelling to the region, this image soon transformed into a more negative portrayal. West Africa became exotic, unfamiliar and frightening. The harsh climate and prevalence of disease provided the anti-imperialists with an argument in favour of Britain's abandonment of west Africa, and such portrayals held sway throughout the middle of the nineteenth century. By the time of the revival of Britain's interest in the region in the 1880s, the image of the west African environment in travel and exploration literature, and in colonial fiction, had become one of pandemonium. Chaotic and confused, it was sadly lacking the order of 'civilization'. This depiction of the physical environment coincided with the desire in some parts of British society to extend its empire in Africa at the time of the Berlin Conference, and notions of 'wilderness' and untamed nature encouraged support for British expansionism and the spread of 'civilization'.

The descriptions of the physical environment by women travellers thus need to be framed within this broader picture of British imperialism, and the changing popular images of west Africa throughout the nineteenth century. The differences in their descriptions are revealing of the women's differing attitudes towards British imperialism in west Africa. Elizabeth Melville's attitude was typical of the 1840s; philanthropic perspectives, anti-slavery concerns, and British anti-colonialism heavily influenced her landscape descriptions at the time. She portrayed west Africa as almost Edenic; it was a land of gardens and cultivation, of flowers, blossoms and perfumes. However, it was not Europe's Eden, but Africa's. She believed west Africa unfit for European colonization, primarily because of climatic conditions; the presence of Britons would be unnecessary once the slave trade had been abolished. Abolishing slavery would ensure that indigenous peoples could be left to live peaceably in their own paradise. Mrs Foote shared Melville's belief that the west African environment was unsuited to European colonization, and the conviction that it was the burden of the British to eradicate what remained of the slave trade. She saw this endeavour in terms of the imperial powers being able to establish legitimate trade that would ultimately benefit Britain. However, like Melville, Foote occasionally constructed Arcadian images of the landscapes of west Africa, and there are similarities in the pastoral paradise the two women envisaged.

Mary Slessor's landscape descriptions continued, to a certain extent, the tradition of romanticising west Africa, but they were also heavily influenced by the realities of living in the region for nearly forty years. The imagery that Slessor deployed was perhaps less influenced by the nature of British attitudes and more informed by her role as a missionary living in Africa. This is not the case with Constance Larymore's descriptions of Nigerian landscapes. Larymore was unique among the women of this study in that she adopted of the 'monarch-of-all-I-survey' position to describe the landscapes she encountered. She even claimed territory as her own in her writings. She was able to do so, because, unlike the other women, she travelled through a part of west Africa that had been conquered by the British and which had been formally incorporated into the British empire. In effect, she was surveying territories that were about to be colonized. Mary Kingsley's landscape descriptions were also unique, not only in their great abundance and poeticism, but also because they challenged many of the images of west Africa that prevailed during the 1890s. Unlike Zélie Colvile, who portrayed west Africa as the 'Land of Death', Kingsley drew on earlier romantic depictions in order to challenge negative visions of west Africa, and to raise interest in the possibilities for British imperialism there. She believed that if she could convince the British public that the region was not a land of darkness, it would encourage the government to increase Britain's trading interests there.

Landscape descriptions by women travellers also need to be viewed in relation to the wider literary and philosophical traditions which persisted throughout the nineteenth century, and which influenced their relationships with, and understanding and depictions of, the environments of west Africa. These traditions include nineteenth-century ideas about 'Nature', Victorian romanticism, and nineteenth-century notions of wilderness and the imperial frontier. Victorian romanticism and ideas about 'Nature' were strongly influenced by late eighteenth- and early nineteenth-century concepts, and in particular by the works of the Romantic poets. However, to those Victorians who adhered to rationality and the spirit of Science, the subjectivity found in such writings was to be avoided. Nature should be objectified. Despite this, many nineteenth-century notions about the physical world remained distinctly conservative. As Knoepflmacher and Tennyson (1977, xxi) argue, 'Though partially discredited and bereft of some of its 'mysteries', it [Nature] would continue to be cherished for its symbolic representations and sacramental meanings in the face of the rapid advances of science into a very different natural order'. Therefore, certain philosophies about the physical environment in nineteenth-century Britain remained essentially backward looking, and 'Nature' remained above all 'a repository of feeling, a sanctuary they were all eager to retain' (ibid., xxi). The cult of Nature was a prominent part of the nineteenth-century experience, and was probably an obverse manifestation of the loss of faith that characterized the period. Many thinkers in Victorian Britain, as in any age, looked back towards a Golden Age and yearned for a countryside which was being swept away by the Industrial Revolution (although there were also utopian optimists, such as John Stuart Mill, who yearned for a new world based on science, rationality and modernity). Contempt for industrialization among some thinkers helped produce a pastoral myth of country cottages and gardens.[1] As discussed in Chapter 3, these developments in philosophies about the physical environment influenced greatly the ways in which non-European landscapes were depicted, and they also influenced the women of this study. Melville and Foote evoked the pastoral myth in their representations of the West African countryside. Slessor and Kingsley both depicted west Africa as a sanctuary, and Slessor in particular painted romantic pictures of the Calabar past. Although most of the women shared a romanticism, this is most clearly expressed in the works of Kingsley, and her portrayals of the landscapes of west Africa owe more to the romanticism of the eighteenth century than that of the nineteenth century.

Portrayals of non-European landscapes were complex, and were influenced not only by nineteenth-century concepts of Nature, but also by imperialist literatures. Thus, on the one hand, non-industrial non-European landscapes could sometimes be depicted as wildernesses and sanctuaries, but on the other hand, these landscapes were also depicted as existing beyond the frontier of 'civilization'. It was the 'duty' of

Britain to push back this frontier and extend 'civilization', commerce and Christianity into these vast wildernesses. The notion of the imperial frontier was particularly powerful in literature concerning Britain's involvement in west Africa. European contact had existed since the fifteenth century, yet it remained a land of mystery. Its extreme climate, high death rate, and dense, unexplored forests ensured that it was perceived by many in Britain as the most nefarious region of the 'dark continent'. The slow progress of British imperialism throughout the nineteenth century ensured that the idea of the imperial frontier endured well into the twentieth century. Thus there are images of the imperial frontier in the narratives of Foote (who wrote in the 1860s), Slessor (who wrote from the 1880s), and in those of Larymore, writing in the first decade of the twentieth century. All alluded to the gradual extension of civilization in west Africa as the influence of the missionaries and the British government increased.

From mid-century onwards, the Edenic Africa of anti-slavery literature was transformed. The failure of expeditions due to the susceptibility of Europeans to fevers and the difficulty of the terrain, the impact of scientific racism from the 1860s onwards, and the descriptions of Africa in exploration literature ensured that the popular image of west Africa darkened. Richard Burton's Africa was 'hideous and grotesque', to Henry Stanley the forests were 'remorseless and implacable' (Hammond and Jablow, 1977, 60). Winwood Reade feminized the continent and its 'horrors' (ibid., 70–1). Africa was represented in exploration literature as a wilderness, the superficial beauty of which concealed the hidden dangers of disease.[2] It was at once fecund, alluring, repulsive, and ultimately destructive. Such portrayals were a feature of nineteenth-century exploration literature, and also of colonial fiction, epitomized by Joseph Conrad's *Heart of Darkness*, published in 1902. They helped legitimize Britain's increasing involvement in the affairs of west Africa during the 1870s and 1880s. Hargreaves (1974, 407) contends that, 'As impressions and prejudices derived from African experience were fed back into Europe a new 'image of Africa' began to emerge, as an incorrigibly barbarous continent, more suited for civilization by conquest than by the old agencies of Christianity and commerce'. These attitudes are certainly apparent in Colvile's portrayal of west Africa in the 1890s, and her descriptions of surrounding landscapes are, at times, almost Conradian in style.

There were, therefore, conventional ways of representing 'other' landscapes during the nineteenth century that influenced the narratives of women travellers. The contrast between the backward-looking romanticism of many nineteenth-century thinkers and the ideas of progress inherent in contemporaneous imperial discourses was apparent in their descriptions of west African landscapes. The physical environment was variously portrayed by these women as a sanctuary, as an Arcadia and refuge from British industrialization, and as a threatening, barbaric, and bewildering wilderness beyond the frontier of 'civilization'. Furthermore, the degree to which landscapes figured in their descriptions is itself indicative of the constraints operating upon and within their texts. There was perhaps a greater emphasis on landscape description in the accounts of women travellers than in those of their male counterparts because of textual constraints, which limited the possibilities for making scientific observations and political comments.

'Race'

Much has been written on race and nineteenth-century Britain (Bolt, 1971; Gilman, 1985a; Huttenbach, 1976; JanMohammed, 1985; Lorimer, 1978; Memmi, 1990; Rainger, 1978), and increasingly studies are combining the issues of gender and racism. While women travellers have become a topic of considerable interest to feminist writers throughout the social sciences, the issue of race and racism has proved a difficult one to tackle. As was discussed in Chapter 1, much of the early feminist research tended either to excuse or ignore the racism of white women in the British empire, or to argue within the confines of a gender dichotomy that women were not, in fact, racist and that white men were the primary purveyors of racism within the empire (Callaway, 1987; Stoler, 1991). As Vron Ware (1992, 36–7) argues, feminist theorists have been reluctant to analyse the nature of the racism apparent in the travel narratives of white women:

> It is still rare ... to find any white feminist history of the nineteenth century that relates to the British Empire, except as a force that touched women's lives in Britain or as a possible escape route for women who failed to make a satisfying life at home. Overlooking the existence of imperialist ideologies suggests that the question of race has no relevance to the history of white women.

Gender was particularly important in organising ideas about 'race' and 'civilization', and women were involved in many different ways in the expansion and maintenance of the empire. This was crucial during the late Victorian period when theories of race and eugenics were used to support the concept of the innate superiority of the white race above all others, and Englishwomen were seen as the 'conduits of the essence of race'. Women were considered to be the guardians of the race in their reproductive capacity, and they also provided – as long as they were of the right class and breeding – a guarantee that British morals and principles were adhered to in the colonies (ibid., 37–8). Thus by the end of the nineteenth and into the twentieth century, the demands of empire began to influence literature on social mores.[3]

The relationship between race and gender is, therefore, of critical importance in the context of British imperial culture. However, there has been relatively little analysis of the ways in which women that actually travelled in the empire negotiated race and racism in the course of their travels. According to Ware (1992, 42–3):

Whereas feminist historians have uncovered many examples of feminists who have braved convention at home to fight to improve the lives and opportunities of women of all classes and backgrounds, there has been little corresponding interest in British women who came face to face with the complexities of racism and male power ... their role in the imperial project and the way they dealt with racism and cultural difference ... The purpose of exploring the histories of ... imperialism is not to bring white women to account for past misdeeds, nor to search for heroines where reputations can help absolve the rest from guilt, but to find out how white women negotiated questions of race and racism – as well as class and gender.

Following Ware, it is clear that the issue of white women and racism within travel texts is highly complex. As Chapter 4 illustrates, there were, in effect, a whole series of different reactions by women travellers that were both informed by, and, in some cases, challenged the prevailing racism at the time of their travels.

The importance of elucidating and understanding images of west Africans in the narratives of white women travellers becomes apparent when one considers Lorimer's (1978, 428) contention that:

Much of the Victorian discussion of race took place in haphazard fashion, mixing the observations of travellers with common prejudices. This was the common-place discourse not only of everyday conversation and of the daily press, but also of scientific gatherings and publications including the organs of the British Association, the Royal Geographical Society, and the Anthropological Institute.

The role of travel narratives in the formulation of racist theories, and the imagery associated with them, was thus of some significance. They played a crucial part in the complex process of the production of images concerning west African peoples; a process which involved the construction of images within Britain, the ever evolving racist theories in Britain, and accounts from those who had travelled in west Africa. Most nineteenth-century travellers shared a fascination with the peoples they encountered in the course of their journeys. As Barnes Stevenson (1982, 10) argues, during the nineteenth century British perceptions of Africans comprised a complex and shifting blend of mythology, ethnocentric prejudice, pseudoscience, and observation. In the early nineteenth century, certain literatures, in particular, anti-slavery literature, mythologized west Africans as 'noble savages' living in an Arcadia being destroyed by slavery. However, the propaganda of abolitionism relied on a dual portrayal of Africa in its efforts to gain support: the revelation of atrocities associated with the slave trade, as well as the evocation of the image of the 'noble savage'.[4] These noble Africans were the counterparts to the English aristocrat. Such images are found occasionally in Melville's account, but are most strongly represented in Kingsley's narratives. Kingsley's evocation of this outmoded stereotype enabled her to challenge the more cynical racist images of Africans that prevailed at the end of the nineteenth century. Melville's humanitarian portrayal of Africans as simple, innocent savages was unintentionally derogatory, and such images were used later in the century by those in favour of extending British imperialism in west Africa. Kingsley herself attempted to undermine such portrayals by proving the intelligence of west Africans. However, during the 1890s, the African 'savage' became analogous not to the English aristocrat, but to the English working classes. Kingsley's response was uncommon; Colvile's contemptuous and condescending tone was more conventional for the time. Negative images of Africans, such as those in Colvile's narrative, persisted throughout the nineteenth century, but gained greater weight from the 1850s onwards. Missionary literature continued to use simplified racial stereotypes that evolved into the more cynical racism of the 1860s. As Lorimer (1978, 77–8) argues, 'the association of Africans with blackness and nakedness, especially in contrast to the fully clothed Victorians, strengthened the impression that Negroes represented unregenerate mankind, sinful and unwashed'. Africans were no longer 'noble savages' living in Eden; they were in the sinful and depraved state of those expelled from Eden, and were crying out for conversion.

Changing attitudes towards Africans were not only constituted by imperial experience, but also by changing attitudes amongst some Victorians at the time of the religious revival in mid-century. There was an increasing interest in Britain in anti-slavery in the United States, which coincided with the wider access to literature and new forms of popular entertainment such as stage and music hall in the 1850s. Popular anti-slavery tracts, such as *Uncle Tom's Cabin* and the minstrel shows, created enduring stereotypes of Africans and Afro-Americans as simple, child-like and amusing. While intended to arouse sympathy for the slaves in the United States, such portrayals also heightened the sense of difference between Britons and black people. This transition in racial attitudes was, therefore, undoubtedly connected to the changing nature of opinions concerning social status in Britain, but it was also, in part, a response to the needs of empire. JanMohammed (1985, 59–87) argues that while the overt aim of the imperial powers, as articulated by imperialist discourse, was to 'civilize' supposedly primitive peoples, there was a hidden aim to create a fixation upon the irrevocable barbarity of the African. By doing so, this provided legitimization for Britain's continued attempts to 'civilize' Africans. Thus, exploitation of Africa's resources could continue indefinitely behind the façade of Britain's position of moral superiority.

By the mid-nineteenth century, at the time of the travels of Foote and Hinderer, many Britons were developing a sense of their own racial uniqueness and, under the influence of the precepts of Social Darwinism and continental racial theories, 'Anglo-Saxonism' began to flourish. As Lorimer (1978, 11) argues, the external reality of expanding European domination over the world and its peoples encouraged some Victorian thinkers to rank racial groups by their power and status. They perceived the

African as the photographic negative of the Anglo-Saxon, and they seemed to get a clearer perception of their own supposed racial superiority from the inverted image of the black African. The notion of the 'gentleman' served to delineate the middle-class man from the working-class labourer, thus making his position in society seemingly unassailable. White skin became an essential mark of a 'gentleman', maintaining the apparent distance between the African and the Anglo-Saxon. These ideas certainly seemed to influence the portrayals of Africans by white women, especially those who were residents in west Africa. Scientific racial theory evolved from what could be termed a pseudoscience in the 1850s and 1860s, into an established science from the 1880s onwards.[5] Evolutionary theory gave this extreme form of racism added weight.

The refusal to acknowledge the richness of African history, philosophy and society can be traced back to the eighteenth century and the works of such 'authorities' as David Hume and Thomas Carlyle (Obichere, 1977, 16). However, by the 1860s the denial of African history and individuality had become an affirmation of African inferiority and backwardness. Evolutionary anthropology, if not portraying Africans as a separate species, placed the African on the lowest rung of the ladder of civilization, and created the myth that the African had more in common with apes than with Europeans. This complemented and legitimated the sense of superiority among some sections of British society, and as Brantlinger (1985, 184) argues, 'evolutionary thought almost seems calculated to legitimate imperialism'. Kingsley's narratives attempted to counter these portrayals of Africa, and her understanding that indigenous peoples had a long and rich history also led her to challenge some of the popular myths about west African customs.

After 1860, the analogy between Africans and children began to be used with increasing frequency. This clearly implied a paternalistic point of view, which denied equality between Africans and Anglo-Saxons by denying the former 'the privileges reserved for adults' (Cairns, 1965, 88).[6] Such portrayals were often used by pro-imperialists to support arguments in favour of establishing formal British imperialism in west Africa, and these images were present in the travel narratives of some women travellers. Larymore referred to west Africans as simple and child-like, and Slessor's authority in Calabar was based upon her 'mother-child' relationship with the local people. Kingsley was the only writer to openly refute and challenge these depictions in her publications.

By the 1890s, at the time of Colvile and Kingsley's travels, the image of west Africa in the imaginations of many Victorians was set. Images in missionary and exploration literature were augmented by colonial fiction, which was extremely popular at the end of the nineteenth century. As Ridley (1983, 70–1) argues, 'the archetypical picture of the cruelty and harshness of Africa [was] repeated *ad nauseum* in all colonial fiction'. Even for critics of European imperialism, such as Joseph Conrad and Paul Vigné, the landscapes of west Africa were accursed, and Europeans had 'succumbed to the evil of Africa herself rather than to the inherent brutality of imperialism'. The preference for strong rule, which arose after 1895, 'sprang from unflattering notions about savagery, infantilism, and general incompetence of the non-white inhabitants of the British Empire' (Bolt, 1971, 215). Attitudes such as these are apparent in Colvile's narrative. They were used by many pro-imperialists to justify the extension of Britain's empire in west Africa, the nature of which, by now, had more to do with strategy and with competition from other European powers than it did with a sense of moral duty to spread civilisation in a supposedly 'savage' land.

Images of west African peoples were, therefore, inextricably linked to both racist theory and imperial policy, and images constructed within Britain had important influences on the opinions of those travelling within the empire. This study has illustrated that great differences were apparent in the ways in which white women related to, and portrayed, the peoples of west Africa. Their views were often influenced by racial theories in Britain, and as these changed and evolved over time, so the attitudes of the women varied and contrasted. Therefore, most of the women formulated their descriptions of west Africans within the conventions of imperial discourse at the time of their travels. However, this was not the case with Mary Kingsley, whose theories on racial difference went completely against contemporary doctrine. As a polygenist, her ideas had more in common with pre-Darwinian ideas about race. Kingsley, and to some extent Slessor, stood apart from the other women travellers in that they acknowledged an African history and attempted, on the whole, to relate to west Africans on an individual basis. Despite this, the fact of racial difference endowed white women travellers with a sense of their own superiority. Although the attitudes of some (for example, Melville, Foote, Larymore and Colvile) were infected with nineteenth-century notions about class superiority, the responses towards west Africans of all the women of this study were premised on racial difference. Whether the women perceived relationships with west Africans in terms of Britain's paternal role (Melville, Foote), or in terms of their own personal maternal role (Hinderer, Slessor), as trading partners (Kingsley), as colonized subjects (Larymore), or whether they treated west Africans with complete contempt (Colvile), a sense of their own racial superiority framed their responses.

Anthropological observations

Informed by racial theories of the time, many nineteenth-century Britons often depicted Africa as a land where human life was particularly cheap. Indigenous African societies appeared to be structured around a random, wanton and arbitrary violence. According to many accounts, west Africa was a land of spectacular and appalling brutality in which slavery, cannibalism, ritual murder and other violent practices were common occurrences. Such visions of landscapes of fear in west Africa were connected to a peculiar Victorian desire to be titillated by tales of savagery and immorality in far-off, exotic places. As illustrated earlier, they were also motivated by a strategic need to represent Africa as a wild and uncivilized place, in need of enlightenment by British imperialism. However, Africans were only savages in the tautological sense that many Victorians were induced by their cultural background to define them as such. As images of Africans transformed from evocations of nobility to bestiality, increasingly to nineteenth-century writers Africa became an accursed land, the Biblical 'land of Cham'. West Africa remained the heart of the 'dark continent'; while travellers and explorers were unravelling the mysteries of the physical geography of west Africa, they were also creating 'clouds which obscured an adequate vision of African life and cultures' (Mazrui, 1969, 668). They were more interested in Africa as a geographical phenomenon than in Africans as social groups. As Mazrui (1969, 675) argues:

> The explorers were enchanted by mountains and rivers but were inadequately sensitised to the ways and customs of the people. Their reports of African societies therefore tended to be offered as a dramatic local background to the adventure of tracking down the sources of great waterways.

Many commentators failed to recognize the complexity of the ethnic structures of the societies that they observed. The same can be said to be true of their representations of customs and cultures. The cultures of west Africa were, and remain, complex, as were systems of beliefs and practices. However, as Idowu (1973, 83) argues, 'In the past this complexity has led would-be scholars on Africa to take refuge in meaningless or insulting terms like 'amorphous', 'savage', 'barbarous', or 'primitive' in describing what they really did not understand'. The spiritual beliefs of indigenous peoples were generally of no interest to Victorian audiences; they were merely 'pagan error'. However, spectacular festivals, human sacrifice, and trials-by-ordeal were 'curiosities', and were, therefore, recounted at length. No traveller wished to return without a story to tell. As Curtin (1965, 23–4) argues, 'The love of the extraordinary was partly the reflection of a much older European interest in the exotic – an interest blending genuine intellectual curiosity with a libidinous fascination for descriptions of other people who break with impunity the taboos of one's own society'.

As the reputation of west Africans grew ever darker, so the popular fascination in certain sections of British society with tales of cannibalism also grew. As Hammond and Jablow (1977, 94) explain, cannibalism was not an important theme in British writing before mid-century, but 'in the imperial period writers were far more addicted to cannibalism than ... Africans ever were'. Stanley was 'carried away in his zealous horror of anthropophagy and repeated every tale of cannibal tribes that he heard in addition to creating quite a number of his own'; Winwood Reade 'sprinkled cannibals around West Africa rather like raisins in a cake'. Although there is little evidence to suggest that cannibalism was widespread in west Africa, the theme provided a new variation on images of the 'beastly savage'. The spiritual beliefs of

Africans, their nakedness and supposed cannibalism formed a syndrome; 'nakedness may well imply that there is also cannibalism and that the people are 'fetish-worshippers'. A clothed cannibal is somehow a contradiction in terms' (ibid., 36–7). These ideas influenced the depictions of African customs by white women travellers, and especially Colvile and Kingsley. Colvile tended to view most customs she witnessed in a negative light, and made several allusions to the supposed savage and cannibalistic tendencies of west Africans. Kingsley, on the other hand, attempted to desensationalize the issue of cannibalism by using humour and irony in her comments about it. She constantly undermined images of Africans as savages in her narratives by referring to their rationality, common sense, and gentle nature. Here again, Kingsley attempted to undermine prevailing preconceptions about west Africans.

Colvile apart, most women travellers tended to avoid the sensational reports of west African customs that were often apparent in other imperialist discourses. Textual constraints may have been a factor in this, prohibiting the women from discussing those violent customs they encountered or had described to them. However, it may be that the nature of the journeys of these women, and the distance between themselves and those women whom they observed, meant that they were unfamiliar with the lifestyles of west Africans. Therefore, they remained unexposed to what many people in Britain perceived to be the most violent of west African customs. Certainly, writers such as Melville, Foote and Colvile did not seem interested in documenting or understanding the customs of the peoples they encountered, and their experiences in the course of their travels merely confirmed their pre-conceptions. However, Kingsley, and to some extent Slessor and Larymore, occasionally challenged European misconceptions about indigenous customs and the depiction of indigenous peoples as barbarous and savage. Therefore, although most of the women of this study were influenced by the racial theories at the time of their travels and the prejudices implicit in these, the images they created of west Africans and their customs were often very different from those found in other imperialist discourses. The complexities of their representations, and the varied nature of their responses suggests that the context of their journeys, and the individual characteristics of each woman, were as significant as gender in shaping their visions.

West African women

A feature of nineteenth-century narratives about Africa was the anonymity of the indigenous peoples themselves; African women were particularly anonymous. Very few travel or exploration accounts referred to African women, and those that did tended to reinforce the twin stereotypes of the oppressed wife in a polygamous household, or the lascivious female, associated with the prostitute in Britain. The middle-class Victorian reverence for the virtuous wife meant that African societies were condemned for condoning infant marriage, for producing child-mothers, for treating women as slaves when they were adults, and for subjecting widows to trial-by-ordeal (Bolt, 1971, 138). The comparative nudity of west African women was considered indicative of their unrestrained sexuality; the blame for the sexual excesses of European men within the imperial setting was thus shifted onto African women. The few descriptions of African women that did exist were, therefore, formulated within the framework of enduring stereotypes. Little effort was made to describe the lives of African women within the context of their own cultures and societies.

Images of women were central to the intellectual and ideological discussion of the non-European 'other'. The 'plight' of African women was depicted, however erroneously, as inferior to the situation of women in Britain. Missionaries, travellers and reformers 'moralised and dramatised rather than analyzed or understood the legal, familial or cultural frameworks of women's lives' (de Groot, 1991). As with other aspects of the popular geographies of west Africa, these images were not rooted in empirical observation but in anthropological theory, fictional writing and imaginative description, as well as the visual images generated in popular journalism, art and advertising. There were, of course, many variations and contradictions in the representations of women in imperialist discourse; they were depicted as exotic, as oppressed victims, as sex objects or as the most ignorant and backward members of primitive societies. As de Groot (1991, 115) argues, these representations of women played a central part in the conceptualization of African societies and European male views of their relationship to those societies.[7] They also obscured the complex circumstances of the lives of African women, and ignored the fact that comparison with the lives of British women could well be to the advantage of the former. Above all, de Groot (1991, 116–7) maintains that images of African women were expressions of power relations rather than expressions of ignorance or bigotry:

> The material and cultural dominance underlying European views of non-Europeans, and in particular non-European women, was a matter not only of the control wielded by powerful groups of European men in a world system, but of connected patterns of gender and class power sustaining male authority over women and the control of propertied and privileged groups over the labouring and popular classes.

The obsessive depiction of these images of 'femininity' and 'foreignness' as simultaneously attractive and subordinate expressed the contradictions inherent in popular geographies of empire, but also the imperatives of class-gender-race which provide the framework for analysis of white women's descriptions of their west African counterparts.

Contemporary constructions of gender were certainly of some importance in white women's portrayals of African women. Their femininity allowed British women access to west African women, and, in turn, their descriptions of the domestic sphere in west African communities facilitated the affirmation of their own impeccable femininity. The transgressive nature of their travels was, therefore, partially concealed by their location of parts of these journeys and of their own interests in the domestic sphere. This is particularly the case with the residents and missionaries. White women travellers could view the lives of west African women in relation to their own lives, and Larymore and Kingsley, in particular, were convinced that in many cases west African women enjoyed greater freedoms than their British counterparts. Therefore, by being able to identify with west African women on the basis of a shared femininity, white women travellers sometimes challenged the representations in other imperialist discourses of the time. However, the fact remains that within the imperial setting, a common female experience did not transcend racial difference in most representations of indigenous women. British women travellers perceived themselves in terms of racial superiority. This is reflected in the fact that few of them developed close personal relationships with west African women, they did not question their right to enter the women's compounds or harems, nor their right to appropriate, objectify and represent indigenous women in their narratives. Furthermore, many British women travellers perceived themselves in terms of class superiority, and this was particularly apparent in the accounts of those women residents who employed west Africans as servants. The only exception to this was, perhaps, Mary Slessor. She did seem to have a profound sense of personal affinity with west African women on the grounds of a common female experience, and spent most of her years in Calabar working with west African women to improve their rights and opportunities. Therefore, representations of west African women by British women travellers were intersected by differences of both 'race' and class, and a knowledge of the personalities of each individual, as well as the context of their travels, is important in gaining an insight into the images that they produced.

Interpretations of the 'dark continent'

The four themes of landscape, 'race', anthropological observations and indigenous women, which recur in women's descriptions of west Africa, formed part of a broader metaphor of the 'dark continent'. This had a particular resonance during the nineteenth century. Unlike the Middle East, where European contact, and thus curiosity, had a very long history, west Africa was a relatively new phenomenon in the imaginations of the British. As a consequence of its novelty, the image of the 'dark continent' had a powerful hold on many nineteenth-century British imaginations. However, this study has illustrated that the 'dark continent' was not a monolithic concept; it was formed by a complex production of knowledge and, therefore, open to a variety of interpretations. The archive used in this study has revealed the complexities of this metaphor.

The images created by women travellers were rooted in relationships of power and formed part of the process by which British scholars, scientists, explorers, administrators, and so on, documented, detailed, mapped and appropriated imperial territories. The fundamental flaw in Said's *Orientalism* was the homogenization of what he referred to as 'the West', which created a binary opposition of Orient/Occident and replicated the very model that he was attempting to critique.[8] The themes of this book have illustrated that there were a variety of interpretations of the 'dark continent' by white women travellers during the nineteenth century. Despite the differences in the periods in which they travelled, all the women of this study referred directly to Africa as the 'dark continent', or used the metaphor in allusions to images of darkness, death, disease or primitiveness in their descriptions of landscapes, peoples and customs. However, their interpretations of this metaphor, as revealed by their narratives, were complex. In the publications of Melville and Foote, west Africa was at once a primitive paradise and land of disease and death. There are similar depictions in Hinderer's narrative. Thus the metaphor of the 'dark continent' was not consistent in these accounts. In particular, the seasonality of the climate played an important role in how women travellers viewed west Africa differently at various times. Colvile's west Africa was the antecedent of Conrad's *Heart of Darkness*, a land of savagery and cannibalism beyond redemption. For Larymore, the 'dark continent' was a land waiting to be civilized and enlightened by British imperialism. Only Slessor, and, in particular, Kingsley challenged the metaphor of the 'dark continent' in any great measure. However, even these women did not resist evoking this metaphor on occasions – Slessor in response to some of the brutality she witnessed and her own sufferings (which were due to climatic conditions and were, therefore, seasonal), and Kingsley in her discussion of Scheele's maps of disease. She wrote (1982, 3), 'There is no mistaking what he means by black ... and black you'll find they colour West Africa from above Sierra Leone to below the Congo'. Despite this, Kingsley proceeded to dismantle her own preconceptions on arrival in west Africa, and through her subsequent publications she challenged more often than she confirmed the metaphor of the 'dark continent'. She tended to be more ambivalent than the other women; west Africa was her kind of place, but she understood that it was not a suitable, or desirable, environment for all.

Women traveller's responses to west Africa: differences and similarities

It is apparent that there are both similarities and contrasts in the travel narratives of British women in west Africa, which go some way towards disrupting essentialist notions of gendered genres of imperial writing. The notion of distance is important when considering these similarities and differences. The relative distance between British women as observers and describers, and the peoples and landscapes that they represented, had important influences on the nature of the imagery they created. In different ways, Kingsley and Slessor attempted to gain in-depth knowledge and understanding by locating themselves within west African landscapes and communities. This was particularly apparent in Kingsley's landscape descriptions, which were almost transcendental in nature, and which demonstrated Kingsley's desire to blend into the landscapes through which she travelled. Kingsley also travelled into the rainforests, accompanied only by African guides, and on a few occasions stayed overnight in west African villages (although for the most part she remained in the coastal towns and mission houses). Her intention was to observe landscapes, peoples and customs from the 'inside' in order to gain an understanding of all things west African; proximity was a primary concern. Similarly, Slessor decided to move away from the European mission stations, to locate in African villages, and to adopt a west African lifestyle in order, firstly, to understand the customs of Calabar and, secondly, to attempt to eradicate the worst of these without destroying the fabric of indigenous social life. This proximity to both the landscapes and peoples of west Africa was in marked contrast to the other women travellers, and it may have been a factor in inspiring the sympathy and fondness that both Kingsley and Slessor held for west Africa and its peoples.

Although the nature of her role in west Africa necessitated that Anna Hinderer live with the peoples of Ibadan, she did not share Slessor's affinity with west Africans, nor did she 'go native' to extent that Slessor adapted her lifestyle. Melville, Foote and Larymore perceived their residences as temporary; west Africa never became 'home' for them in the same way as it did in material terms for Slessor, who lived there for most of her life and who died there, or as it did in spiritual terms for Kingsley. Kingsley's travels were a fundamentally liberating experience and she seemed, from her writings between 1895 and 1900, never to lose her desire to return to west Africa. The only way that Larymore could make Nigeria feel a little like home was by attempting to impose English gardens upon the landscape. Zélie Colvile was the most removed from west Africa, viewing it from the decks of a steamer, and taking only brief excursions inland by way of the Oil Rivers. As a pure tourist travelling during the period of high imperialism in Africa, it is perhaps of no surprise that Colvile was the most dismissive and contemptuous among British women travellers in west Africa. Whereas Kingsley and Slessor could understand and even empathize with indigenous customs, and could feel at home in the unfamiliar physical environments, many of the other women remained detached and critical. The distance between observer and observed, therefore, had enormous implications for the images contained in the travel accounts of British women.

The relationships between several of the women in this study and the peoples and environments that they encountered were often deeply ambivalent.[9] For example,

Slessor, Kingsley and Larymore did not wish to see the landscapes of west Africa altered and spoiled by the presence of the British, but they failed to account for the impact they themselves were having on these landscapes. Larymore was aware of her own ambivalence; she was part of a British military expedition to establish an administrative network in Nigeria, and she was aware that this would alter drastically the landscapes and pace of life in Nigeria, yet at the same time she bemoaned these changes. Women travellers realized that their presence in west Africa was facilitated by the same British imperialism that posed a threat to those very features of west Africa that they took pleasure in. This ambivalence was apparent in Kingsley's expressed desire to see indigenous customs remain unchanged. She paid no attention to the impact that she, as a white woman who employed guides and engaged in trade, had on these customs. She did not consider the impacts that her support for drawing west Africa into Britain's trading sphere would have on these customs, and believed naively that market forces and capitalism would benefit Britain and west Africa equally. Finally, Kingsley did not contemplate what the effects of closer contacts with European anthropologists and other scientists, which she also advocated, would have on west African cultures. Similarly, Slessor regretted the changes that the British had wrought in southern Nigeria, but did not consider that she herself, by establishing mission stations in the interior and a network of 'native courts', had helped lay the foundations for these very changes. Therefore, these women may have been critical of certain aspects of British imperialism and the effects they were having on west Africa, but ultimately they shared in British imperial power and authority, and this facilitated their own liberation during their time in west Africa.

One obvious reason for the differences in the geographical knowledges created by these women lies in the fact that they travelled in different regions of west Africa. These included Sierra Leone, the region of Lagos, Calabar and the Oil Rivers further to the east, Fernando Po and the Congo Français to the southeast, the central areas of Yoruba, and the emirates in the sub-Saharan regions to the north. These geographical variations, and the different landscapes and peoples encountered would obviously create variations in description. However, this would not necessarily produce variations in how the women reacted to and represented west African environments and peoples. The attitudes of the women themselves, and the external factors informing these attitudes, are of critical importance. Thus, as discussed previously, the temporal variation of their journeys becomes significant, particularly in relation to the changing nature of British imperial culture throughout the nineteenth century.

In addition to these external differences, there were also differences in the women themselves as individuals that influenced their writings. Social class was an important factor. It was suggested in Chapter 1 that the backgrounds of these women varied significantly. Zélie Colvile and Elizabeth Melville both had aristocratic backgrounds; Mrs Foote, Anna Hinderer, Constance Larymore and Mary Kingsley were very much middle class; Mary Slessor had a working-class upbringing. These differences in social class were compounded by such factors as marital status (Kingsley and Slessor were both unmarried), and whether or not the women had children with them in west Africa (Elizabeth Melville actually gave birth to her first child in Sierra Leone). Furthermore, there were different reasons behind their decisions to travel to west Africa. Some were missionaries, some were the wives of military men or administrators, and some were independent travellers. These varying roles in turn influenced their motives for travel. Many travelled out of a sense of duty. Some, like Zélie Colvile travelled as tourists. Others such as Mary Kingsley undertook scientific research during their travels. Many, if not all, were seeking some measure of personal liberation and an extension of their experiences that would not have been possible in Victorian Britain. What becomes clear is that the personal motives for travelling to west Africa were often complex and, therefore, unique to each woman. The various roles that the women performed and the personal motivations for their journeys had some bearing on the geographical knowledges of west Africa that each woman constructed.

Subaltern histories of geography and imperialism?

Perhaps the major geographical significance of travel narratives in any period of history lies in the images they contain, and the ways in which the authors' visions are projected onto the lands through which they travel. Leading geographers at the end of the nineteenth century recognized the importance of descriptive material in securing Britain's empire, and the ways in which it augmented the hard, empirical, geographical facts based on measurement and mapping. As Richards (1993, 21) argues, geography was a necessary but not sufficient tool for realizing territory; it must always be accompanied by 'thick' description (this was discussed in Chapter 3). Richards states that the British empire was loose and fragmented, and was not controlled by any central authoritative body (the Foreign Office at this time was small and overworked). The 'knowledge' that was collected about the empire, both empirical and descriptive, was critical to British imperial culture; the 'control of knowledge' was clearly allied to the 'control of the empire', and helped produce the 'myth' of the British Empire as a controllable and manageable whole (ibid., 1–9).

In the light of this, although it may be difficult to make a case for the inclusion of women in historiographies of geography in the disciplinary sense during the late-nineteenth century, women certainly contributed to geographical thought and knowledges at this time. Women travellers may not have 'discovered', mapped and explored 'new' territories, but they did add to the imagery constructed about the empire. Moreover, they influenced how this imagery was mapped onto the imaginations of the majority of people in Britain who did not have first-hand experience of areas of the world such as west Africa. The fact that they experienced places that many people in Britain could never experience, and that they conveyed impressions of these places to their readers, makes the work of these women 'geographic'. They are not the 'heroines' of the foundation of the discipline of geography – they did not define themselves as geographers and they cannot be claimed in any disciplinary sense. Several feminist geographers have attempted to define women travel writers as geographers, but one could argue that they could equally be claimed by other disciplines such as literary criticism, anthropology or history. It is the contention here that they should not be 'claimed' by any single discipline, but that the narratives they produced can be analyzed within and across a range of disciplines. However, their works are important to geographers today because of the geographical knowledges of imperial lands that they contain, and because of their contribution to British imperial culture at the time of publication. An emphasis on the creation of images of territories beyond Europe, their importance to imperial culture, and the part that women played in their construction, perhaps facilitates a more critical analysis of histories of geographical thought than those that have gone before. Women travellers were not feminist heroines whose narratives can be viewed uncritically; they were deeply involved in the production of 'knowledge' and, therefore, of 'power' in Britain. The publications by these women, and their own liberation and achievements, must be viewed within the context of British imperial culture.

A study of the imaginative geographies of empire is not only significant in an historical context; the production of imagery of territories beyond Europe also has some relevance today. The power to label and to define what constitutes 'the Other' still lies in the developed world, which has produced what some scholars refer to as a 'crisis of representation' within geography (Duncan and Sharp, 1993; Radcliffe, 1994). This study has focused upon representations of west Africa during the nineteenth century, a period in which it tended to be depicted in various imperialist discourses as the heart of the 'dark continent'. It has analyzed, particularly, how women travellers constructed west Africa as a place in their travel narratives. As Jarosz (1992, 105) argues, the authority to construct Africa in various discourses is still located in the former imperial powers, and the tradition continues today. Historical images of Africa inform contemporary representations of the continent; 'the metaphor of Africa as the Dark Continent continually (re)makes and represents the continent as Other'. Images of famine and a Malthusian population crisis, and images of Africa as a land of environmental catastrophe, disease and death still have a resonance today. The most recent re-emergences of this metaphor have occurred in academic and popular mass media accounts of AIDS in Africa (ibid., 111–13); they have also re-emerged in images of the appalling violence in Rwanda, which is portrayed not as in some part a legacy of imperialism, but as a symptom of spectacular African barbarity.[10] Thus the validity of exploring historical constructions of west Africa as a place is apparent since this process continues to a large extent in contemporary academic and popular discourses.

This book perhaps has rather limited ambition, and is based on a small sample of women who travelled in a particular area during a specific historical period. However, this has allowed for a detailed understanding of the broader context of each travel narrative, it permits a more specific exploration of the geographical knowledges contained therein, and it avoids references to an essential 'feminine' experience of empire and 'feminine' genre of travel writing. It also facilitates the incorporation of women and their experiences in histories of geographical thought and imperialism. The archive explored here is a valuable one; many of the narratives have not been reprinted and have rarely been studied. Few women wrote about west Africa during the nineteenth century; the fact that the women studied here were among the few to have travelled in west Africa, and to have recounted their experiences in published travel accounts, makes these all the more valuable. They provide scholars today with a unique insight into the complexities of women's experiences of empire and the ways in which they contributed to imperial culture during the nineteenth century. The travel accounts analyzed in this study are important for this reason alone.

In addition, the chapters of this book have attempted to produce a more nuanced reading of one aspect of imperial culture than has often been formulated to date. The focus is primarily on difference, on the intersections of various relationships of power, and on the breaking down of binary oppositions frequently articulated in histories of imperial culture. Femininity is viewed as complex and contested arena, a fractured and disputed state in which women had an important and even formative role to play. Chapter 7 also deals with the possibilities of the agency and resistance of colonized peoples, evidence of which is apparent within dominant discourses. Regarding imperial discourse as multivocal and heterogeneous allows for the uncovering of evidence of different agencies that may, in fact, contest the power relations of hegemonic discourse. White women's gender-specific representations did not have counter-hegemonic potential because these women were all automatically anti-racist. Rather, 'it is the very contradictions thrown up by the assumption (then and now) that women made no contribution to, or had no active role in, imperial expansion that allowed women the positionality from which a counter-hegemonic discourse could be enunciated' (Lewis, 1996, 20). The women of this study certainly did play an important role in the history of imperialism in west Africa, and in the construction of geographical knowledges from the mid-nineteenth century onwards. However, they did so in ways that were often very different and that were shaped by a variety of motivations. One thing all these women shared, however, was their position of authority vis-à-vis indigenous peoples. As Ware (1996, 154) argues:

> In order to be alert to these multi-layered images of femininity and to understand their relationship to the past, feminism needs to reconstruct histories of ideas

217

about women with a perspective that takes in not just the shifting parameters of gender itself but also the interrelated concepts of ethnic, cultural and class difference. The danger that arises from overlooking the 'often silent and hidden operations' of racial domination throughout women's histories poses a threat to the survival of feminism as a political movement. For it is partly through the past that we are able to understand how those categories of difference between women and men, white and non-white, have emerged and how, why and where they continue to retain significance today.

It is in this spirit that this book has attempted to bring together ideas about critical histories, the debates surrounding feminist histories, and postcolonial theories about the production of knowledge, to suggest ways in which we might construct critical and less exclusive histories of geography and imperialism. It has endeavoured to recount those 'minor pasts', primarily of white women but also, to some extent, of those people that they discursively represented, that have previously been hidden from history. These histories are subordinated or 'subaltern' pasts (Chakrabarty, 1998, 18). As Chakrabarty argues:

> They are marginalised not because anyone consciously intends to marginalise them but because they represent moments or points at which the very archive that the historian of a (marginalised) group mines in order to bring the history of that group into a relationship with a larger narrative (of class, of the nation, etc.) develops a degree of intractability with respect to the very aims of professional history.

In other words, to return to a point made in the Introduction, disciplinary boundaries and practices (be they in history, geography, ethnography, etc) by their very existence sometimes prohibit the inclusion of marginalized identities and knowledges. This book has attempted to explore strategies through which these boundaries can be overcome, whilst always being aware of the contradictions in these strategies. Ultimately, perhaps all one can do is test the limits of theory and the implications of all critical practice, including our own.

With this in mind, there is a need for continual questioning of the ways in which the discipline of geography is territorialized and bounded, and the implications this has for those left on the outside. As Barnett (1997, 137) suggests, questions about institutional positionality and academic authority have to be kept squarely in sight when discussing the problems of representing the struggles and agency of marginalized social groups. Chapter 7 suggests strategies to avoid the epistemic violence that inflects histories of geography and imperialism, and simultaneously writes out the agency of white women and of colonized peoples. These strategies are not without problems and contradictions, but they need not be disabling. Indeed, it is important that they are not disabling, since a history of white women, nineteenth-century geography and imperialism is a poor one if it continues to erase the agency of colonized peoples.

There is, of course, a final paradox. Postcolonial theory, upon which I draw and which I feel is of political significance, originated in the Third World as a critique of western hegemony. The question remains, is the engagement by western academics with postcolonial theory simply a form of re-colonization, or is it now a case that 'we' are more willing to recognize the limits of our knowledge and be receptive to different ideas and different voices? Does this engagement de-centre hegemonic knowledge forms, or does it merely incorporate and appropriate marginal voices into the centre? These questions are rhetorical, and there are a variety of opinions about such questions within current debates. The point remains that feminist geographers have been successful in critique from within, in employing alternative strategies to bring about change within the discipline in terms of epistemologies, theories and practice. However, there is still a long way to go before the old imperial discipline of geography can be said to have engaged fully with critiques of hegemonic knowledge production. Barnett (1995, 419) suggests that those claiming to explore the history of geography in order to cast light on the state of the discipline today are perhaps avoiding looking in the most obvious places. As Bhabha (1994) argues, we can re-read the past by looking more critically at the present. Analyzing critically the contemporary construction of histories of geography and how the past is still discursively constituted in masculine and eurocentric terms is thus of importance. Reflecting on our own ambivalent positions as critical academics, both in terms of the research process and in relation to broader questions about power and knowledge, is only a beginning.

Notes

1. Despite this some writers, such as George Eliot, elucidated the fantasy of this vision of the past. Eliot pointed out that there were rural slums among the tidy hamlets, and that the poor, who were now trapped in urban slums, had never lived in cottages with gardens, but had worked other people's land whilst burdened by the poor rates.
2. The image of 'feminine' beauty concealing hidden danger paralleled the image of the syphilitic prostitute that was powerful throughout the nineteenth century. This was epitomized in Émile Zola's *Nana*, where Nana's alluring face/mask eventually succumbs to the disease, and Zola describes at the end of the novel in gruesome detail how her face putrefies and decomposes before she dies. Where Zola's imagery was symbolic of the disease at the heart of French

society, images of putrefaction and decomposition were integral to representations of west Africa as the heart of the 'dark continent' (Gilman 1985, 234–7).

3. Anna Davin (1978) documents the changing attitudes from the middle of the nineteenth century to the early twentieth century towards the role of women in the empire. For example, she notes that the recommended reasons for marriage changed from the 1860s, when a woman was advised to seek a partner who would support, protect, guide and help her, to 1914, when the three main objects of marriage were the reproduction of the race, the maintenance of social purity, and the mutual comfort of the couple.

4. The latter image had a long history. Shakespeare's Othello and Marlow's Tamburlaine were both barbaric noblemen. As Hammond and Jablow (1977, 18) suggest, Aphra Behn brought the 'noble savage' to Africa with her novelette *Oroonoko*, whose main character, as the victim of white men, became the model for the 'noble savage'. As Miller (1985, 5) argues, in the late eighteenth and early nineteenth centuries, Africa was 'made to bear a double burden, of monstrousness and nobility, all imposed by a deeper condition of difference and instability'.

5. For a full account of the formation of the Anthropological Society, see Rainger, 1978, 51–70.

6. There was also an association between blackness and madness. As Gilman (1985a, 140) argues, it was believed that 'the 'simple nature' of blacks and their 'child-like essence' did not permit them to function well in the complexities of the modern world and predisposed them to insanity'.

7. De Groot also offers an interesting (and at present under-researched) link between these depictions, imperial policies towards women, and policies that shape the lives of women in contemporary 'Third World' societies.

8. Said (1994, xi–xii) himself has since recognized this problem, and has explored it in some depth.

9. On ambivalence, see Alison Blunt (1994, 23–6), who draws extensively on the work of Homi Bhabha (1985).

10. The social inequities that exist between the Tutsi and the Hutu are not far removed from those that existed between the aristocracy and the proletariat in early nineteenth-century Britain, although in the Rwandan case they are complicated by ethnicity. However, British society was allowed to evolve naturally. The working classes gradually gained more rights and freedoms, primarily through parliamentary reform, and the threat of revolution was abated. In contrast, Rwandan ethnic and social divisions were frozen in time, first by Germany and then by Belgium; they were even encouraged in a policy of divide and rule. When the European colonists withdrew in the middle of the twentieth century, they left a country in which social inequalities had been

frozen and exacerbated for at least 150 years. Although the story of Rwanda is a complex one, this must play a major part in explaining the continual ferment since independence, and the atrocities that occurred in the country during the 1990s. Disturbingly, right-wing historians and political commentators such as Andrew Roberts (1994) see such tragedies as a justification for a new imperialism. Roberts writes, 'Imperialism, were we able to throw off our politically correct notions of national self-determination for people who patently cannot exercise it properly, is an idea whose time has come'.

Archival sources

Zélie Colvile

Blackwood Papers (1893–1900), National Library of Scotland, Mss. 4598, 4628, 4672, 4698, 26490–560

Mrs Henry Grant Foote

Letter from John Abel Smith to Layard on her behalf, Foreign Office Papers, British Library, Ms. 39106 f. 425
Foote to Foreign Office, 9/5/1861 and 10/5/1861, Public Records Office
Foote to Lord John Russell, 8/5/1861, Parliamentary Papers 1862, Public Records Office

Anna Hinderer

David Hinderer Collection, Yoruba Mission/C.M.S. Papers, Birmingham University Library, CA 2/049/9, 12, 14, 20, 27
Church Missionary Intelligencers, 1857–69, British Library
Proceedings of the Church Missionary Society, 1851–71, British Library

Mary Kingsley

Chamberlain Papers, Birmingham University Library
Matthew Nathan Papers, 1868–1939, Bodleian Library, Oxford
Miss E.M. Bowdler Sharp Papers, 1893–99, British Library
Macmillan Correspondence, Macmillan Archive, British Library, Mss. 54914, 54915
Günther Collection, British Museum (Natural History) Library
Letters to Mrs. Brownlow, Cambridge University Library, Ms. Add. 7649 (E)
Letters to Mrs. Cowell, Cambridge University Library, Ms. Add. 6377 (E)
Letters to James Frazer and wife, Cambridge University Library
A.C. Haddon Papers, Cambridge University Library
Microfilm of material in National Library of Ireland, letters to Alice Stopford Green, Cambridge University Library, Ms. 117

Letters to Mrs Evans, Highgate Literary and Scientific Institution
Letters to Mrs Rose, Highgate Literary and Scientific Institution
Dennett, R.E, 'Miss M.H. Kingsley's visit to Cabinda 1893', unpublished manuscript, Highgate Literary and Scientific Institution
St Loe Strachey Papers, House of Lords Record Office
John Holt Papers, Rhodes House Library, Oxford, Mss. Afr. s. 1525, boxes 16, 23, 24
Letters to E.B. Tylor and wife, Rhodes House Library, Oxford
Letters to J. Saxon Mills, Rhodes House Library, Oxford, Mss. Afr. s. 4.ff, 37–59
Lugard Papers, Rhodes House Library, Oxford
Letters from R.B. Blaize to A.S. Green, Royal African Society
Mary Kingsley, 'Gardening in Africa', Scraps 894, Royal African Society
Reviews of Mary Kingsley's publications, Royal African Society
Reviews of Mary Kingsley's publications, Royal Commonwealth Society Library
Obituaries and reminiscences, Royal Commonwealth Society Library
Letters to John Keltie and Marion Farquarson, Royal Geographical Society, Correspondence 1881–1910
Letters from John Keltie to Mary Kingsley, Royal Geographical Society, Correspondence 1881–1910
Letters to Violet Roy, Royal Geographical Society, Correspondence 1881–1910
Letters to Reginald Maudslay, Royal Geographical Society, Correspondence 1881–1910
Letters to Gertrude Bradbury, Royal Geographical Society, Correspondence 1881–1910
Beth Urquhart's Collection: Correspondence with Joseph Chamberlain, Christy, Edward Clodd, Lord Cromer, Thiselton Dyer, James Frazer, Mrs Frazer, Professor Haddon, Mrs Haddon, Hartland, Alice Stopford Green, Dr Günther, Stephen Gwynn, Mrs Gwynn, Ling Roth, Mrs Ling Roth, Sir Alfred Lyall, E.D. Morel, John Holt, Matthew Nathan, St Loe Strachey, Sir Edward Tylor, Mrs Tylor

Constance Larymore

Colonial Office List, Public Records Office

Mary Slessor

Missionary Record of the United Presbyterian Church, 1854–1879, British Library

The Women's Missionary Magazine of the United Free Church of Scotland, 1901–15, British Library, P.P. 1030 bh

Mary Slessor Collection, Dundee City Archives

Audio tape of Mary Slessor (1906), Dundee City Library

Correspondence with Charles Partridge, Dundee City Library

Diaries, 1912 and 1914, Dundee Museum, McMannus Galleries

Letters from Calabar 1878–1915, Dundee Museum, McMannus Galleries

Cairns Papers, National Library of Scotland, Ms. Acc. 6825, 5932: letters from Mary Slessor to Mrs Findlay

Scottish Foreign Missions Record: letters to Mary Slessor from United Presbyterian Church, National Library of Scotland, Mss. 7654–7959

Presbyterian Church of Nigeria Papers: letters from Mary Slessor to Mrs Peebles 1884–1891, National Library of Scotland

Kathleen A. Goldie Papers: three scripts of broadcasts on Slessor, 1914, 1953–4, National Library of Scotland, Acc 8078, nos. 401, 413, 573

Scottish United Presbyterian Church Missionary Record 1847–57, 1881–99, National Library of Scotland

Missionary Record of the United Church of Scotland 1900–1916, National Library of Scotland

Edward Morris Falk Correspondence, Rhodes House Library, Oxford

Letter from Slessor to Irvine, 1903, St. Andrew's Hall Missionary College, Selly Oak, Birmingham

Bibliography

Adewoye, O. (1977), *The Judicial System in Southern Nigeria, 1854–1954*, London: Longman

Agiri, B. (1981), 'Slavery in Yoruba society in the nineteenth century', in Lovejoy, P. (ed.), *The Ideology of Slavery in Africa*, London: Sage

Ahmad, A. (1992), *In Theory: Classes, Nations, Literatures*, London: Verso

Aitken, M. (1987), *A Girdle Round the Earth*, London: Constable

Aitken, S.C. and Zonn, L.E. (eds) (1994), *Place, Power, Situation and Spectacle: A Geography of Film*, Lanham, Maryland: Rowman and Littlefield

Ajaji, J.F.A. and Crowder, M. (eds) (1974), *History of West Africa, Volume 2*, London: Longman

Ajayi, W.O. (1959), *A History of the Yoruba Mission 1843–1880*, unpublished. M.A. thesis, Bristol University

Alatas, S.H. (1977), *The Myth of the Lazy Native*, London: Cass

Alexander, C. (1989), *One Dry Season: In the Footsteps of Mary Kingsley*, London: Bloomsbury

Alloula, M. (1986), *The Colonial Harem*, Manchester: Manchester University Press

Amos, V. and Parmar, P. (1984), 'Challenging imperial feminism', *Feminist Review*, 17, 3–19

Arens, W. (1979), *The Man-Eating Myth. Anthropology and Anthropophagy*, London: Oxford University Press

Ashcroft B., Griffiths, G. and Tiffin, H. (1989), *The Empire Writes Back. Theory and Practice in Post-Colonial Literatures*, London: Routledge,

Ashfar, H. (ed.) (1991), *Women, Development and Survival in the Third World*, London: Tavistock

Auerbach, N. (1986), *Romantic Imprisonment*, New York: Columbia University Press

Ayendele, E.A. (1966), *The Missionary Impact on Modern Nigeria, 1842–1914. A Political and Social Analysis*, London: Longman, Green and Co.

Barnes, T. and Duncan, J. (eds) (1992), *Writing Worlds: Discourse, Text and Metaphor in the Representation of Language*, London: Routledge

Barnes Stevenson, C. (1982), *Victorian Women Travel Writers in Africa*, Boston: Twayne

Barnett, C. (1995), 'Awakening the dead: who needs the history of geography?' *Transactions of the Institute of British Geographers*, 20, 4

Barnett, C. (1997), '"Sing along with the common people": politics, postcolonialism, and other figures', *Environment and Planning D: Society and Space*, 15, 137–54

Barnett, C. (1998), 'Impure and worldly geography. The Africanist discourse of the Royal Geographical Society', *Transactions of the Institute of British Geographers*, 23, 2, 239–52

Beidelman, T.O. (1982), *Colonial Evangelism: A Socio-Historical Study of an East African Mission at the Grassroots*, Bloomington: Indiana University Press

Bell, M., Butlin, R. and Heffernan, M. (eds) (1995), *Geography and Imperialism 1820-1940*, Manchester: Manchester University Press

Bell, M. (1995) 'A woman's place in "a white man's country". Rights, duties and citizenship for the "new" South Africa, ca.1902', *Ecumene*, 2, 129–48

Bell, M. (1995) '"Citizenship not charity": Violet Markham on nature, society and the state in Britain and South Africa', in Bell, M., Butlin, R. and Heffernan, M. (eds), *Geography and Imperialism 1820-1940* Manchester: Manchester University Press, 189–220

Bell, M. and McEwan, C. (1996) 'The admission of women Fellows to the Royal Geographical Society, 1892-1914: the controversy and the outcome', *The Geographical Journal*, 162, 3, 295–312

Berman, E. (1995), 'The abnormal distribution of development policies for southern women and children', *Gender, Place and Culture*, 2, 1, 21–36

Bertens, H. (1995), *The Idea of the Postmodern. A History*, Routledge, London

Bhabha, H. (1984), 'Of mimicry and man: the ambivalence of colonial discourse' *October*, 28, 125–33

Bhabha, H. (1985), 'Signs taken for wonders: questions of ambivalence and authority under a tree outside Delhi, May 1817', *Critical Inquiry*, 12, 144–165

Bhabha, H. (1994), *The Location of Culture*, London: Routledge

Birkett, D. (1987a), 'An Independent Woman in West Africa: the Case of Mary Kingsley', unpublished. Ph.D. thesis, School of Oriental and African Studies, University of London

Birkett, D. (1987b), 'West Africa's Mary Kingsley', *History Today*, May, 10–16

Birkett, D. (1987c), 'Networking West Africa', review article, *African Affairs*, 87, 115–19

Birkett, D. (1989), *Spinsters Abroad: Victorian Lady Explorers*, Oxford: Blackwell

Birkett, D. and Wheelwright, J. (1990), '"How could she?" Unpalatable facts and feminist heroines', *Gender and History*, 2, 1, 49–57

Birkett, D. (1992), *Mary Kingsley. Imperial Adventuress*, London: Macmillan

Bishop, P. (1989), *The Myth of Shangri-La*, London: Athlone Press

Blake, S.L. (1990), 'What difference does gender make?' *Women's Studies International Forum*, 13, 4, 347–55

Blaut, J.M. (1993), *The Colonizer's Model of the World: Geographical Diffusionism and Eurocentric History*, New York: Guilford Press

Blunt, A. (1994a), *Travel, Gender, and Imperialism. Mary Kingsley and West Africa*, New York and London: Guilford Press

Blunt, A. (1994b), 'Mapping, authorship and authority: reading Mary Kingsley's landscape descriptions', in Blunt, A. and Rose, G. (eds), *Writing Women and Space: Colonial and Post-Colonial Geographies*, New York: Guilford Press, 51–72

Blunt, A. and Rose, G. (eds) (1994), *Writing Women and Space: Colonial and Post-Colonial Geographies*, New York: Guilford Press

Blyden, E.W. (1901), *The African Society and Miss Mary H. Kingsley*, London

Bolt, C. (1971), *Victorian Attitudes to Race*, London: Routledge & Kegan Paul

Bonnett, A. (1997), 'Geography, race and Whiteness: invisible traditions and current challenges', *Area* 29, 3, 193–99

Bradley, I. (1976), *The Call to Seriousness. The Evangelical Impact on the Victorians*, London: Cape

Brantlinger, P. (1985), 'Victorians and Africans: the genealogy of the myth of the Dark Continent', *Critical Inquiry*, 12, 166–203

Brantlinger, P. (1988), *The Rule of Darkness: British Literature and Imperialism, 1830-1914*, Ithaca: Cornell University Press

British Commonwealth Leaflets (1948)

Broks, P. (1990), 'Science, the press and empire: Pearson's publications, 1890-1914', in MacKenzie, J.M. (ed.), *Imperialism and the Natural World*, Manchester: Manchester University Press

Brydon, L. and Chant, S. (1989), *Women in the Third World: Gender Issues in Rural and Urban Areas*, London: Edward Elgar

Buchan, J. (1980), *The Expendable Mary Slessor*, Edinburgh: Saint Andrew Press

Buchan, J. (1984), *Peacemaker of Calabar: The Story of Mary Slessor*, Exeter: Religious and Moral Education Press

Bushong, A.D. (1984), 'Ellen Churchill Semple 1863-1932', in Freeman, T.W. (ed.), *Geographers: Bio-Bibliographic Studies, 8*, London: Marshall Publications, 87–94

Butchart, A. (1998), *The Anatomy of Power. European Constructions of the African Body*, London: Zed

Cairns, A.C. (1965), *Prelude to Imperialism. British Reactions to Central African Society 1840–1890*, London: Routledge and Kegan Paul

Callan, H. and Ardener, S. (eds) (1984), *The Incorporated Wife*, London: Croom Helm

Callaway, H. (1987), *Gender, Culture and Empire. European Women in Colonial Nigeria*, London: Macmillan

Callaway, H. and Helly, D.O. (1992), 'Crusader for Empire. Flora Shaw/Lady Lugard', in Chaudhuri, N. and Strobel, M., (eds), *Western Women and Imperialism. Complicity and Resistance*, Bloomington: Indiana University Press, 79–97

Campbell, O. (1957), *Mary Kingsley. A Victorian in the Jungle*, London: Methuen

Carby, H. (1982), 'White women listen! Black feminism and the boundaries of sisterhood', in *Centre for Contemporary Cultural Studies, The Empire Strikes Back, Race and Racism in 70's Britain*, London: Hutchinson, 212–32

Chakrabarty, D. (1994), 'Postcoloniality and the artiface of history: who speaks for 'Indian' pasts?' in Veeser, H.A. (ed.), *The New Historicism Reader*, London: Routledge, 342–65

Chakrabarty, D. (1998), 'Minority histories, subaltern pasts', *Postcolonial Studies*, 1, 1, 15–30

Chamberlin, C. (1978), 'The migration of the Fang into central Gabon during the nineteenth century: a new interpretation', *International Journal of African Historical Studies*, 2, 429–56

Chambers, I. and Curti, L. (eds) (1995), *The Post-Colonial Question*, London: Routledge

Chappell, J. (1927), *Three Brave Women*, London: Partridge

Chaudhuri, N. and Strobel, M. (eds) (1992), *Western Women and Imperialism. Complicity and Resistance*, Bloomington: Indiana University Press

Childs, P. and Williams, P. (1997), *An Introduction to Post-Colonial Theory*, London: Prentice Hall

Christian, C. and Plummer G. (1970), *God and One Redhead. Mary Slessor of Calabar*, London: Hodder and Stoughton

Church Missionary Society (1911), *The Yoruba Mission*, London: C.M.S. Publications

Clifford, J. (1992), 'Travelling Cultures', in Grossberg, L. (ed.), *Cultural Studies*, London: Routledge, 96–116

Cline, C.A. (1980), *E.D. Morel 1873–1924 - The Strategies of Protest*, London: Blackstaff Press

Coetzee, J.M, (1988), *White Writing: On the Culture of Letters in South Africa*, New Haven: Yale University Press

Colvile, Z.E. (1893), *Round the Black Man's Garden*, Edinburgh: Blackwood

Colvile, Z.E. (1893b), 'Ten days on an Oil River', *Blackwood's Magazine*, March, 372-82

Colvile, Z.E. (1896), *History of the Colvile Family*, Edinburgh: printed privately

Colvile, Z.E. (1908) Obituary: 'Major-General Sir H.E. Colvile, K.C.M.G., C.B.', *Geographical Journal*, 31, 113

Comaroff, J. and Comaroff, J. (1988), 'Through the looking-glass: colonial encounters of the first kind', *Journal of Historical Sociology*, 1, 1, 6–32

Corbey, R. (1995), 'Ethnographic Showcases 1870-1930', in Pieterse, J.N. and Parekh, B. (eds), *The Decolonization of Imagination*, London: Zed, 57–80

Crosby, C. (1991), *The Ends of History: Victorians and the 'Woman Question'* Routledge, London

Crowder, M. (1981), *West Africa Under Colonial Rule*, London: Hutchinson

Crush, J. (1994), 'Gazing on Apartheid: Post-Colonial Travel Narratives of the Golden City', in Simpson-Housley, P. and Preston, P. (eds), *Writing the City*, London: Routledge

Curtin, P. (1965), *The Image of Africa. British Ideas and Action 1780–1850*, London: Macmillan

Davin, A. (1978), 'Imperialism and motherhood', *History Workshop*, 5, 9–65

de Groot, J. (1991), 'Conceptions and misconceptions: the historical and cultural context of discussion on women and development', in Mohanty, C., Russo, A. and Torres, L. (eds), *Third World Women and the Politics of Feminism*, Bloomington: Indiana University Press, 107–35

Deutsch, R. (1991), 'Boys Town', *Environment and Planning D: Society and Space*, 9, 5–30

Dictionary of National Biography

Di Leonardo, M. (ed.) (1991), *Gender at the Crossroads of Knowledge: Feminist Anthropology in the Post-modern Era*, Oxford: University of California Press

Domosh, M. (1991a), 'Towards a feminist historiography of geography', *Transactions of the Institute of British Geographers*, 16, 1, 95–104

Domosh, M. 1991b), 'Beyond the frontiers of geographical knowledge', *Transactions of the Institute of British Geographers*, 16, 4, 488–90

Donaldson, L.E. (1992), *Decolonizing Feminisms. Race, Gender and Empire-Building*, London: Routledge

Driver, F. and Rose, G. (eds) (1992), *Nature and Science: Essays in the History of Geographical Knowledge*, Historical Geography Research Series, 28, London

Driver, F. (1992), 'Geography's empire: histories of geographical knowledge', *Environment and Planning D: Society and Space*, 10, 23–40

Driver, F. (1995), 'Submerged. identities: familiar and unfamiliar histories', *Transactions of the Institute of British Geographers*, 20, 4, 410–13

Duncan, N and Sharp, J.P. (1993), 'Confronting representation(s)', *Environment and Planning D: Society and Space*, 11, 473–86

Dusgate, R. (1985), *The Conquest of Northern Nigeria*, London: Frank Cass

Edwards, E. (1992), *Anthropology and Photography 1860–1920*, London: Yale University Press

Elam, D. (1994), *Feminism and Deconstruction*, Routledge, London

Etienne, M. and Leacock, E. (1980), *Women and Colonization. Anthropological Perspectives*, New York: Bergin

Fage, J.D. (1961), *Introduction to the History of West Africa*, London: Cambridge University Press

Ferguson, M. (1992), *Subject to Others. British Women Writers and Colonial Slavery, 1670–1834*, London: Routledge

Flint, J.E. (1960), *Sir George Goldie and the Making of Nigeria*, London: Oxford University Press

Flint, J.E. (1963), 'Mary Kingsley – a reassessment', *Journal of African History*, 4, 95–104

Flint, J.E. (1964), *Introduction to new edition of West African Studies*, London, Cass

Flint, J.E. (1965), 'Mary Kingsley', *African Affairs*, 64, 150–61

Foote, H.G. (1869), *Recollections of Central America and the West Coast of Africa*, London: Newby

Foster, S. (1991), *Across New Worlds: Nineteenth Century Women Travellers and their Writings*, London: Harvester Wheatsheaf

Frank, K. (1986a), *A Voyager Out: The Life of Mary Kingsley*, London: Hamish Hamilton

Frank, K. (1986b), 'Voyages out: nineteenth-century women travelers in Africa', in Sharistanian, J. (ed.), *Gender, Ideology and Action. Historical Perspectives on Women's Public Lives*, Connecticut: Greenwood

Fussell, P. (1982), *Abroad. Literary Travelling Between the Wars*, Oxford: Oxford University Press

Fyfe, C. (1962), *A History of Sierra Leone*, London: Oxford University Press

Gartrell, B. (1984), 'Colonial wives: villains or victims?' in Callan, H. and Ardener, S. (eds), *The Incorporated Wife*, London: Croom Helm

Gaunt, M. (1912), *Alone in West Africa*, London: T. Werner Laurie

Gikandi, S. (1996), *Maps of Englishness. Writing Identity in the Culture of Colonialism*, New York: Columbia University Press

Gilman, S.L. (1985a), *Difference and Pathology. Stereotypes of Sexuality, Race and Madness*, Ithaca: Cornell University Press

Gilman, S.L. (1985b), 'Black bodies, white bodies: toward an iconography of female sexuality in late nineteenth-century art, medicine, and literature', *Critical Inquiry*, 1, 12, 202–42

Gittins, C. (ed.) (1996), *Imperialism and Gender. Constructions of Masculinity*, Hebden Bridge: Dangaroo Press

Godlewska, A. and Smith, N. (eds) (1994), *Geography and Empire*, Oxford: Blackwell

Graham-Brown, S. (1988), *Images of Women. The Portrayal of Women in the Photography of the Middle-East 1860–1950*, New York: Columbia University Press

Grampian (1965), *Great Scot*, issue 482

Green, A.S. (1901), 'Mary Kingsley', *African Society Journal*, 1, 1–16

Greenstein, S. (1982), 'Sarah Lee: the woman traveller and the literature of Empire', in Dorsey, A., Egejuru, K. and Arnold, N. (eds), *Design and Intent in African Literature*, Washington: Three Continents Press

Gregory, D. (1995), 'Between the book and the lamp: imaginative geographies of mid-nineteenth century Egypt', *Transactions of the Institute of British Geographers*, 20, 1, 29–57

Griffin, A. (1977), 'The Interior Garden and John Stuart Mill', in Knoepflmacher, V.C. and Tennyson, G.B. (eds), *Nature and the Victorian Imagination*, Berkeley: University of California Press

Grossberg, L, Nelson, C. and Treicher, P. (eds) (1992), *Cultural Studies*, London: Routledge

Gwynn, S. (1932), *The Life of Mary Kingsley*, London: Macmillan

Haggard, H.R. (1885), *King Solomon's Mines*, London: Cassell

Haggis, J. (1990), 'Gendering colonialism or colonising gender? Recent Women's Studies approaches to white women and the history of British colonialism', *Women's Studies International Forum*, 13, 1(2), 105–15

Hall, C. (1992), 'Missionary Stories, Gender and Ethnicity in England in the 1830s and 1840s', in Grossberg, L., Nelson, C. and Treicher, P. (eds), *Cultural Studies*, London: Routledge, 240–76

Hall, C. (1996), 'Histories, Empires and the Post-Colonial Moment', in Chambers, I. and Curti, L. (eds), *The Post-Colonial Question*, London: Routledge , 65–77

Hall, S. (1995), 'When was the "Post-Colonial"? Thinking at the limit', in Chambers, I. and Curti, L. (eds), *The Post-Colonial Question*, London: Routledge, 242–60

Hamalian, L. (1981), *Ladies on the Loose. Women Travellers of the Eighteenth and Nineteenth Centuries*, London: Dodd, Mead and Co.

Hammond, D. and Jablow, A. (1977), *The Myth of Africa*, Library of Social Science

Hargreaves, J.D. (1966), *Prelude to the Partition of West Africa*, London: Macmillan

Hargreaves, J.D. (1974), 'The European partition of West Africa', in J.F.A. Ajayi and Crowder, M. (eds), *History of West Africa, Volume 2*, London: Longman

Harrison, B. (1978), *Separate Spheres: The Opposition to Women's Suffrage in Britain*, London: Croom Helm

Hayford, Rev. M.C. (1901), *Mary H. Kingsley: From an African Standpoint*, London: Bear and Taylor

Heffernan, M.J. (1989), 'The limits of Utopia: Henri Duveyrier and the exploration of the Sahara in the nineteenth century', *The Geographical Journal*, 155, 465–80

Helly, D.O. (1969), 'Informed. opinion on tropical Africa in Great Britain 1860–1890', *African Affairs*, 68, 195–217

Hewat, E.G.K. (1960), *Vision and Achievement 1796-1956. A History of the Churches United in the Church of Scotland*, Edinburgh: Nelson

Hinderer, A. (1872), *Seventeen Years in the Yoruba Country*, London: Seeley, Jackson and Halliday (with a foreword by Richard B. Hone)

Hodgkin, T. (1960), *Nigerian Perspectives. An Historical Anthology*, London: Oxford University Press

Hogg, G. (1958), *Cannibalism and Human Sacrifice*, London: Pan Books

Hogg, Jessie F. (1915), 'Mary M. Slessor', *Women's Missionary Magazine of the United Free Church of Scotland*, February, 53–54

Holmes, I.M. (1949), *In Africa's Service. The Story of Mary Kingsley*, London: Saturn Press

hooks, b. (1982), *'Ain't I a Woman?' Black Women and Feminism*, London: Pluto

hooks, b. (1989), 'Travelling theories, travelling theorists', *Inscriptions*, 5

hooks, b. (1991), *Yearning: Race, Gender and Cultural Politics*, London: Turnaround

Horner, A. and Zlosnik, S. (1990), *Landscapes of Desire*, London: Harvester Wheatsheaf

Howard, C. (1957), *Mary Kingsley*, London: Hutchinson

Hudson, B. (1977), 'The new geography and the new imperialism: 1870–1918', *Antipode*, 9, 2, 12–19

Hudson, S., Jarvie, T.W. and Stein, J. (1978), *'Let the Fire Burn'. A Study of R.M. McCheyne, Robert Annan, Mary Slessor*, Dundee: Hansell

Hunt, N.R. (1990), '"Single ladies on the Congo": Protestant missionary tensions and voices', *Women's Studies International Forum*, 13, 4, 395–403

Hurtado, A. (1989), 'Relating to privilege: seduction and rejection in the subordination of white women and women of color', *Signs*, 14, 833–55

Huttenbach, A. (1976), *Racism and Empire. White Settlers and Coloured Immigrants in the British Self-Governing Colonies, 1830–1910*, London and Ithaca: Cornell University Press

Hyam, R. (1990), *Empire and Sexuality. The British Experience*, Manchester: Manchester University Press

Idowu, E.B. (1973), *African Traditional Religion. A Definition*, London: S.C.M. Press

Jackson, P. (1989), *Maps of Meaning*, London: Unwin Hyman

Jackson, P. (1991), 'The cultural politics of masculinity: towards a social geography', *Transactions of the Institute of British Geographers*, 16, 2, 199–213

Jackson, P. (1998), 'Constructions of "whiteness" in the geographical imagination', *Area* 30, 2, 99–106

JanMohammed., A.R. (1985), 'The economy of Manichean allegory: the function of racial difference in colonialist literature', *Critical Inquiry*, 12, 1, 59–87

Jarosz, L. (1992), 'Constructing the Dark Continent: metaphor as geographic representation of Africa', *Geografiska Annaler*, 74 B, 2, 105–15

Jarosz, L. (1994), 'Agents of power, landscapes of fear: the vampire and heart thieves of Madagascar', *Environment and Planning D: Society and Space*, 12, 4, 421–36

Jeffreys, M.D.W. (1950), 'Mary Slessor – Magistrate', parts 1 and 2, *West African Review*, June, 628–9, 802–5

Johnson, Douglas H. (1991), 'Criminal secrecy: the case of the Zande 'secret societies", *Past and Present*, 130, 170–200

Jubilee Booklet (1948), *The Life of Mary Slessor, Pioneer Missionary, 1840–1915*, Dundee

Kabbani, R. (1986), *Europe's Myths of Orient. Devise and Rule*, London: Macmillan

Kay, J. (1991), 'Landscapes of women and men: rethinking the regional historical geography of the United. States and Canada', *Journal of Historical Geography*, 17, 4, 435–52

Kearns, G. (1997), 'The imperial subject: geography and travel in the work of Mary Kingsley and Halford Mackinder', *Transactions of the Institute of British Geographers*, 22, 4, 450–72

Keay, J. (1985), *Explorers Extraordinary*, London: John Murray

Keay, J. (1989), *With Passport and Parasol*, London: B.B.C. Books

Keith, W.J. (1974), *The Rural Tradition. A Study of the Non-Fiction Prose Writers of the English Countryside*, Toronto: University of Toronto Press

Kennedy, D. (1996), 'Imperial history and post-colonial theory', *The Journal of Imperial and Commonwealth History*, 24, 3, 345–63

Kiernan, V.G. (1969), *The Lords of Human Kind*, London: Weidenfeld and Nicolson

Kingsley, M.H. (1896a), 'The development of Dodos', *National Review*, March, 66–79

Kingsley, M.H. (1896b), 'Travels on the western coast of equatorial Africa', *Scottish Geographical Magazine*, 12, 113–24

Kingsley, M.H. (1896c), 'The ascent of Cameroons Peak and travels in French Congo', *Transactions of the Liverpool Geographical Society* 1, 36–52

Kingsley, M.H. (1897a), 'The fetish view of the human soul', *Folklore*, 8, 138–51

Kingsley, M.H. (1897b), 'West Africa, from an ethnologist's point of view', *Transactions of the Liverpool Geographical Society*, 1, 58–73

Kingsley, M.H. (1897c), 'The forms of apparitions in West Africa', *West Africa*, 14, 35, 331–42

Kingsley, M.H. (1898a), 'Introduction' in Dennett, R.E. *Notes on the Folklore of the Fjort – French Congo*, London: Folklore Society

Kingsley, M.H. (1898b), 'The liquor traffic with West Africa', *Fortnightly Review*, April, 537–60

Kingsley, M.H. (1898c), 'A lecture on West Africa', extracts from an address given at the S.P.G.   and S.P.C.K., from *Cheltenham Ladies' Magazine*, 38, 264–80

Kingsley, M.H. (1899a), *West African Studies*, London: Macmillan

Kingsley, M.H. (1899b), 'The administration of our West African colonies', *Manchester Chamber of Commerce Monthly Record*, 30, March, 63–65

Kingsley, M.H. (1899c), 'Life in West Africa', in Shoewring, W. (ed.), *The British Empire Series*, 2, 366–80

Kingsley, M.H. (1900a), *The Story of West Africa*, London: Horace Marshall

Kingsley, M.H. (1900b), 'Memoir', in Kingsley, G.H. *Notes on Sport and Travel*, London: Macmillan

Kingsley, M.H. (1900c), 'Nursing in West Africa', *Chambers Journal*, 3, 369–71, 393–6

Kingsley, M.H. (1900d), 'West Africa from an Ethnological Point of View', *Imperial Institute Journal*, 6, April, 82–97

Kingsley, M.H. (1982), *Travels in West Africa, Congo Français, Corisco and Cameroons*, London: Virago (first published. in 1897)

Knoepflmacher, V.C. and Tennyson, G.B. (eds) (1977), *Nature and the Victorian Imagination*, Berkeley: University of California Press

Kolodny, A. (1984), *The Land Before Her. Fantasy and Experience of the American Frontiers 1630–1860*, London: University of Carolina Press

Koster, D. (1975), *Transcendentalism in America*, Boston: Twayne

Kowalewski, M. (1992), *Temperamental Journeys: Essays on the Modern Literature of Travel*, Athens, Georgia: University of Georgia Press

Larymore, C. (1908), *A Resident's Wife in Nigeria*, London: Routledge

Lewis, J. (1991), *Women and Social Action in Victorian and Edwardian England*, Aldershot: Elgar

Lewis, R. (1996), *Gendering Orientalism. Race, Femininity and Representation*, London: Routledge

Light, A. (1991), *Forever England. Femininity, Literature and Conservation Between the Wars*, London: Routledge

Livingstone, D.N. (1992), *The Geographical Tradition*, Oxford: Blackwell

Livingstone, D.N. (1995), 'Geographical traditions', *Transactions of the Institute of British Geographers*, 20, 4, 420–22

Livingstone, D.N. (1998), 'Reproduction, representation and authenticity - a re-reading', *Transactions of the Institute of British Geographers*, 23, 1, 13–20

Livingstone, W.P. (1916), *Mary Slessor of Calabar. Pioneer Missionary*, London: Hodder and Stoughton (6th edition)

Loomis, C.C. (1977), 'The Arctic Sublime', in Knoepflmacher, V.C. and Tennyson, G.B. (eds), *Nature and the Victorian Imagination*, Berkeley: University of California Press, 95–112

Lorimer, D.A. (1978), *Colour, Class and the Victorians. English Attitudes to the Negro in the Mid-Nineteenth Century*, Leicester: Leicester University Press

Lorimer, D.A. (1988), 'Theoretical racism in late Victorian anthropology, 1870-1900', *Victorian Studies*, 31, 405–30

Lovejoy, P. (ed.) (1981), *The Ideology of Slavery*, London: Sage

Low, G. (1996), *White Skins/Black Masks. Representation and Colonialism*, London: Routledge

McClintock, A. (1995), *Imperial Leather. Race, Gender and Sexuality in the Colonial Conquest*, London: Routledge

McEwan, C. (1994), 'Encounters with West African Women: Textual Representations of Difference by White Women Abroad', in Blunt, A. and Rose, G. (eds), *Writing Women and Space. Colonial and Postcolonial Geographies*, New York: Guilford Press, 73–100

McEwan, C. (1995a) 'How the 'seraphic' became 'geographic': women travellers in west Africa, 1840-1915', unpublished. Ph.D. thesis, Loughborough University

McEwan, C. (1995b), "The Mother of All the Peoples' – Geographical Knowledge and the Empowering of Mary Slessor) in Bell, M., Butlin, R.A. and Heffernan, M.J. (eds) *Geography and Imperialism*, Manchester: Manchester University Press, 125–150

McEwan, C. (1996), 'Paradise or pandemonium? West African landscapes in the travel accounts of Victorian women', *Journal of Historical Geography*, 22, 1, 68–83

McEwan, C. (1998a), 'Cutting power lines in the palace? Countering paternity and eurocentrism in the 'geographical tradition'', *Transactions of the Institute of British Geographers*, 23, 3, 371–84

McEwan, C. (1998b), 'Gender, science and physical geography in nineteenth century Britain', *Area*, 30, 3, 215–24

McFarlan, D.M. (1946), *Calabar. The Church of Scotland Mission, 1846–1946*, London: Nelson

McFarland, T. (1969), *Coleridge and the Pantheist Tradition*, Oxford: Clarenden Press

MacGregor, J.K. (1917), 'Mary Mitchell Slessor, 1848-1915', *The East and the West*, 1, 15, 143–63

MacKenzie, J.M. (ed.), *Imperialism and the Natural World*, Manchester: Manchester University Press

McKenzie, P.R. (1976), *Inter-Religious Encounters in West Africa*, Leicester Studies in Religion I, Leicester: Blackfriars

Madge, C. (1993), 'Boundary disputes: comments on Sidaway', *Area*, 25, 3, 294–9

Mallory, W.E. and Simpson-Housley, P. (eds) (1987), *Geography and Literature. A Meeting of the Disciplines*, Syracuse: Syracuse University Press

Mander, A.M. (1995), 'Geography, gender and the state: a critical evaluation of the development of geography 1830-1918', unpublished. D.Phil. thesis, University of Oxford

Mani, L. (1992), 'Cultural Theory, Colonial Texts: Reading Eyewitness Accounts of Widow-Burning', in Grossberg, L., Nelson, C. and Treicher, P. (eds), *Cultural Studies*, London: Routledge, 392–408

Matless, D. (1991), 'Nature, the modern and the mystic: tales from early twentieth century geography', *Transactions of the Institute of British Geographers*, 16, 3, 272–286

Matless, D. (1995), 'Effects of history', *Transactions of the Institute of British Geographers* 20, 4, 405–9

Matthews, W. (1947), *Dauntless Women*, London: Edinburgh House Press

Mazrui, A.A. (1969), 'European exploration and Africa's self-discovery', *Journal of Modern African Studies*, 7, 4, 661–76

Melman, B. (1992), *Women's Orients: English Women and the Middle East 1718–1918. Sexuality, Religion and Work*, London: Macmillan

Melville, E. (1968), *A Residence at Sierra Leone: described from a journal kept on the spot, and from letters written to friends at home* (edited by Mrs Norton), London: Frank Cass (first published anonymously in 1849)

Memmi, A. (1990), *The Colonizer and the Colonized*, London: Earthscan

Mermin, D. (1982), 'Browning and the primitive', *Victorian Studies*, 25, 2, 211–37

Middleton, D. (1965), *Victorian Lady Travellers*, London: Macmillan

Middleton, D. (1973), 'Some Victorian lady travellers', *The Geographical Journal*, 139, 65–75

Midgley, C. (1992), *Women Against Slavery. The British Campaigns, 1780–1870*, London: Routledge

Miller, B. (1946), *Mary Slessor. Heroine of Calabar*, Michigan: Zondervan

Miller, C. (1985), *Blank Darkness. Africanist Discourse in French*, London: University of Chicago Press

Miller, D.P. and Reill, P.H. (eds) (1996), *Visions of Empire. Voyages, Botany and Representations of Nature*, Cambridge: Cambridge University Press

Millett, K. (1970), 'The debate over women: Ruskin versus Mill', *Victorian Studies*, September, 63–73

Mills, S. (1991), *Discourses of Difference. An Analysis of Women's Travel Writing and Colonialism*, London: Routledge

Mills, S. (1994), 'Knowledge, Gender and Empire', in Blunt, A. and Rose, G. (eds), *Writing Women and Space. Colonial and Postcolonial Geographies*, New York: Guilford Press, 29–50

Mills, S. (1996), 'Gender and colonial space', *Gender, Place and Culture*, 3, 2, 125–48

Mishra, V. and Hodge, B. (1993), 'What is Post(-)colonialism?', in Williams, P. and Chrisman, L. (eds), *Colonial Discourse and Post-Colonial Theory*, London: Harvester Wheatsheaf, 276–90

Mitchell, T. (1988), *Colonising Egypt*, Cambridge: Cambridge University Press

Mizuoka, F. (1998), 'The development and demise of alternative geography in Japan', Discussion Paper Series, 13, Graduate School of Economics, Hitotsubashi University

Mohanty, C.T. (1991), 'Cartographies of struggle, Third world women and the politics of feminism', in Mohanty, C., Russo, A. and Torres, L. (eds), *Third World Women and the Politics of Feminism*, Bloomington: Indiana University Press, 1–47

Monicat, B. (1994), 'Autobiography and women's travel writings in nineteenth century France: journeys through self-representation', *Ecumene*, 1, 1, 61–70

Moore, H.L. (1988), *Feminism and Anthropology*, Cambridge: Polity

Moore-Gilbert, B. (1997), *Postcolonial Theory. Contexts, Practices, Politics*, London: Verso

Morin, K. (1995), 'A "Female Columbus" in 1887 America: marking new social territory', *Gender, Place and Culture*, 2, 2, 191–208

Nair, K.K. (1972), *Politics and Society in South-Eastern Nigeria 1841-1906. A Study of Power, Diplomacy and Commerce in Old Calabar*, Northwestern University Press

Nast, H.J. *et al* (1994), 'Women in the field: Critical feminist methodologies and theoretical perspectives', *Professional Geographer*, 46, 1, 54–102

Nathan, M. (1907), 'Some reminiscences of Miss Mary Kingsley', *Journal of the African Society*, 7, 25, 28–32

Nicholson L (ed..) (1990), *Feminism/Postmodernism*, Routledge, London

Noor, F. (1996), 'Innocents abroad? The ab/uses of (white) innocence in contemporary feminist and "nostalgic" travelogues', unpublished paper presented at the British Sociological Association Annual Conference, University of Reading

Northrup, D. (1981), 'The ideological context of slavery in southeastern Nigeria in the nineteenth century', in Lovejoy, P., (ed.), *The Ideology of Slavery in Africa*, London: Sage

Nussbaum, F.A. (1995), *Torrid Zones. Maternity, Sexuality, and Empire in Eighteenth-Century English Narratives*, Baltimore and London: John Hopkins University Press

Nwabughuogu, A.I., (1981), 'The role of propaganda in the development of Indirect Rule in Nigeria, 1880-1929', *International Journal of African Historical Studies*, 14, 1, 65–93

Nworah, K.D. (1971), 'The Liverpool 'Sect' and British West African policy 1895-1915', *African Affairs*, 3, 349–64

Obichere, B. (1977), 'African critics of Victorian imperialism: an analysis', *Journal of African Studies*, 4, 1, 16

Oduyoye, M. (1969), *The Planting of Christianity in Yorubaland*, Ibadan: Daystar Press

Oliver, C. (1982), *Western Women in Colonial Africa*, Westport, Connecticut: Greenwood

Ong, A. (1988), 'Colonialism and modernity: feminist re-presentations of women in non-western societies', *Inscriptions*, 3, 4, 79–93

Orr, C. (1965), *The Making of Northern Nigeria*, London: Frank Cass [first published in 1911]

Padwick, C.E. (1916), *White Heroines in Africa*, London: United Council for Missionary Education [2nd edition]

Pateman, C. (1988), *The Sexual Contract*, Cambridge: Polity

Pearce, R.D. (1988), 'Missionary education in colonial Africa: the critique of Mary Kingsley', *History of Education*, 17, 4, 283–94

Pearce, R.D. (1990) *Mary Kingsley, Light at the Heart of Darkness*, Oxford: The Kensal Press

Peet, R. (1985), 'The social origins of environmental determinism', *Annals of the Association of American Geographers*, 75, 309–33

Phillips, R. (1997), *Mapping Men and Empire. A Geography of Adventure*, London: Routledge

Pieterse, J.N. and Parekh, B. (eds) (1995), *The Decolonization of Imagination. Culture, Knowledge and Power*, London: Zed

Ploszajska, T. (1995), 'Making all the difference in the world: geography's popular school texts, 1870–1944', Department of Geography Research Papers, 3 Royal Holloway, University of London

Poovey, M. (1989) *Uneven Developments. The Ideological Work of Gender in Mid-Victorian*, London: Virago

Porter, B. (1968), *Critics of Empire*, London: Macmillan

Porter, D. (1991), *Haunted Journeys. Desire and Transgression in European Travel Writing*, Princeton: Princeton University Press

Pratt, M.L. (1985), 'Scratches on the face of the country; or, what Mr. Barrow saw in the land of the Bushmen', *Critical Inquiry*, 12, 119–43

Pratt, M.L. (1992), *Imperial Eyes: Travel Writing and Transculturation*, London: Routledge

Radcliffe, S. (1994), '(Re)presenting post-colonial women: authority, difference and feminisms', *Area*, 26, 1, 25–32

Rainger, R. (1978), 'Race, politics and science: the Anthropological Society of London in the 1860s', *Victorian Studies*, 22, 1, 51–70

Ramusack, B. (1990), 'Cultural missionaries, maternal imperialists, feminist allies: British women activists in India, 1865–1945', *Women's Studies International Forum*, 13, 4, 309–21

Rich, P.B. (1986), *Race and Empire in British Politics*, Cambridge: Cambridge University Press

Richards, T. (1993), *The Imperial Archive. Knowledge and the Fantasy of Empire*, London: Verso

Ridley, H. (1983), *Images of Imperial Rule*, London: Croom Helm

Roberts, A. (1994), 'When the East was a career for the West', review article, *The Times*, October

Robertson, C. and Klein, M. (eds) (1983), *Women and Slavery in Africa*, University of Wisconsin Press

Robinson, J. (1991), *Wayward Women. A Guide to Women Travellers*, Oxford: Oxford University Press

Robinson, J. (1994), 'White Women Researching/Representing 'Others': From Antiapartheid to Postcolonialism', in Blunt, A. and Rose, G. (eds), *Writing Women and Space. Colonial and Postcolonial Geographies*, New York: Guilford, 197–226

Robinson, R. and Gallagher, J with Denny, A. (1981), *Africa and the Victorians. The Official Mind of Imperialism*, London: Macmillan

Rose, G. (1992), 'Geography as a Science of Observation: the Landscape, the Gaze and Masculinity', in Driver, F. and Rose, G. (eds), *Nature and Science: Essays in the History of Geographical Knowledge*, Historical Geography Research Series, 28, London, 8–18

Rose, G. (1993), *Feminism and Geography. The Limits of Geographical Knowledge*, Cambridge: Polity

Rose, G. (1995), 'Tradition and paternity: same difference?' *Transactions of the Institute of British Geographers*, 20, 4 , 414–16

Rothenberg, T. (1994), 'Voyeurs of imperialism: The National Geographic Magazine before World War II', in Godlewska, A. and Smith, N. (eds), *Geography and Empire*, Oxford: Blackwell, 155–72

Russell, M. (1988), *The Blessings of a Good Thick Skirt*, London: Collins

Russett, C.E. (1989), *Sexual Science. The Victorian Construction of Womanhood*, Cambridge, Mass.: Harvard University Press

Ryan, J.R. (1994), 'Visualizing imperial geography: Halford Mackinder and the Colonial Office Visual Instruction Committee, 1902-11', *Ecumene*, 1, 2, 157–76

Said, E. (1978), *Orientalism*, London: Peregrine

Said, E. (1990), 'Narrative, geography and interpretation', *New Left Review*, 180, 81–97

Said, E. (1994), *Culture and Imperialism*, London: Vintage

Semple, E.C. (1911), *Influences of Geographic Environments. On the Basis of Ratzel's System of Anthropo-Geography*, New York: Holt

Seth, S., Gandhi, L. and Dutton, M. (1998), 'Postcolonial studies: a beginning...' *Postcolonial Studies*, 1, 1, 7–11

Sharistanian, J. (ed.) (1986), *Gender, Ideology and Action*, Connecticut: Greenwood Press

Short, J.R. (1991), *Imagined Country. Environment, Culture and Society*, London: Routledge

Sidaway, J.D. (1992), 'In other worlds: on the politics of research by 'First World' geographers in the 'Third World'', *Area*, 24, 4, 403–8

Sidaway, J.D. (1997), 'The (re)making of the western 'geographical tradition': some missing links', *Area*, 29 1, 72–80

Simpson-Housley, P. and Preston, P. (eds) (1994), *Writing the City*, London: Routledge

Slessor, M. (1901), 'Triumphing over superstition', *Women's Missionary Magazine*, May, 109

Slessor, M. (1905), 'The awakening in the Cross River', *Women's Missionary Magazine*, April, 81–2

Slessor, M. (1905), 'How the seeds grow in Itu', *Women's Missionary Magazine*, June, 125–6

Slessor, M. (1908), 'Concerning advance work in West Africa', *Women's Missionary Magazine*, January, 4

Slessor, M. (1909), 'Calabar snapshots', with Mrs. Lindsay, *Women's Missionary Magazine*, November, 257

Slessor, M. (1910), 'A missionary's testimony', *Women's Missionary Magazine*, March, 66–68

Spivak, G.C. (1985), 'Subaltern Studies: Deconstructing Historiography' in Guha, R. (ed.), *Subaltern Studies IV*, New Delhi: Oxford University Press, 330–63

Spivak, G.C. (1986), 'Imperialism and sexual difference', *Oxford Literary Review* 8: 1-2, 225–40

Spivak, G.C. (1988), *In Other Worlds. Essays in Cultural Politics*, London: Routledge

Spivak, G.C. (1988), 'Can the Subaltern Speak?' in Nelson, C. and Grossberg, L. (eds), *Marxism and the Interpretation of Culture*, Urbana: University of Illinois Press, 271–313

Spivak, G.C. (1991), 'Theory in the Margin: Coetzee's Foe Reading Defoe's Crusoe/Roxana', in Arac, J. and Johnson, B. (eds), *Consequences of Theory*, Baltimore: John Hopkins University Press, 154–80

Spivak, G.C. (1992), 'Interview', *Ariel* 23, 3

Steen, S.L.M. (1980), *European and African Stereotypes in Twentieth-Century Fiction*, London: Macmillan

Stock, E. (1899), *History of the Church Missionary Society, 2*, London: Church Missionary Society Publications

Stoddart, D. (1991), 'Do we need. a feminist historiography of geography - and if we do, what should it be?' *Transactions of the Institute of British Geographers*, 16, 4, 484–7

Stoler, A.L. (1991), 'Carnal Knowledge and Imperial Power. Gender, Race and Mortality in Colonial Asia', in Di Leonardo (ed.), *Gender at the Crossroads of Knowledge: Feminist Anthropology in the Post-Modern Era*, Oxford: University of California Press, 1–76

Stott, R. (1989), 'The Dark Continent: Africa as female body in Haggard's adventure fiction', *Feminist Review*, 32, 69–89

Strobel, M. (1991), *European Women and the Second British Empire*, Bloomington: Indiana University Press

Sunday Mail Story of Scotland (1988), 3, 39, 1091–2

Tabor, M. (1930), *Pioneer Women, 3*, London: Sheldon Press

Tannahill, R. (1975), *Flesh and Blood. A History of the Cannibal Complex*, London: Hamish Hamilton

Thornton, A.P. (1965), *Doctrines of Imperialism*, London: Wiley and Sons

Thorp, E. (1950), *Swelling of Jordan*, London: Lutterworth Press

Thorp, E. (1967), *Ladder of Bones*, London: Collins Fontana

Tiffin, C. and Lawson, A. (eds) (1994), *De-Scribing Empire. Postcolonialism and Textuality*, London: Routledge

Tinling, M. (1989), *Women into the Unknown. A Sourcebook on Women Explorers and Travellers*, London and Connecticut: Greenwood Press

Trinh, T. (1989), *Woman, Native, Other. Writing Postcoloniality and Feminism*, Bloomington: Indiana University Press

Tuhiwai Smith, L. (1999), *Decolonising Methodologies. Research and Indigenous Peoples*, London: Zed

Walford, E. (1874), *The County Families of the United Kingdom*, London: Robert Harwicke

Walkowitz, J. (1986), *Science and the Seance: Transgressions of Gender and Genre in Late Victorian London*, Cambridge University Press, Cambridge

Ware, V. (1992), *Beyond the Pale. White Women, Racism and History*, London: Verso

Ware, V. (1996), 'Defining Forces: "Race", gender and memories of empire', in Chambers, I. and Curti, L. (eds), *The Post-Colonial Question*, London: Routledge, 142–68

Whitehead, A. (1981), '"I'm hungry, mum". The politics of domestic budgeting', in Young, K. et al. (eds), *Of Marriage and the Market*, London: Routledge, 93–116

Williams, P. and Chrisman, L. (eds) (1993), *Colonial Discourse and Post-Colonial Theory*, London: Harvester Wheatsheaf

Williams, R. (1973), *The Country and the City*, London: Chatto and Windus

Winstone, H.V.F. (1978), *Gertrude Bell*, London: Cape

Young, K. et al. (eds) (1981), *Of Marriage and the Market*, London: Routledge

Young, R. (1995), Colonial Desire. Hybridity in Theory, Culture and Race, London: Routledge

Youngs, T. (1994), *Travellers in Africa. British Travelogues, 1850–1900*, Manchester: Manchester University Press

Index